THE SERMON ON THE MOUNT THROUGH THE CENTURIES

THE SERMON ON THE MOUNT THROUGH THE CENTURIES

EDITED BY

JEFFREY P. GREENMAN
TIMOTHY LARSEN
STEPHEN R. SPENCER

BrazosPress
Grand Rapids, Michigan

Published by Brazos Press
a division of Baker Publishing Group
P.O. Box 6287, Grand Rapids, MI 49516-6287
www.brazospress.com

Printed in the United States of America

Library of Congress Cataloging-in-Publication Data
Reading the Sermon on the Mount through the centuries / edited by Jeffrey P. Greenman, Timothy Larsen, Stephen R. Spencer.
    p.   cm.
   Includes bibliographical references.
   ISBN 10: 1-58743-205-6 (pbk.)
   ISBN 978-1-58743-205-7 (pbk.)
   1. Sermon on the mount—Criticism, interpretation, etc.—History. I. Greenman, Jeffrey P. II. Larsen, Timothy, 1967- III. Spencer, Stephen R. IV. Title.
BT380.3.R43 2007
226.9′0609—dc22   2007004772

For Jill Peláez Baumgaertner

Contents

Contributors

Dr. William T. Cavanaugh is associate professor of theology at the University of St. Thomas in St. Paul, Minnesota. His PhD is from Duke University. He is the coeditor of *The Blackwell Companion to Political Theology* and is the author of *Theopolitical Imagination* and *Torture and Eucharist: Theology, Politics, and the Body of Christ*.

Dr. Boyd Taylor Coolman is assistant professor of theology at Boston College. He has previously taught at Duke Divinity School and Yale Divinity School. He received his PhD from the University of Notre Dame. He is the author of *Knowing God by Experience: The Spiritual Senses in the Theology of William of Auxerre*. His current projects include a book on Hugh of St. Victor's theology of Reformation.

Dr. Jeffrey P. Greenman is professor of Christian ethics and associate dean of biblical and theological studies at Wheaton College (Illinois). His PhD dissertation at the University of Virginia dealt with seventeenth-century Anglican practical divinity. He is the coeditor of *Reading Romans through the Centuries: From the Early Church to Karl Barth* and coauthor of *Unwearied Praises*. His research interests include theological ethics, the English Reformation, and Anglican intellectual history.

Dr. Stanley Hauerwas is the Gilbert T. Rowe Professor of Theological Ethics at Duke University. He delivered the prestigious Gifford Lectureship at the University of St. Andrews in Scotland in 2001, published as *With the Grain of the Universe: The Church's Witness and Natural Theology*. He is the author of numerous books, including *The Peaceable Kingdom, A Community of Character, In Good Company: The Church as Polis*, and *Performing the Faith: Bonhoeffer and the Practice of Nonviolence*.

Dr. David Lyle Jeffrey is Distinguished Professor of Literature and Humanities at Baylor University. His doctorate is from Princeton University. He is general editor and coauthor of *A Dictionary of Biblical Tradition in English Literature*. Among his other books are *The Early English Lyric and Franciscan Spirituality, By Things Seen: Reference and Recognition in Medieval Thought, Chaucer and Scriptural Tradition, People of the Book*, and *Houses of the Interpreter*. In 2003 he received a Lifetime Achievement Award from the Conference on Christianity and Literature/Modern Language Association.

Dr. Timothy Larsen, a fellow of the Royal Historical Society, is the McManis Professor of Christian Thought at Wheaton College (Illinois). He is the editor of the *Biographical Dictionary of Evangelicals*. His books include *Contested Christianity: The Political and Social Contexts of Victorian Theology* and *Crisis of Doubt: Honest Faith in Nineteenth-Century England*.

Dr. Margaret M. Mitchell is professor of New Testament and early Christian literature at the University of Chicago Divinity School. She received her PhD from the University of Chicago. She is recognized as a specialist in patristic exegesis. She is the author of *The Heavenly Trumpet: John Chrysostom and the Art of Pauline Interpretation* as well as *Paul and the Rhetoric of Reconciliation*. She is coeditor of the *Cambridge History of Christianity: Origins to Constantine*, volume 1.

Dr. Mark Noll is Francis A. McAnaney Professor of History at the University of Notre Dame. He obtained his PhD in the history of

Christianity from Vanderbilt University. He is the author of numerous books, including *A History of Christianity in the United States and Canada*, *The Princeton Theology, 1812–1921*, *America's God: From Jonathan Edwards to Abraham Lincoln*, *The Rise of Evangelicalism*, and *The Civil War as a Theological Crisis*.

Dr. Susan E. Schreiner is associate professor of the history of Christianity and theology at the University of Chicago Divinity School. She earned her PhD at Duke University. Her academic interest is historical theology, with specialization in the era of the Protestant and Catholic Reformations. She teaches courses in the history of exegesis. Her publications include *Theater of His Glory: Nature and the Natural Order in the Thought of John Calvin* and *Where Shall Wisdom Be Found? Calvin's Exegesis of Job from Medieval and Modern Perspectives*.

Dr. Stephen R. Spencer is Blanchard Professor of Theology at Wheaton College (Illinois). His PhD is from Michigan State University. He is the author of essays in systematic and historical theology. He teaches courses on theological exegesis. His research interests include Thomas Aquinas, Calvin, and Reformation theology.

Dr. Robert Louis Wilken, a fellow of the American Academy of Arts and Sciences, is the William R. Kenan Jr. Professor of the History of Christianity at the University of Virginia. He is past president of both the North American Patristic Society and the American Academy of Religion. He is the author of highly acclaimed studies, such as *John Chrysostom and the Jews*, *The Christians as the Romans Saw Them*, *Remembering the Christian Past*, *The Land Called Holy*, and *The Spirit of Early Christian Thought*.

Introduction 1

Timothy Larsen

S uch is the fame of the Sermon on the Mount that it seems almost redundant to stress its significance in this introduction. It
is quite simply the most celebrated discourse by Jesus of Nazareth,
the incarnate Word. The Sermon on the Mount as recorded in
Matthew 5–7 is widely considered to be the heart of Jesus's teaching. Its influence runs through the centuries like a majestic river,
giving life to new crops everywhere it goes. Indeed, so rich is this
discourse that these claims could even be made for just a small
portion of it. A volume such as this would still have a cornucopia
to offer if its scope was confined, for example, to only the Lord's
Prayer or the Beatitudes. As Luke Timothy Johnson succinctly puts
it, "In the history of Christian thought—indeed in the history of
those observing Christianity—the Sermon on the Mount has been
considered an epitome of the teaching of Jesus and therefore, for
many, the essence of Christianity."[1] In this book, we see some of
the most influential Christian leaders and theologians from the
early church to the present reflecting on this biblical encapsula-
tion of the spirit of Christianity.

1. Luke Timothy Johnson, "The Sermon on the Mount," in *The Oxford Companion
to Christian Thought*, ed. Adrian Hastings (Oxford: Oxford University Press, 2000),
654.

As was its predecessor in this series, *Reading Romans through the Centuries*,[2] this volume is based on the assumption that an ideal way to explore the history of Christian thought is as a conversation with Holy Scripture. Listening to Christians from different ages and different traditions speak about the same biblical passages is a particularly effective way to measure where they differ as well as—what for some of us is perhaps an even more important reminder—the many substantial things they share in common. It is also a promising way for us to learn from one another as we are challenged by what others stress that we have ignored, take seriously that we have evaded, and see clearly that we have glimpsed blurred.

Christian studies—like all areas of learning—is becoming increasingly fragmented into self-contained subdisciplines. The structure of this volume works against this unhelpful segregation and compartmentalization. These essays follow trajectories that inclusively draw together aspects of biblical studies, church history, historical theology, constructive theology, pastoral theology, spiritual and moral formation, and ethics. In any given chapter, one can witness how a figure in Christian history wrestled with the meaning of Scripture and—while being molded in some measure by their historical situatedness—went on to think theologically about the themes raised by Christ's words and to implement a pastoral vision for moral formation in the light of them.

Toward this end, we have assembled a suggestive sequence of major Christian figures ranging from the early church to the present. Augustine is indisputably the most influential church father in the West, and John Chrysostom is a laudable representative of the East. Hugh of St. Victor, from that center of the renewal of biblical studies, provides a quintessentially medieval treatment of the Sermon on the Mount. A chapter exploring Dante and Chaucer also represents the millennium between the early church and the Reformation. These two preeminent authors remind us that the influence of the Sermon on the Mount extends well beyond theologians and ministers to permeate Western culture more

2. Jeffrey P. Greenman and Timothy Larsen, eds., *Reading Romans through the Centuries: From the Early Church to Karl Barth* (Grand Rapids: Brazos, 2005).

generally—including some of the most exquisite heights of its literary canon. Two giants of the Protestant Reformation—Martin Luther and John Calvin—are here, while other Reformation traditions appear further downstream in the Anabaptist identity of John Howard Yoder and the Anglican identity of John R. W. Stott. John Wesley not only embodies a major Christian movement that arose in the eighteenth century, but also serves as a contrast to the Reformed identities of his neighbors in this volume. A chapter on Charles Haddon Spurgeon is an apt way to discover what the "prince of preachers" made of this greatest of all sermons. This leads on to the twentieth century and beyond. Lutheran martyr Dietrich Bonhoeffer continues to shape profoundly theology and moral formation, decades after his death. Pope John Paul II and Leonardo Boff offer two contrasting (as well as sometimes similar) versions of modern Roman Catholic thought. The volume concludes with the international evangelicalism of the venerable John R. W. Stott who—at the time this is being written—is still active in ministry.

In other words, the diversity of the Christian tradition is well on display here. Indeed, this is underlined by the disquieting polemics of so many of these figures against the Christian identities of others in this volume. Luther, Calvin, and Spurgeon, for example, all provide examples of anti-Catholic rhetoric. The Baptist Spurgeon, himself a Calvinist, would have regretted Calvin's attacks on the Anabaptists—a camp more fully represented by Yoder. Once again, however, the affinities are arguably what are truly surprising. Augustine teaches the "deification" of believers, a doctrine often thought to be uniquely Eastern. Spurgeon's anti-Catholicism does not prevent him from appropriating Catholic medieval mysticism to an astonishing degree—making his reading of the Beatitudes much closer to that of Hugh of St. Victor than one would ever have imagined. Likewise, evangelicals might find Hugh of St. Victor's elaborate scheme of interconnected sevens strangely appealing as they share with him a deep commitment to expounding Scripture with Scripture. Hugh's work may best be viewed as a reverent reveling in intrabiblical exegesis. John Chrysostom's resolute attack upon wealth reemerges in as different a context as the Methodism of Wesley—making one wonder what both the Eastern father and the evangelical pioneer would have thought of Boff's unequivocal siding with the poor.

Inevitably, some basic challenges or choices in reading this biblical passage are perennial ones. One example of this is what to do about the absolutist language of some of Christ's statements and demands. Many of the figures presented here, beginning with John Chrysostom and Augustine, affirm that the Sermon on the Mount is not an impossible ideal, but rather a genuine charge to all believers, while Calvin notably softens several points. A range of stances are taken on specific points, however. Many of the other figures in this volume, for example, would not read Christ's words as demanding the thoroughgoing pacifism that Yoder challenges us to hear in them. Another issue is the relationship between law and gospel. Luther, of course, was attentive to this, and Wesley was particularly concerned to exclude both works-righteousness and antinomianism. Calvin insisted on the continuity of law and gospel, based on God's unchanging character. Boff was quite willing to read the Sermon on the Mount as an affirmation of love in contrast to law, while Pope John Paul II emphasized that the law was not abolished but rather fulfilled in the gospel.

Such contrasts notwithstanding, much of the theological reflection offered in these chapters is complementary rather than competitive. One does not need to choose, for example, between Wesley's emphasis on "gracious holiness" and Stott's highlighting of "Christian counter-culture." The counter-culture of a life of unceasing confrontation with the world is found in John Chrysostom and Augustine, in Luther and Calvin, as well in Bonhoeffer's well-known warning against cheap grace. All of these comments are merely suggestive rather than exhaustive. The reader will no doubt wish to add to these lists of comparisons, contrasts, and complementary themes.

The genesis of this volume was a conference on the theme "Reading the Sermon on the Mount: Classic Christian Resources for Moral Formation," held at Wheaton College (Illinois), in November 2005. We are grateful to everyone who participated in and helped with that conference. We owe a special debt of gratitude to Liz Klassen, graduate administrative assistant in the Biblical and Theological Studies Department. Not only did she serve as the conference secretary, but she also assisted us in the preparation of this manuscript. We are very grateful to the Center for Applied Christian Ethics at Wheaton College, directed at the time by Lindy Scott, for providing the primary funding for the conference. Crucial additional funding was also kindly given by the following endowed chairs: Carl Armerding and Hudson T. Armerding, Blanchard Theology, Gunther H. Knoedler, and Carolyn and Fred McManis. Finally, additional funding was providing by the dean of humanities and theological studies, Dr. Jill Peláez Baumgaertner. In addition to her support for this specific project, each of us is thankful to Jill for her ongoing leadership and support of us as members of the department of biblical and theological studies. We dedicate this volume to her as an expression of our gratitude.

John Chrysostom

Margaret M. Mitchell

How did John Chrysostom (ca. 347–407) interpret the Sermon on the Mount? In one respect, one could say that he did not interpret the Sermon on the Mount, in that Chrysostom never devoted a separate treatment (homily, treatise, or commentary) to this literary composition.[1] But he does provide an exegesis and representation of those chapters as homilies 15–24 in his set of ninety sermons on the whole of Matthew's Gospel. One could easily enough extract Chrysostom's interpretation of this part of Matthew's Gospel; but would that necessarily mean we were seeing Chrysostom's interpretation of the Sermon on the Mount, per se, as we think of it as a classic text of the Christian tradition in its own right? As I hope to show in this essay, we are justified in that inference, for in his interpretation of the Sermon, John is acutely aware of Matthew 5–7 being an oratorical or rhetorical unit, and he tries to find the structural clues to this most famous teaching discourse of Jesus within the speech itself. This is not just a matter of the literary unit, but also of genre. John interprets the Sermon on the Mount *as a sermon*, an integrated oral argument by Jesus, and—as one would expect from a late antique Christian orator who had had a rich rhetorical education from the greatest teacher of his day, Libanius—John is acutely attuned to the way in which

---

1. Compare, e.g., Gregory of Nyssa's eight homilies on the Beatitudes.

Jesus has so carefully crafted each word of this masterpiece to maximal persuasive purpose.

In 170 pages of Greek text (in the Field edition of 1839) John Chrysostom[2] has some remarkable moments of intense emotion and profound admiration of the words of Jesus, exhibits keen exegetical insight and deep moral psychology of his own, and is responsible for some lengthy digressions and arresting visual comparisons (such as the Mosaic law compared to the breast from which babies are nourished and Jesus's antitheses, which by the rhetorical form of *synkrisis*[3] move the law toward the "solid food" of adult moral engagement, said to be akin to the bitter salve a weaning mother smears on her breast to keep the child from turning back to it when words of persuasion are not sufficient).[4] Jesus in the antitheses ("you have heard it said, but I say to you") is compared to the wise doctor who prescribes preventive treatments but also attends to the pathology when it erupts (hence, the prohibition of anger, in relation to the command against murder, is a prophylactic; the prescription to be reconciled with the neighbor is the medicine for the affliction which inevitably occurs at some point).[5] In speaking of prayer in relation to Matthew 6:33 ("seek first the kingdom of God and its righteousness, and all these things will be added to you"), John explores a set of biblical characters he regards as embodying the right approach to prayer (the Syro-Phoenician woman, the friend at night, the importunate widow, the prodigal son) and then calls on his congregation to go forth in prayer *eukairōs akairōs* ("in a timely, nontimely fashion"). He resolves the paradox of his own pun in this manner: prayer, like breathing, is never "untimely."[6] Chrysostom's exegesis of the

2. For the purposes of this paper I have had to forego long discussion of John's life and historical context. I refer the reader to the excellent guides by Wendy Mayer and Pauline Allen, *John Chrysostom* (London: Routledge, 2000), and J. N. D. Kelly, *Golden Mouth: The Story of John Chrysostom—Ascetic, Preacher, Bishop* (Ithaca: Cornell University Press, 1995).

3. Frederick Field, *S. Joannis Chrysostomi homiliae in Mattheum* (Cambridge: Cambridge University Press, 1839), hom. 16.210B (1:222). All citations in this chapter are from volume 1; all translation into English are the author's.

4. hom. 17.230A–B (Field 249).

5. hom. 16.218A–C (Field 233).

6. hom. 22.283A (Field 323).

Sermon on the Mount is furthermore a canonical interpretation, in that he continually seeks to show that Jesus's teaching was echoed and affirmed also by Paul (the refrain *kai ho Paulos* occurs fully fifty times in the course of his exegesis of the Sermon).[7] And it very much bears the marks of Nicene Christology, as John explains that Jesus only appears to hide his divine nature for the sake of his hearers, Jews who might be offended if he were to name directly his relationship with the Father.[8] In this regard we should mention his derogatory characterization of "Jews" for their stubborn disobedience, vainglory, and murderous nature[9] and other moments of rather forced exegesis that quite overtly serve his contemporary purposes and biases (i.e., that Jesus's words in Matt. 6:16 against putting on a gloomy face in fasting direct a lesson against women who disfigure their faces with makeup).[10] And no survey of his interpretation would be complete without highlighting the continual exhortative refrains of John's own that

7. On the importance of Paul for Chrysostom, see Margaret M. Mitchell, *The Heavenly Trumpet: John Chrysostom and the Art of Pauline Interpretation*, Hermeneutische Untersuchungen zur Theologie 40 (Tübingen: Mohr/Siebeck, 2000; Louisville: Westminster John Knox, 2002). This has special hermeneutical weight in regard to the Sermon on the Mount, for John sees absolutely none of the tension that contemporary scholars may find between the attitude of Jesus toward the law and that of Paul or any inkling that *dikaiosynē* may not mean the same thing in both. Paul and Christ are in some sense not even separate voices for Chrysostom, as he states in hom. 23.284A, in introducing Pauline words: "For Paul, too, says this same thing [about not judging; Matt. 7:1]; but, rather, there, too, Christ was speaking through Paul . . . [Rom. 14:10]."

8. Jesus would have started with the first commandment ("the Lord your God is one God") but if he had he would have then introduced his own identity, and "it was not yet time to give any such instruction about himself" (hom. 17.222B [Field 238–39]; see also hom. 18.239A–B [Field 262]).

9. See, e.g., hom. 17.227A–C (Field 245), on how God allowed the writ of divorce in the Mosaic law to block the Jews from worse crimes, like adultery or murder: "For if God had commanded the husband to retain the hated wife in his house, the hating husband would have slaughtered her. For such is the nation of the Jews. For those who do not spare their own children, and kill prophets, and pour out blood like water, how much more would they not spare women? That is why he makes concession in a small matter, to cut off the greater."

10. Of many examples of Chrysostom's reflexive misogyny, see how in discussion of the sixth antithesis he invokes as the example of forgiveness how women childbirth attendants do not hold grudges when the laboring woman inveighs against them. This leads to the exhortation (obviously addressed to a man): "You, too, emulate them and don't be weaker than women!" (hom. 18.240C–D [264]).

21

show the pastor at work, such as the repeated call: "Let us not consider that these commandments are impossible!"[11]

These few assorted examples will, I hope, serve as a sufficient reminder that John was interpreting the Sermon on the Mount *in sermons of his own*;[12] he sought not only to explicate these words as an exegetical task of decoding their meaning, but to repreach them, to issue forth the Sermon's exhortations into his own context in the great city of Antioch in the 390s.[13] The utmost seriousness with which he takes this responsibility should not escape us. He sees his own eschatological salvation at stake in whether he presses his case urgently enough and can even envision with a shudder the possibility of his ultimate failure to repreach the Sermon on the Mount effectively: "For none of the people who are rich now will protect me then, when I am indicted and accused of not having defended the laws of God with suitable vehemence."[14] At one point in his own sermon after inveighing against swearing oaths, his audience breaks into applause. John rebukes them by saying, "This clapping for me is praise? If you praise what is said but do not do what you praise, then the punishment is greater, the accusation more severe, and for us it is shame and ridicule."[15]

But within his extended and multifaceted repreaching of Jesus's Sermon on the Mount, I wish to demonstrate that Chrysostom works from and expounds an integrated sense of the overall purpose and import of Matthew 5–7. He understands the Sermon on the Mount as the foundational speech—now become the charter document—of the Christian *politeia* that constitutes the life of

11. hom. 18.236D–E (Field 258); hom. 21.273A (Field 310); also "for none of the things he has commanded are burdensome or odious" (hom. 22.280E [Field 320]).

12. On the problem with treating Chrysostom as a commentator akin to modern critical commentaries, see my *Heavenly Trumpet* and "Reading Rhetoric with Patristic Exegetes: John Chrysostom on Galatians," in *Antiquity and Humanity: Essays on Ancient Religion and Philosophy Presented to Hans Dieter Betz on His 70th Birthday*, ed. Adela Yarbro Collins and Margaret M. Mitchell (Tübingen: Mohr/Siebeck, 2001), 333–55.

13. So Johannes Quasten, *Patrology*, vol. 3: *The Golden Age of Greek Patristic Literature* (Westminster, MD: Newman, 1960), 437, with reference to the statement in hom. 7 that "our city was the first to have the name 'Christians' attached to it" (cf. Acts 11:26).

14. *hotan enkalōmai kai katēgorōmai hōs mē meta tēs prosēkousēs sphodrotētos tous tou theou diekdikēsas nomous*; hom. 17.233B (Field 254).

15. hom. 17.232D (Field 253).

all Christians, who are called to a philosophical life lived always within an eschatological horizon. It is a *logos peri politeias*.[16] In the Sermon Jesus, through both protreptic and apotreptic rhetoric,[17] with a focus on the rewards and punishments of the future and those of the present, instructs (*didaskein, paideuein*) his disciples in the life-forms of a Christian philosophy, what he terms a greater philosophy (*pleiōn philosophia*) or "the height of philosophy" (*akros philosophias*).[18] Chrysostom's interpretation of the Sermon on the Mount in this way is fashioned by two major, prevailing concerns: his attention to the rhetorical composition of the Sermon (viewing Christ as, like Chrysostom himself, a skilled and deliberate speaker whose intent can be discovered through the *akolouthia*, or logical progression of the discourse)[19] and his apologetic concern to demonstrate that the Christian way of life is superior to all others in the history of humankind.

Chrysostom's careful attention to the composition of the Sermon on the Mount can be seen immediately in his homily 15. He insists first that the placement and introduction Matthew has given to the mountaintop discourse (Matt. 5:1–2) are meant to demonstrate the integrated but dual-pronged ministry of Jesus both to heal bodies (*sōmata therapeuein*, as indicated in the summary statement about Jesus's miracles in 4:23–24) and to correct souls (*psychas diōrthoun*,

16. This aspect of Chrysostom's interpretation is surprisingly not represented in Jaroslav Pelikan, *Divine Rhetoric: The Sermon on the Mount as Message and as Model in Augustine, Chrysostom, and Luther* (Crestwood, NY: St. Vladimir's Seminary Press, 2000), 139–44, which focuses on the Sermon's language of *basileia*, but not how Chrysostom aligns it with *politeia*.

17. The rhetorical terms *protrepein* and *apotrepein* are frequently used in these homilies; see, e.g., hom. 15.188C (Field 191): *oute gar apo tōn mellontōn agathōn protrepei monon, alla kai apo tōn parontōn* ("for he persuades them not only by appeal to future goods, but also to present ones"). In hom. 21.270D, 271C (Field 306–7) John analyzes the rhetorical heads Jesus uses: not only an appeal to advantage (*ta sympheronta*) but also to what is possible (*dynata*), and appeals to *paradeigmata*, or examples (in reference to Matt. 6:25). This language is found throughout the homilies.

18. Of many instances see, e.g., hom. 17.222A (Field 238), hom. 18.235B (Field 256), and hom. 18.238D (Field 261) for *hypsos philosophias*; and hom. 21.273D–E (Field 310) for *meizōn philosophia*.

19. See hom. 16.213D (Field 227): *anankaion de epi to prokeimenon elthein, kai tēs akolouthias echesthai tōn emprosthen eirēmenōn* ("but it is necessary to go to what stands before this, and to attend to the logical progression of the things that were said previously").

which is the essential purpose of the Sermon).[20] Jesus's care for both body and soul explains a variegated ministry that combines, for maximal benefit (*ōpheleia*), "the teaching of his words and the demonstrable proof from his deeds" (*anamignys tē tōn logōn didaskalia tēn apo tōn ergōn epideixin*).[21] The rhetorical commonplace of *logos/ergon* ("word/deed") is used by John not only to demonstrate consistency in the ministry of Jesus (i.e., he practiced what he preached), but also perhaps to draw a direct contrast that his own audience would recognize, but we might miss: between Plato and Jesus, for it was a commonplace that, while Apollo gave the power to heal souls to Plato, he gave the ability to heal bodies to Asclepius.[22] Christ bests both by combining philosopher and healer in a holistic ministry to save soul *and* body. (Full demonstration that this comparison may be in effect will be given below.)

As often in late antique Christian oratory, John seeks to fight on two fronts—against unbelievers and against heretical Christians. He claims that by this providential divine care (*pronoia*) of bodies and souls Jesus was proleptically "muzzling the shameless mouths of the heretics" (*ta anaischynta tōn airetikōn emphrattōn stomata*)[23] of John's own day, whose ontological dualism denies the essential unity of the human person by attributing to God responsibility for only one half of the creature (the soul) and not the other (the body) (he has in mind Marcionites and possibly Manichees or Gnostics).

But this is a passing concern. John returns to the word/deed contrast when he confronts the introductory phrase in Matthew 5:2: *kai anoixas to stoma autou edidasken autous*. What we might regard as a Semitic pleonasm in Matthew (probably due to the Septuagint translation of such phrases as *pt /p h ph* with *anoigein to stoma*)[24] is for John an opportunity for more emphasis on this

20. hom. 15.184E (Field 186).
21. hom. 15.184E (Field 186).
22. See the epigrams preserved in Diogenes Laertius 3.45: *kai gar ho toude gegōs Asklēpios estin iētēr sōmatos, hōs psychēs athanatoio Platōn* ("for [Phoebus's] son Asclepius is a healer of the body, and Plato of the immortal soul"); *Phoibos ephyse brotois Asklēpion ēde Platōna, ton men hina psychēn, ton d' hina sōma saoi* ("Phoebus brought forth for mortals Asclepius and Plato, the one that he might save the soul, the other the body").
23. hom. 15.184E (Field 186).
24. E.g., Ps. 38:14 MT (= 37:14 LXX); Prov. 31:8, 9; Job 35:16; Isa. 53:7; cf. Acts 8:35; 10:34. On the "Semitic redundancy" see W. D. Davies and D. C. Allison Jr., *Matthew*

integrated psychology as the basis for human ethical conduct: "Why did he [Matthew] add the phrase 'and opening his mouth'? So that you might learn that even when silent Christ was teaching, not only when giving utterance, but at one time he teaches by opening his mouth, and at another by giving voice through his deeds."[25] So, for Chrysostom, the Sermon on the Mount is the "open-mouthed" portion of the teaching of Jesus.

It is at this point that John takes up for the first time what has always been and remains still one of the most famous hermeneutical cruxes of the Sermon on the Mount—to whom was it addressed, and hence for whom does its ethical guidelines apply? The exegetical issue for John is simply named: what is the antecedent of the pronoun *autous* in "he was teaching them" (*edidasken autous*)? The immediate context of Matthew 5:1 provides two possibilities: *hoi ochloi* ("the crowds"; cf. 7:28) or *hoi mathētai* ("the disciples"), who had approached Jesus after he went up onto the mountain and had taken a seat. John has a deft solution to what appears a difficult dichotomy, which he bases upon the educational elitism of his day. As often in these homilies, John's rhetoric is cast in apotreptic form, warning his audience against what he takes to be a false or at least inadequate interpretation:

> When you hear that "he was teaching them," don't think that he was speaking to the disciples alone, but also through them to all. For since the crowd was common folk [*dēmōdes*], and still composed of people who are dragged down to the ground,[26] by setting the chorus of the disciples as a foundation, he addresses his words to them. In his discourse to them he provides also to all the rest—who are greatly in need[27] of what was being said—instruction in philosophy [*tēs philosophias hē didaskalia*] which is not burdensome.[28]

1–7, International Critical Commentary (Edinburgh: Clark, 1988), 1.425–26.

25. hom. 15.185A (Field 186–87).

26. Other manuscripts read *erchomenōn* ("coming to the ground"), apparently taking this to mean that the crowd stayed at the bottom of the mountain.

27. The Greek phrase *tois sphodra apodeousi tōn legomenōn* could also mean that they "were greatly inferior to what was being said"; see Henry George Liddell, Robert Scott, and Henry Stuart Jones, *A Greek-English Lexicon*, 9th ed. (Oxford: Clarendon, 1976), 196, s.v. *apodeō* (B).

28. hom. 15.185A–B (Field 187).

John substantiates his interpretation that Jesus intentionally instituted a kind of two-tiered philosophical *paideia* by recourse to the introduction that Luke places on the Sermon on the Plain: "And Jesus, after raising his eyes to his disciples, was saying," which John takes as a "hint" (*ainittesthai*) from the evangelist that "he was diverting his teaching to them [i.e., the disciples]."[29] Matthew was doing the same thing, John says, by his introduction (Matt. 5:1–2). Both evangelists in John's eyes captured accurately Jesus's own intention, that by this stratagem of focusing on the better-equipped disciples "the rest [*hoi loipoi*] would attend more fervently than if Jesus had extended his speech to them all."[30]

What John means by the philosophical instruction (*tēs philosophias hē didaskalia*) Jesus offers becomes clear in what follows. He asks a leading question that is at once exegetical and philosophical: "From where then does Jesus begin [*pothen archetai*],[31] and what sort of foundations [*themelia*] does he lay down for us for the new *politeia* [*hē kainē politeia*]?"[32] In one sense the question is about the *prooimion* to Jesus's speech; in another it is about the cornerstone of the philosophical curriculum that he teaches. Before answering this crucial leading question, John enunciates two brief hermeneutical principles that readers of his vast corpus of writings will find immediately familiar: *akousōmen meta akribeias tōn legomenōn* ("let us listen with precision to what is said") and *eirētai men gar pros ekeinous, egraphē de kai dia tous meta tauta hapantas* ("for these things have been said to them, but they were written also for all those who come after").[33] The first methodological standard means that the Sermon on the Mount

---

29. hom. 15.185B (Field 187).

30. hom. 15.185B (Field 187).

31. Throughout his treatment of the Sermon on the Mount John emphasizes the importance of "beginnings": the Beatitudes as beginning of the whole, the first beatitude's call to humility as the appropriate beginning (hom. 15.188B [Field 190]); the first commandment treated in the antitheses (hom. 16.210D–E [Field 223]; hom. 17.222B–D [Field 239]); the second "beginning" of *how* to carry out the philosophical life to which he calls them in Matt. 5, through the practices of Matt. 6: *kai hora pothen archetai apo nēsteias, kai euchēs, kai eleēmosynēs* (hom. 19.244B–C [Field 269]).

32. hom. 15.185C (Field 187).

33. hom. 15.185C (Field 187). In another context John emphasizes that, unlike Zeno or Plato, Jesus did not write his *politeia* (*Adversus Judaeos* 48.886: *ho de Christos ouk egrapse politeian monon, alla kai pantachou tēs oikoumenēs autēn katephyteuse*).

as recorded in Matthew must be read with absolute attention for exact details (*akribeia*), because that is the way in which it was composed.[34] John frequently insists that Jesus did not say anything *haplōs* ("simply") or in any offhand fashion,[35] but chose his words with exquisite, deliberate care at each turn.

The second principle zeroes in on a third dimension of the exegetical chasm John had just sought to bridge (the speech was not directly to *either* the disciples or the crowds, but to all through the mediating role of the disciples). The transference of the Sermon from the oral to the written medium, John celebrates, brought about also a tremendous shift of audience. Spoken aloud, the Sermon had a particular set of historical auditors; once written, it stands as philosophical teaching for all those who live later. John finds this ecclesiological scriptural hermeneutic etched in the very words of the text, for the Matthean Beatitudes, written in the third person, pronounce not just the disciples blessed, but all in the future who fit the various designations ("blessed are the poor in spirit"). Perhaps because he remembers that the Lukan Beatitudes *are* in second person, John quickly corrects himself by saying that even if Jesus had said "blessed are you," and so on, the meaning would still have accrued to all people in common down the ages, as it must for the final line of Matthew's Gospel, spoken to the eleven disciples on a mountaintop once more: "Behold I am with *you* all the days, until the completion of the age" (28:20).[36] John finds confirmation of the principle of open addressees also in particular exegetical details of the Sermon itself, such as the blessing on the poor in spirit, which seems unnecessary as an exhortation to the disciples who, as lowly fishermen, unnotable and unskilled, would hardly need warning off from the braggadocio that is the opposite of *tapeinophrosynē* ("humility"): *hē tapeinophrosynē philosophias hapasēs archē* ("humility is the

34. See Robert C. Hill, "Akribeia: A Principle of Chrysostom's Exegesis," *Colloquium* 14 (1981): 32–36.
35. All interpreters use this "text-focusing mechanism" to lay claim to a particular element of the writing as a hermeneutical key. It is equally useful for readings that are literal and those that are allegorical, as well as the many that are somewhere on the spectrum between.
36. hom. 15.185C (Field 187).

beginning of all philosophy").[37] The clear explanation of this apparent anomaly, John thinks, is that Jesus said this with others in mind—both at that time and all who would come later—who might by life-position and achievements regard themselves too highly and hence needed to be persuaded to humility. Indeed, he says, Jesus even was speaking proleptically to the later state of the disciples in the success of their future mission years, after they had distinguished themselves by signs and wonders, worldly honor, and boldness before God and might be tempted to boast in their efforts. Hence the Sermon on the Mount is a speech spoken, and then written, with a simultaneous holographic eye on all times and circumstances in which it may pertain.

But what is the *politeia* that John imagines that Jesus fashioned here orally to be set down in written form for all generations? If we look at the full scope of Chrysostom's homilies on Matthew's Gospel, we can see that for John this *politeia* is a comprehensive vision of human life and society that has utterly vanquished every other option, in particular that of Plato's famous *Republic* (in Greek, *Politeia*). For proof of this contention we must go back to the first homily in the set of *homiliae in Matthaeum*. John begins his treatment of Matthew's Gospel by taking on the apologetic task, necessitated both by anti-Christian polemic[38] and "heretical" Christian complaint that the four canonical gospels vary from one another. John seeks to turn that apparent deficit into proof of their veracity, by insisting that the extent to which the four agree with one another is unaccountable proof that they gave true testimony to the same historical events. John allows that there is variability in wording and expression (*mē rhēmata ta auta . . . eipein, kai tropous lexeōn*), but insists this does not amount to discord (*diaphōnia*) or contradiction. It is at this point that he offers, by way of *paraleipsis* (pretended omission), a rhetorical comparison (*synkrisis*) with the unruly "canon" of Greek philosophical writings, which can hardly live up to the expectation of complete accord:

37. hom. 15.186D (Field 189).
38. Such as Porphyry and Julian (whom John has in his sights in other writings [*On Babylas*, for example] as the metonymy of the "pagan" critic, probably because Julian was resident in Antioch when John was a teenager).

And I have not yet mentioned that the men who are so greatly celebrated for rhetorical and philosophical prowess [*hoi mega epi rhētorikē kai philosophia kompazontes*], when they wrote so many books about the same topics [*polloi polla biblia grapsantes peri tōn autōn pragmatōn*], also disagreed, not only incidentally, but they even spoke in contradictory fashion to one another [*ou monon haplōs diephōnēsan, alla kai enantiōs allēlois eipon*].[39] Now, it is one thing to say something in different words, and another to engage in a war of words [*kai gar heteron esti diaphorōs eipein, kai machomenous eipein*]! But may I not compose a defense from the madness of those philosophers [*ek tēs ekeinōn paranoias*], since I certainly do not wish to establish what is true from what is false.

Having introduced and then dropped the comparison for the moment, John goes on to rejoice in the triumph of the Christian gospel in his time, issuing a giddy declaration of the paradoxical success of worldwide Christianity in the late fourth century (indeed, remember, he is speaking in the very years in which Theodosius I was promulgating laws against traditional cults and rites):

For, after they composed the gospels, they did not bury them in a single corner, but they were spread out everywhere on land and sea by the ears of all. And even in the presence of enemies these things were being read, just as is the case even now, and none of the things said was a stumbling block to anyone. And that is rightly so. For a divine power was attending all and ensuring success in all ventures. Since if this were not the case, how was it that the tax collector, and the fisherman, and men who were illiterate were teaching a philosophy of such caliber [*epei ei mē touto ēn, pōs ho telōnēs, kai ho alieus, kai ho agrammatos toiauta ephilosophei*]? For that which the outsiders could not ever have imagined, not even in a dream, that is what these very men proclaim and persuade with such assurance [*tauta*

39. The divergence among the philosophers and philosophical schools was itself a philosophical problem that needed to be accounted for; see, e.g., the discussion in Cicero, *de Finibus* 4.3; and Numenius of Apamea, frags. 24–28, from his treatise *Peri tēs tōn akadēmaikōn pros Platōna diastaseōs* (E. des Places, *Numénius, fragments* [Paris: Les Belles Lettres, 1973]). For discussion in relation to second- and third-century Christian apologetic texts, see A. J. Droge, "Self-Definition vis-à-vis the Graeco-Roman World," in *Cambridge History of Christianity*, vol. 1: *Origins to Constantine*, ed. Margaret M. Mitchell and Frances M. Young (Cambridge: Cambridge University Press, 2006), 235–37.

houtoi meta pollēs tēs plērophorias kai apangellousi kai peithous]—and not only when living, but also after they died. Not 22 men, nor 100, or 1,000 or 10,000s, but cities and nations and peoples, both land and sea, both Greek and barbarian, both civilized and uninhabited territories.[40]

So, John claims, the gospel has converted all of humanity. But what was the philosophical message brought by these unlikely apostolic envoys?

They spoke about matters that very much transcend our nature [*kai peri pragmatōn sphodra tēn hēmeteran hyperbainontōn physin*]. For having left the earth, they discoursed entirely about matters in heaven [*tēn gar gēn aphentes, panta peri tōn en ouranois dialegontai*], introducing another life [*hetera zōē*] to us and another lifestyle [*bios allos*], both wealth and poverty, freedom and slavery, life and death, cosmos and *politeia*, everything transformed [*kai ploutos kai penia, kai eleutheria kai douleia, kai zōē kai thanatos, kai kosmos kai politeia, panta exēllagmena*].[41]

At this point John brings the full force of the *synkrisis* to bear:

Not like Plato, who composed that ridiculous *politeia* [*ou kathaper Platōn, ho tēn katagelaston ekeinēn politeian syntheis*], and Zeno, and anyone else who wrote a *politeia* [*kai Zēnōn, kai ei tis heteros politeian egrapsen*], or laid down laws [*ē nomous synethēken*]. Indeed, inadvertently these men were showing that an evil spirit and some wild demon combats against our nature and is an enemy of moderate behavior, one who battles against good order; doing everything from start to finish, he resounded in their soul. For when they make wives common to all,[42] and stripping virgins naked they lead them to the *palaestra* before the eyes of men,[43] and they confirm clandestine marriages, mixing and shaking up everything together, and overturning the boundaries of nature, what else can one say? . . . And, mind you, these things came not with persecutions, with dangers, or with wars, but with security and complete freedom they

40. hom. 1.8B–C (Field 7).
41. hom. 1.8C–9A (Field 8).
42. *Republic* 5.449D–450C.
43. *Republic* 5.452A–B.

30

wrote them and gave them polish for the many from many angles. But it was the things spoken by the fishermen, who were dragged about, whipped, in constant danger, that both the untrained and the wise, both slaves and free, both kings and soldiers, both barbarians and Greeks received with complete favor.[44]

Although in passing John offers some moralistic barbs here against Plato for wife-swapping and other stereotypical deficits (dismissing his *politeia* as "laughable" [*katagelastos*]),[45] John's essential point is that the Christian message is the preeminent philosophy as proven by the fact that it has done what none other in history has—met with worldwide acceptance. What Chrysostom means by a philosophy (*philosophia*) is both a system of thought and a characteristic set of practices constituting a *bios* (as Pierre Hadot stresses is true of Greek philosophy generally).[46]

44. hom. 1.9C–10A (Field 8).

45. Chrysostom is turning the rhetoric of the dialogue back on itself in this insult, for Socrates introduced these teachings on the matters of women with an acknowledgement that, in the light of present custom, they seem *geloia* ("laughable") (*Republic* 5.452A). Most of the elements that Chrysostom mentions about Plato's *Politeia* are found in the brief summary at the beginning of the *Timaeus* (17A–19C). On Chrysostom's knowledge of Plato, see Chrysostomos Baur, *John Chrysostom and His Time*, trans. M. Gonzaga (Westminster, MD: Newman, 1959), 1.305–14; and the important earlier work of Anton Naegele, "Johannes Chrysostomos und sein Verhältnis zum Hellenismus," *Byzantinische Zeitschrift* 13 (1904): 73–113, who did much to overturn earlier scholarship that took Chrysostom's rhetorical repudiation of Plato and classical learning literally and at face value. A partial advance on the influence of Plato in particular was represented by P. R. Coleman-Norton, "St. Chrysostom and the Greek Philosophers," *Classical Philology* 25 (1930): 305–17, but his approach—just listing Chrysostom's statements on various philosophers extracted from their contexts—prohibited precisely what is needed: an analysis of the rhetorical uses that John was making of any mention of the Greek philosophers. But the force of Chrysostom's polemics was not easily overturned; Jean Dumortier, for instance, allowed for knowledge and admiration of Plato in John's youthful ascetic writings, but thought he eschewed it in later life; "La culture profane de S. Jean Chrysostome," *Mélanges de science religieuse* 10 (1953): 53–62. More recent scholarship recognizes that Chrysostom tensively wishes to both draw upon and praise Plato in order to make the comparison with Christian communities who come off as his better; see E. A. Clark "The Virginal Politeia and Plato's Republic: John Chrysostom on Women and the Sexual Relation," in her *Jerome, Chrysostom, and Friends: Essays and Translations*, Studies in Women and Religion 2 (New York: Mellen, 1983), 1–34; further discussion and literature in Mitchell, *Heavenly Trumpet*, 240–50.

46. Pierre Hadot, *Philosophy as a Way of Life: Spiritual Exercises from Socrates to Foucault*, trans. M. Chase (Oxford: Blackwell, 1995); and idem, *What Is Ancient Philosophy?* trans. M. Chase (Cambridge: Harvard University Press, 2002).

The Christian philosophy as John sees it has answers to the same topics as the great philosophical dialogues of old—ethics (life, lifestyle),[47] politics (freedom and slavery, the *politeia*), metaphysics ("cosmos" = cosmogony/cosmology), life and death, and "nature" (*physis*)—and better, more persuasive answers, at that. The *politeia*, correspondingly, is the sphere within which this Christian *philosophia* is carried out. Here the multivalence of the term, in both the Greek philosophical writers and the Christians who take it up, works so nicely, for it can refer to "citizenship," "the daily life of a citizen," "body of citizens," "government," "civil polity or the state," or "republican government, free commonwealth."[48] In Chrysostom *politeia* means both the company of citizens in their civil polity and the behavior appropriate to that polity. But it is not the earthly empire of the Roman emperor Theodosius I (379–95) that he has in mind. His concept of the Christian *politeia* is a "heavenly *politeia*" (which can be traced back at least to Paul in Phil. 3:20: *hēmōn gar to politeuma en ouranois hyparchei*; cf. 1:27: *monon axiōs tou euangeliou tou Christou politeuesthe*),[49] one that is also defined in relation to its opposite.

As we have seen, John invokes Plato and Zeno—the two most famous authors of *politeiai* in Greek antiquity—as just two representatives of the whole of Greek thought. But that John has Plato's *Republic* in an even more specific sense in mind is clear by where he returns to the theme of Jesus's *politeia* in his homilies on the Sermon on the Mount proper. Where he does so is in regard to the eighth beatitude: *makarioi hoi dediōgmenoi heneken dikaiosynēs* ("blessed are those who have been persecuted for the sake of justice"). Plato's *Republic*, of course, arguably the most fa-

47. Even where the practices may overlap (in regard to placing limits on possessions, like the Cynics, or cultivating an attitude of *apatheia*, like the Stoics), the Christian *philosophia* is superior, John says, because of the rationale and judgment behind it (hom. 21, 273E–274A [Field 311]).

48. Glosses as listed in Liddell, Scott, and Jones, *Greek-English Lexicon*, 1434. Compare G. W. H. Lampe, *A Patristic Greek Lexicon* (Oxford: Clarendon, 1961), 1113–14: "citizenship, citizen rights," "polity, constitution," "regulation, order, for conduct of civil affairs," organized society, commonwealth, state," "civil affairs," "way of life," "ascetic practice, act of religious behaviour."

49. See also Epistle to Diognetus 5.9: *epi gēs diatribousin, all' en ouranō politeuontai*.

mous dialogue on the political order produced by the Greeks, was entitled *Peri dikaiou, politikos*—"a political discourse concerning justice" (*to dikaion* or, virtually interchangeably in the dialogue, *hē dikaiosynē*).[50] John regards this justice (*hē dikaiosynē*), as did Plato, as rooted in one's theory of the soul. Jesus, he says, "was accustomed always to say that the entire philosophy of the soul is justice" (*dikaiosynēn gar eiōthen aei tēn hapasan legein tēs psychēs philosophian*).[51] And it is here again that John returns to the motif of the triumph of the Christian philosophy—as enscripted in the words of Jesus:

> What could be more new than these commands, when Jesus says that things which others flee from are to be desired—I mean, to live in poverty, to mourn, to be persecuted, and to hear calumny against oneself. But nevertheless, Jesus both said it and he convinced, not 2 or 10 or 20 or 100 or 1,000 people, but the entire world! For even as they heard things that were burdensome and vexing, thoroughly opposed to the customs held by many, "the crowds were amazed."[52]

Collapsing the narrative auditors of Matthew 7:28 (*hoi ochloi*) into the rising Christian demographics in his own late-fourth-century context, John proclaims Jesus's *politeia* to be Plato's conqueror. For a final time later in his homilies on Matthew, when treating Matthew 24:13 ("the one who endures to the end will be saved"), Chrysostom will dance on the grave of Greek philosophy with the following taunts:

> Where now is Plato? Where Pythagoras? Where the string of Stoics? For the former [Plato], having enjoyed great honor, was so reproved as even to be sold off, and he accomplished none of the things he wished, not even in the case of a single tyrant [i.e., Dionysius of Sicily]. But after even betraying his students, mercifully he left this life. Also the Cynic "offscourings" have all passed away like a dream and a shadow. Although such never completely be-

---

50. See, e.g., *Republic* 331C–E; 332B. It is unclear precisely when this title comes into the manuscript traditions, but no reader of the dialogue could miss this thematic focus on justice.

51. hom. 15.190C (Field 194).

52. hom. 15.190C–D (Field 194–95).

fell them, but on account of the "outsiders'" philosophy they were considered even luminaries; the Athenians publicly dedicated the letters of Plato sent when he was with Dion, and they lived at rest their whole lives, endowed with no small amount of riches. Indeed in this way Aristippus used to buy himself expensive prostitutes; he wrote a will, leaving no chance inheritance. After his disciples had built a bridge, he strode upon it. They say that the man of Sinope [Diogenes the Cynic] even used to publicly perform disgraceful things in the marketplace. For to them these acts are dignified. But we find no such thing here [in the Christian *politeia*], but appropriate modesty [*sōphrosynē*] is commanded and decorum [*kosmiotēs*] precisely kept.[53]

Chrysostom's overarching image of the Christian *politeia* that Jesus offers is that it is an angelic *politeia*, a "heavenly *politeia*." This, too, is a trumping of Plato, for his *politeia* was also described—in one of the most well-known passages in the dialogue that comes at the end of book 9—by Socrates in these terms:

"I understand," he [Glaucon] said, "you are speaking of the city in which we have now come to set up our dwelling, the city which is established in words [*polei . . . tē en logois keimenē*], since I do not suppose it exists anywhere on earth [*epei gēs ge oudamou oimai autēn einai*]." "But," I [Socrates] said, "perhaps a pattern of it is laid up in heaven for the person who wishes to look at it, and by gazing upon it to settle him or herself there [*en ouranō isōs paradeigma anakeitai tō boulomenō hopan kai hopōnti heauton katoikizein*]." (*Republic* 9.592B)

Chrysostom dwells on the paradox that Christians are called to live the heavenly *politeia* already now on earth. What are its contours? Jesus's *politeia*, for John, is both an ethical template and heavenly polity, characterized by *aretē* ("excellence, virtue"). This aggregate concept refers to a hybrid table of virtues formed from the Platonic cardinal virtues, Jewish-Christian cultic practice, and the popular Stoicism that informed Christian asceticism from early on. He is able to find them all on the lips of Jesus in the Sermon on the Mount. *Aretē* ("excellence in virtue") includes

---

53. hom. 33.382A–C (Field 465–66).

agapē ("love," "the root of all virtues"),[54] *dikaiosynē* ("justice"), *eleēmosynē* ("almsgiving"), *aktēmosynē* ("living without possessions"),[55] *tapeinophrosynē* ("humility"), *sōphrosynē* ("moderation" or "chastity"), and *hyperopsia tōn chrēmatōn* ("disdain for possessions"). Yet this Christian *politeia*, John stresses, is not just a laundry list of unconnected commands. He insists that the very order and priority in the literary progression of the Sermon demonstrates that Jesus taught an integrated moral psychology. The key to this is John's understanding of the Beatitudes as the "beginning" (*archē*) that describes the disposition of the citizen of heaven:

> For the one who is humble also will mourn over his own sins; and the one who mourns will also be meek and just and merciful; the one who is merciful and just and contrite is also completely pure in heart; and such a person is also a peacemaker; and the one who has succeeded in all these things will be well positioned in the face of danger and will not be perturbed when they hear badly of themselves or suffer countless terrible things.[56]

The Sermon on the Mount gives the building blocks of the life of virtue (*hē aretē tou biou*), the proof for which is outward deeds.[57] John adds his exhortation to Jesus's own in Matthew 5:14–16: "So shine your whole life, and take no account of those who slander you. For it is not possible—it is not possible—for the one who attends to virtue not to have many enemies."[58] Again here he draws the polemical comparison with the Greek philosophers:

> For what will be our defense, finally, when human glory had such a strong pull on the Greek philosophers [*para tois Hellēnōn philosophois*], but among us the fear of God does not? For even some of them divested of their possessions and despised death [*chrēmata apedysanto, kai thanatou katephronēsan*], so that they might make an appearance before people. And therefore their hopes have been in vain. Then what argument will rescue us—when such great things

54. hom. 19.255B (Field 284).
55. hom. 20.261D (Field 294).
56. hom. 15.193B–C (Field 198).
57. hom. 15.197B (Field 205).
58. hom. 15.197E (Field 205).

lie before us, and such a great philosophy has been opened to us [*tosautēs philosophias hēmin anoichtheisēs*]—if we are not able to do the same things they did, but we destroy both ourselves and others. For nothing so destroys Greek folly as a Christian doing these things. And rightly so. For the glory of those philosophers has perished; but our glory, for the sake of the grace of God, is both distinguished and widely manifest among the impious.[59]

The glory (or "reputation," *doxa*) of the Greek philosophers was all they had, for their "hopes" were unjustified. On that basis even virtuous deeds by those sages (including some of the same practices that John sees as crucial to the Christian *politeia*, like *aktēmosynē* and *apatheia*) are bankrupt. The comparison here serves not just as pretext for the celebration of the demise of Greek philosophy (which, we should at least pause to mention, is more than a bit premature on John's part!), but it is meant to goad John's own audience of Christians to live up to the expectation of the "open philosophy" now set before them by Jesus.[60]

Part of that "open philosophy" is Jesus's clear declaration of laws greater than those of old (*meizona tōn palaiōn . . . nomothetein parangelmatōn*), which "make the path that leads to a divine and heavenly *politeia*" (*kai theias tinos kai ouraniou politeias temnein hodon*).[61] In striking contrast to the earlier discussion, in which even similarities in virtue-theory and praxis between Christians and Greek philosophers are deemed disjunctive, here John does not declare Jesus's *politeia* the vanquisher of the old, the Mosaic law.[62] Rather, it is the "breast" from which the followers of the old law must now be weaned, as they move into adulthood in the new

59. hom. 15.198B–C (Field 205).

60. This strategy is used again, e.g., in John's interpretation of Matt. 6:25–26 on *aktēmosynē* ("living without possessions"): "Although among the Greeks some even accomplished this—except without the right meaning—and divested themselves of all the goods they had. . . . But if we don't do even this, what kind of excuse would we deserve, we who are commanded to go beyond the laws in the Old [Covenant], and appear as less than the Greek philosophers? What might we say, when, though we should be angels and sons of God, we don't manage to maintain being human?" (hom. 21.273E–274A [Field 311]).

61. hom. 16.203B (Field 212).

62. This is why we do not find in these homilies any trace of the commonplace argument in Jewish and Christian apologetics that Plato had learned from Moses.

politeia.[63] Crucial to John's interpretation is the observation (held also by many modern scholars) that Matthew 5:17–20 is a crucial pivot from the cornerstone of the Beatitudes into the antitheses that follow. John takes the negative phrasing of 5:17 ("do not think that I have come to destroy the law or the prophets") as an "anticipatory correction" (terming it the rhetorical figure *prodiorthōsis*)[64] of a possible misreading by his audience of the antithetical statements that will follow. Against Marcionites and others, John wants to insist that Jesus's lawgiving (which is also God's) is *not* a contradiction of the Mosaic laws, but rather stands in complete continuity with those divine ordinances.[65] Otherwise, John notes, the suspicion might take hold that Jesus is *antitheos* ("against God").[66] Indeed (as John will insist throughout these homilies) Jesus customarily spoke words of humility in the Sermon (as contrasted with John's Gospel, with which Chrysostom compares this) so as to cloak his divine nature (*theotēs*) by condescension so that the Jews might be receptive to what he says.[67] Jesus is a lawgiver (*nomothetēs*), not an interpreter of the law of Moses. The new laws issued by Jesus effect a weaning process for the religiously mature who are ready for solid food (surely 1 Cor. 3:1–3 is behind his image).

John also exegetes the positive side of the statement ("not to destroy . . . but to fulfil"), arguing that Christ did so in three ways:

63. hom. 17.230A–231A (Field 249–50).

64. Defined by the rhetorician Alexander (second century) as "when we are going to say something which requires some curative attention so that the hearer does not receive it with great difficulty" (*prodiorthōsis estin, hotan mellōmen ti toiouton legein, ho deitai tinos therapeias, hōste mē chalepōs auto prosdexasthai ton akroatēn*); Leonard Spengel, *Rhetores graeci* (Leipzig: Teubner, 1856), 3.14. I here have to disagree with Pelikan's blanket statement: "On theological as well as historical grounds, Christian rhetors expounding the Sermon on the Mount would have rejected any notion that Christ, the Only-begotten Son and immortal Word of God, was subject to the rhetorical principles of Classical Greece and Rome" (*Divine Rhetoric*, 97). Indeed, Chrysostom thinks Jesus used these techniques, and he praises him for it.

65. "He begins the lawgiving, finally, in no simple fashion, but by way of a comparison [*synkrisis*] with the old legal ordinances [*ta palaia nomima*], wishing to show two things: that he lays down these laws [*tauta nomothetei*] not contradicting [*machomenos*] the former, but very much in harmony with them [*symphōnōn*], and in a very timely fashion he adds [*prostithei*] the second ones [*ta deutera*] to the former" (hom. 16.210B [Field 222]).

66. hom. 16.203D–E (Field 213).

67. hom. 16.203E–205C (Field 211–13).

(1) by never transgressing a commandment, (2) by answering the foretellings of the prophets and being a source of *dikaiosynē* for his followers (by way of Rom. 10:4), and (3) by handing on a *nomothesia* ("lawgiving") for the future, one that was not a destruction of the old (*ou . . . anairesis*), but an extension (*epitasis*)[68] and fulfillment (*plērōsis*) of it.[69] John insists that the command against becoming angry does not destroy that prohibiting murder, but fulfils and secures it; this is the case with all the other antitheses, as well. That "heaven and earth will not pass away before all these things come to pass" is a deliberate "hint" (*ainittesthai*) from Jesus that the universe is being transformed, which is meant to stir the hearer and show justly that Jesus is introducing a new *politeia*, which involved the calling of humanity to a new (heavenly) *patris* ("homeland") and *biou paraskeuē hypsēloterou* ("provision for a higher life").[70]

We can see this overarching concept of *politeia* ("Christian republic") at work also in Chrysostom's exegesis of the Lord's Prayer (Matt. 6:9–13). Taking up the first line, John says, "For the person who has called God 'Father,' indeed, 'common Father' [*patēr koinos*], might be sufficiently just [*dikaios*] to demonstrate such a great *politeia* as not to appear unworthy of this noble family, and show an eagerness equal to the gift."[71] The fourth petition in the prayer ("let your will come to pass on earth as in heaven") serves perfectly John's view that while living on earth (*entautha diatribontes*) believers are called "to eagerly demonstrate the same *politeia* as those above" (*spoudazein tēn autēn tois anō politeian epideiknysthai*).[72] Here John urges a *politeia* that simultaneously overcomes both the cosmological *and* chronological divide that he assumes stands between heaven and earth: "Even *before heaven* [Christ] commands us *to make earth heaven*, and while living on earth to conduct ourselves as citizens [*politeuomenoi*] there [*hōs ekei*]."[73] Whereas Plato's heaven was inhabited by the gods (and,

---

68. Or "intensification"; see Liddell, Scott, and Jones, *Greek-English Lexicon*, 664.
69. hom. 16.206C (Field 216–17).
70. hom. 16.207C–D (Field 218, taking the variant reading for *hypsēloteran*).
71. hom. 19.250B (Field 278).
72. hom. 19.251A–B (Field 279).
73. hom. 19.251B (Field 279).

at least theoretically, by pure souls), John's heaven is inhabited by active and real citizens (angels),[74] who live the *politeia*, rather than the ideas of which the earthly is an imperfect counterpart.[75] The demand is that Christians live like the angels, who, in John's eyes, do not heed the divine command in only a selective fashion, but yield and obey them all. The theological anthropology involved in the claim that human beings *can* be like the angels is for John a consistent (if rather ambitious) one; *arete* consists in two things: human zeal and heavenly grace *ou tēs hēmeteras spoudēs hē aretē monon, alla kai tēs anōthen charitos*.[76] He offers this theory (as often throughout his huge corpus of orations)[77] as a proleptic rebuttal to expressions by his congregation of discouragement in the face of such a daunting ethical expectation. John characterizes Jesus's teaching as "moderate" in this regard (*metriazein edidaxe*). Yet, as the request for daily bread in the next petition shows, John believes, Jesus anticipated this problem and conceded that humans, unlike angels, are wrapped in flesh (*sarka perikeimenoi*) and subject to the constraint of nature (*anankē physeōs hypokeimenous*), which means that they cannot have the same *apatheia* ("lack of desire" or "imperturbability") as angelic beings.[78] Christ issues the same commands (*epitagmata*) to both angels and humans, but he shows consideration (*synkatabainein*, "accommodating" or "condescending") to the weakness of human nature. In a neat wordplay Chrysostom sums up this line of thinking: "Christ says, 'I ask for *akribeia*, but not *apatheia* [ethical accuracy but not impassivity].'" Here Christ concedes to human hunger the need for daily bread, for daily sustenance, but not money, luxury, fine garments, or such things. Jesus wishes his followers to be *euzōnoi* and *epterōmenoi* ("unencumbered and winged"), yielding to nature only in its absolute necessities.[79] The allusion suggests that John would agree with Plato in principle that "in a just manner only

---

74. See hom 19.257D (Field 288), where this is said explicitly: *angeloi kai archangeloi, kai hoi tōn ouranōn dēmoi*.

75. In *Phaedrus* 247D it is the mind alone that is able to see heaven and there will gaze upon *talēthē*, i.e., *dikaiosynē, sōphrosynē, epistēmē*.

76. hom. 19.251C (Field 279).

77. See Mitchell, *Heavenly Trumpet*, 135–99.

78. hom. 19.251D (Field 279–80).

79. hom. 19.252B (Field 280).

the mind of the philosopher is winged" (*dikaiōs monē pteroutai hē tou philosophou dianoia*).[80] That philosopher, for John, is the Christian who on earth lives like the angels above.

The next petition of the Lord's Prayer, for forgiveness, shows that even the baptismal bath does not offer a guarantee of sinlessness for those who call upon God as Father. God's gift of forgiveness John can only pronounce *philanthrōpias hyperbolē* ("a superabundant love for humanity").[81] Here Jesus "instructs us to live out philosophically God's inexpressible love for humanity" (*kai peri tēs aphatou tou theou philanthropias philosophein hēmas paideuōn*).[82] The whole prayer thus comes around to the first petition: "The sanctification of God's name is the precise expression of the *politeia* having been brought to perfection" (*kai gar to hagiasthēnai to onoma autou apērtismenēs esti politeias akribeia*).[83]

In the rest of his homilies on the Sermon the theme of the Christian *politeia* continues to be a constant baseline of Chrysostom's exhortations. John finds much that he can approve in the teachings of Matthew 6:19–34, for they exemplify what is for him the monastic virtue of *aktēmosynē* ("living without possessions"). He castigates the rich because "though they will risk much for possessions, they suffer themselves to endure neither small nor big things for the sake of the philosophical life [*hyper tou philosophein*]."[84] For this reason they in turn must endure a "double darkness"—one of their own doing and one from not heeding their teacher (*didaskalos*). These tragic, unphilosophical rich are not even able to hear when "the sun of justice shines its light, because their wealth has shut tight

---

80. *Phaedrus* 249C. Indeed, the mark of such a one is that he "stands apart from human pursuits and is directed toward the divine" (*existamenos de tōn anthrōpinōn spoudasmatōn kai pros tō theiō gignomenos*) (*Phaedrus* 249D). Lying behind this may well be an allusion to the famous Platonic image of the soul as a pair of winged horses (*hypopterou zeugoi*) (*Phaedrus* 246A; cf. 246C: of the *psychē* as *epterōmenē*).

81. hom. 19.252B (Field 280).

82. hom. 19.252D (Field 281).

83. hom. 19.252E (Field 281). The antithesis is expressed by the last line of the prayer, which is an unremitting summons to the Christian athlete (qua philosopher) to be properly anointed to wage war against "the evil one," the devil, who is subordinate to God (hom. 19.253E–254D [Field 282–83]).

84. hom. 20.266B (Field 300). Plato, of course, saw three categories in a democracy: the people (*dēmos*), the rulers (*archontes*), and the rich (*hoi plousioi*) (*Republic* 8.564C–565B).

their eyes." John (like Jesus and Plato) prescribes vision therapy: "Let's attend now with precision, so that late in the day we might then see again [*hina opse goun pote anablepsōmen*]. And how is it possible to see again? If you learn how you were blinded. And how were you blinded? By evil desire." What can penetrate this pathology? Only "if we receive the shining ray of the teaching of Christ" (*ean tēn aktina tēs tou Christou dexōmetha didaskalias*).[85] The final parable of the men building on sand and on rock is for John the heart of the Sermon expressed in metaphor. He exhorts his Antiochenes that, like the apostles, "you, too, if you want to do things with complete accuracy, must laugh off earthly troubles. And if you have been fortified with the philosophy of these pieces of ethical advice, then nothing will be able to grieve you [*kan gar hēs ōchyrōmenos tē tōn paraineseōn toutōn philosophia, ouden se lyēsai dynēsetai*]."[86]

Chrysostom was not the first to present the Christian message as a philosophy.[87] Although that view is not found within the New Testament, per se (the only use of the term *philosophia* in the New Testament is a disparaging one at Col. 2:8), already in the mid-second century with Justin the movement had self-consciously taken on the mantle and the vocabulary of Greek philosophy in its self-expression, representation, and development. In the writings of Clement of Alexandria, Origen, and Eusebius (think especially of the *praeparatio evangelica*) this quest and claim for a Christian philosophical theology was self-consciously being constructed. Chrysostom, in contrast, is famous for his *lack* of philosophical acumen, by which scholars mostly mean his relative disinterest

---

85. hom. 20.266C–D (Field 300–301).

86. hom. 24.303A (Field 352).

87. Two classic works documenting this development are A. M. Malingrey, *"Philosophia": étude d'un groupe de mots dans la literature grecque, des présocratiques au IVe siècle après J. C.* (Paris: Klinksieck, 1961); and W. Jaeger, *Early Christianity and Greek Paideia* (Cambridge: Harvard University Press, 1961); see also the more recent summary treatment by J. A. McGuckin, "Philosophy, the Church and," in *The Westminster Handbook to Patristic Theology*, ed. J. A. McGuckin (Louisville: Westminster John Knox, 2004), 270–72.

in metaphysical speculation (indeed, at such times, as in his discourses on the Anomoeans, he insists on resisting what he considers *periergia*, "being a busybody" about divine mysteries). But what is sometimes seen as its alternative, Chrysostom's famous moralizing, can also be regarded—as indeed he presented it—as a philosophical pursuit of the virtuous life. And it was all in service of his overall program of democratizing monastic virtues onto the urban laity of Antioch and Constantinople around the turn of the fifth century. It is in these homilies that we have the first full-scale exposition of Jesus's Sermon on the Mount as providing the principal foundation of the Christian *politeia*. This commonwealth is a very earthly concern, even as it has its eyes fixed on the life of heaven and its "angelic *politeia*" as well as on such "also-rans" as Plato, pronounced dead and yet still very much in play.

Augustine

3

Robert Louis Wilken

> Seeing the crowds, he went up on the mountain, and when he sat
> down his disciples came to him. And he opened his mouth and
> taught them, saying, "Blessed are the poor in spirit, for theirs is
> the kingdom of heaven."

Before Jesus went up on the mountain he had been moving
about Galilee teaching in the synagogues and preaching the
good news of the coming of the kingdom of God. Crowds of people
followed him, some of whom brought to him their sick and infirm
to be healed. But then, according to the Gospel of Matthew, Jesus
went up to a mountain to teach his disciples. For Augustine, the
reason Jesus went up on a mountain is clear: he wanted to teach
them about higher things. Seated on a mountain they were lifted
above the quotidian affairs of their towns and villages, the cares
and trials of life with family and friends and neighbors. On the
mountain they could gaze on the great expanse of the heavens
stretching above them, look down on the comings and goings of
merchants and travelers and fishermen, stand in awe before God's
majesty and power, and say with the psalmist, "O Lord, our Lord,
how excellent is thy name in all the earth." On the mountain they

could hear what was said in a way that was not possible in the towns and villages on the plain.

So the first key to understanding the Sermon on the Mount is to keep in mind where it was delivered, on a mountain. The second, as Augustine observes, is to take note of how it ends, for in the final words we learn what is meant by the word *sermon* in the title "Sermon on the Mount," what kind of discourse Jesus delivered to his followers. At the conclusion of his sermon Jesus says: "Everyone . . . who hears these words of mine and does them will be like a wise man who built his house upon the rock." Augustine observes that Jesus did not say, "Whoever hears my words," but "whoever hears *these* words of mine."[1] Not any words, mind you, but these particular words, ones fitting for a discourse on a mountain, select words that have to do with the higher precepts of the Christian life.

Finally, if one is to hear and heed these words one must ask who it is that speaks them? Augustine also provides an answer to this question. The words of the Sermon on the Mount are given by the Lord, the Son of God, and the title of Augustine's commentary is *De sermone domini in monte* ("The Lord's Sermon on the Mount"); and it is addressed, says Augustine, to a people whom he has "set free by his love."[2] These are the words of the divine Word who in the last days took on human flesh and lived among us. In the past God spoke through the mouths of his holy prophets, but now through his Son he opens "his own mouth."[3] And he addresses those whom he has called to be his own, his holy church.

This then is an agenda for interpreting the Sermon on the Mount: It is a sermon on higher things. Its words are unique among the words of Jesus for they are addressed to the mature Christian, not to beginners. They are not simply the words of an extraordinary

1. Augustine, *The Lord's Sermon on the Mount* 1.1.1, in Augustine, *Commentary on the Lord's Sermon on the Mount: With Seventeen Related Sermons*, trans. Denis J. Kavanagh, Fathers of the Church 11 (Washington, DC: Catholic University of America, 1951), 20 (hereafter FC); *De sermone domini in monte*, Corpus christianorum: series latina 35 (Turnhout: Brepols, 1967), 2 (hereafter CCSL); see also *The Lord's Sermon on the Mount*, trans. John J. Jepson, Ancient Christian Writers 5 (New York: Newman, 1948).

2. *Lord's Sermon on the Mount* 1.1.2 (FC 11.20; CCSL 35.2).

3. *Lord's Sermon on the Mount* 1.1.2 (FC 11.21; CCSL 35.3).

rabbi or the oracles of a renowned prophet or the sayings of a venerable sage; they are the words of the second person of the Holy Trinity addressed to his faithful people.

If that is the framework in which the Sermon on the Mount is to be interpreted, it should be obvious that we have before us a quite different kind of discourse than what is expounded in modern commentaries, for if we take Augustine as our *magister* Jesus's sermon must be read not in light of what came before, what can be derived from the study of ancient Jewish or Greek sources, but in light of what came after, the new things that came to be through Christ's suffering, death, and resurrection. That is to say, the Sermon will be understood in a Christian way only if one reads it through the prism of the Christ confessed in the creeds and expounded in the church's faith.

When Augustine left Italy after his mother's death in 387 to return to his hometown, Thagaste in North Africa, he had hoped to establish a monastic community on his family's estates and continue his philosophical studies and writing. For a brief period he was able to live a tranquil life among friends, but he grew restless and seemed no longer satisfied to "live sweetly with the mind."[4] On a visit to Hippo Regius, in the midst of a service in the church he was forcibly pushed to the apse where the bishop (who had talked about the need for a priest in Hippo) was sitting and peremptorily ordained priest. As he was being ordained Augustine wept—and some wag has suggested he was weeping not because of the burdens of his new office but because he was being made only a priest, not a bishop.

Augustine thought he was unprepared for his responsibilities, and shortly after his ordination he asked Valerius the bishop to grant him a period of leisure to study the Scriptures. He had already written a treatise on Genesis and some notes on the Psalms, but the first book to come out of his sabbatical was a commentary on the Sermon on the Mount, his first extended exegetical work on the New Testament. It is not a major work, and Platonic

---

4. Letter 10.1 in *Works of Saint Augustine*, trans. Edmund Hill et al., ed. John E. Rotelle (Hyde Park, NY: New City Press, 1990–), II/1.23 (hereafter WSA) = Corpus scriptorum ecclesiasticorum latinorum 34.1.22–25.

language of the ascent of the soul colors his treatment, but it is a verse-by-verse commentary on every pericope in the Sermon, and it anticipates themes that will be developed over the course of his lifetime. The date was 393–95, hence it belongs among his earliest writings, along with *On True Religion* and the *Usefulness of Believing*, and it predates the *Confessions* by about five years.

For Augustine then the Sermon on the Mount was a key text in the Scriptures. This is borne out in his later writings where passages from it are often cited. What this means is that in offering an Augustinian interpretation of the Sermon on the Mount one has to draw on two quite different bodies of material, this early commentary and scattered references to the Sermon in his later writings. The commentary has the virtue of completeness, but it is a first reading and sometimes strikes the reader as thin. Like any good commentator (and preacher) Augustine grew in understanding as he studied the Scriptures more seriously (and preached on them). When one reads a text is often a key to its interpretation, and Augustine's experience entered deeply into his exegesis. For example, he passes over "forgive us our debts as we forgive our debtors" quickly in the early essay, but explains it again and again in his writings against Pelagius. In any presentation of Augustine's interpretation of the Sermon on the Mount both bodies of material have to be examined, and I will move freely between them.

As I have already indicated, Augustine views the Sermon on the Mount through the prism of the church's faith, that is, the confession of God as Father, Son, and Holy Spirit. So it is not surprising that he begins his exposition by presenting the Beatitudes as gifts of the Holy Spirit. As the dry earth cannot bring forth fruit without moisture, so we, who were once a dry tree, cannot bring forth fruits in our lives unless we have been watered by the dew of the Holy Spirit, the gracious rain from above.

Christians have sung about the seven gifts of the Spirit for centuries in the words of *Veni Creator Spiritus*:

> Come, Holy Ghost, our souls inspire,
> and lighten with celestial fire.
> Thou the anointing Spirit art,
> who dost thy sevenfold gifts impart.

The seven gifts of the Spirit are found in Isaiah 11: "And the Spirit of the Lord shall rest upon him, the spirit of wisdom and understanding, the spirit of counsel and might, the spirit of knowledge and godliness, and the spirit of the fear of God will fill him." So reads the Septuagint version of that passage, the translation that was used in the early church and on which Augustine's Latin is based. In Hebrew there are only six gifts. In the Septuagint, the sixth gift is translated piety or godliness, and the next verse, which reads, "his delight shall be in the fear of the Lord," becomes the seventh gift, the "spirit of the fear of God." Hence the seven gifts are wisdom, understanding, counsel, might, knowledge, godliness, and fear of God.

Like other early Christian commentators, Augustine was attracted to the passage in Isaiah because it did not speak in general about the work of the Spirit, but made his bounty concrete by enumerating his gifts. The difficulty of seeing the Beatitudes and the gifts of the Spirit in Isaiah as complementary is that there are eight beatitudes, not seven. Obviously Augustine knew this, and he meets the objection at the outset. His answer is that the eighth beatitude, "happy are those who are persecuted for righteousness' sake for theirs is the kingdom of heaven," recapitulates the first, for it repeats the refrain "theirs is the kingdom of heaven." The other six have different endings: "shall be comforted," "inherit the earth," "see God," and so on. As Augustine puts it, "The eighth maxim returns, as it were, to the beginning, because it shows and commends what is *perfect* and complete."[5]

The number seven is a perfect number. It is reasonable then to talk of seven gifts, and by gifts Augustine means attitudes and actions that lead to perfection, as Jesus says later in the Sermon: "Be ye perfect as your Father in heaven is perfect." Augustine is thinking in terms of the virtues, but instead of using the philosophical terms, for example, prudence, justice, fortitude, temperance, he uses biblical language, for example, compassion, fear of the Lord, meekness.

Once Augustine has established that there are seven gifts or "virtues" presented in the Beatitudes, he turns to the "sevenfold

5. *Lord's Sermon on the Mount* 1.3.10 (FC 11.26; CCSL 35.9).

operation of the Holy Spirit of which Isaiah speaks." But then he meets another difficulty. The prophet begins with the most excellent among the gifts, wisdom, but in the Sermon on the Mount Jesus begins with the "more lowly," the "poor in spirit." Augustine suggests that the order in which the virtues are given is reversed.[6] The first beatitude reads: "Blessed are the poor in Spirit," and this is identified with the last gift in Isaiah, namely "fear of the Lord." The first beatitude, "Blessed are the poor in Spirit," is talking about humility, another way of speaking about fear or awe. In support he cites Romans 11:20: "Do not become proud, but stand in awe" (Revised Standard Version).

Augustine then proceeds to show the correspondence between each beatitude and the corresponding gift of the Spirit in Isaiah. The "meekness" of the second beatitude corresponds to "godliness" in Isaiah; "fortitude" to those who "hunger and thirst for righteousness"; "merciful" to the "spirit of counsel," that is, one who overcomes burdensome evils by forgiving others; "understanding" to "purity of heart"; "wisdom" to "peacemaking." The eighth beatitude, ending "theirs is the kingdom of heaven," hearkens back to the first and points to the final goal: the kingdom of heaven. Echoing Ephesians 3, Augustine says that it announces the "perfect human" or "mature human" who is able to bear all things for the sake of truth and righteousness.[7]

Admittedly Augustine's scheme is somewhat artificial and contrived, but that is hardly an argument against it. What is significant is that he gives the Beatitudes a Trinitarian reading, and by linking them with Isaiah's enumeration of the gifts of the Spirit he helps his readers to sort out the different ways in which the Scriptures depict the life to which Christ's followers aspire. If one makes a serious attempt to set forth a model of the Christian life from the Scriptures—and that means all the Scriptures—one is confronted by a bewildering range of terms and images. In the passages before us we find wisdom, fear, godliness, understanding, meekness, peacemaking, mercy, and so on.

6. *Lord's Sermon on the Mount* 1.4.11 (FC 11.27; CCSL 35.9).
7. *Lord's Sermon on the Mount* 1.4.12 (FC 11.30; CCSL 35.13).

And if one would throw St. Paul into the mix, things would become even more complicated. In Galatians Paul speaks not about gifts but about the "fruit of the Spirit" and mentions love, joy, peace, patience, kindness, goodness, faithfulness, gentleness, self-control. To relate this list to the other two will require a great deal of bending and molding and shaving, but it will also deepen and broaden the meaning of the terms, interpreting one set in light of the other. Augustine's aim, of course, is to come up with a scheme that is simple and memorable. As a teacher of the church he wishes to present the Sermon not as a body of general moral principles but a workable guide to life.

Note too that Augustine holds fast to the biblical language. A less gifted preacher—and especially a contemporary one—might be inclined to translate the biblical language into the current cultural idiom. Augustine, however, translates one set of biblical terms into terms from elsewhere in the Bible. He knew that the language of the Bible is more resonant, more affective, more enduring (because it will be heard again), richer in spiritual and moral content, and more edifying than any local idiom.

There is more here, however, than practiced rhetoric. Augustine's exegesis is profoundly theological and anticipates a theme that will run throughout his writings. One of the texts he cites most frequently is Romans 5:5: "The love of God has been poured into our hearts through the Holy Spirit which has been given to us" (note the word *given* for the Holy Spirit). Augustine took the phrase *love of God* in this passage to be a reference to our love toward God, what grammarians call an objective genitive. For Augustine the Christian life was an affair of growing fellowship with God through love. Through the gift of the Spirit there arises in the soul the delight and love of God by which we cleave to God, as it is written in the psalm: "It is good for me to cleave to God" (Ps. 73:28). There can be no true devotion, no good life, without love of God, and this is possible only through the gift of the Spirit.

In this view the individual beatitudes become stages on the way that lead to God: humility, meekness, compassion, hunger and thirst for righteousness, purity of heart, zeal for justice. The exhortations in Augustine's *Sermon on the Mount* depict those attitudes and actions that bring us into more intimate fellowship to God. They do so not because our works earn merit before God—though they certainly do that—but because the doing of them makes us into different kinds of persons by remaking us in the image of God.

It must be remembered—and Augustine saw this clearly—that the first main section of the Sermon on the Mount ends with the injunction, "Be ye perfect as your Father in heaven is perfect" (Matt. 5:48). In fact one might say that this is the central theme of the Sermon. Jesus's statement of this theme, "be ye perfect," comes hard on the heels of his words: "You have heard that it was said, 'You shall love your neighbor and hate your enemy.' But I say to you, Love your enemies and pray for those who persecute you, so that you may be sons of your Father who is in heaven."

Augustine also noticed that Jesus here calls God "Father" and his followers "children." So he proposes that these words be understood in light of John 1:12: "He gave them power to be made sons of God." The term *father* is not simply a term of endearment; it implies that one is the offspring of the Father, that one has been reborn and made into someone new. Augustine puts it this way:[8] There is only one Son of God by nature, and that is Christ who was without sin. We, however, "are made sons." This kind of sonship is possible only by being united to Christ, for the apostle Paul wrote that we become children of God through the Holy Spirit, and if we are God's children, then we are "coheirs with Christ" (Rom. 8:17). The only way to become God's children is by undergoing a "spiritual rebirth" through an act of love of the God who created us. Redemption is always restoration and renewal of what we once were. Adoption is a coming home, a return, rather than a new beginning.

Augustine also notes a curious feature of Jesus's language. He observes that Jesus did not say, "Do these things because you are children [of God]," but "do these things *in order that* you may be children [of God]" (*itaque non ait: Facite ista, quia estis filii, sed: Facite ista, ut sitis filii*).[9] His interpretation of the Sermon hinges on this insight. For Augustine the works one does as a Christian are

8. *Lord's Sermon on the Mount* 1.23.78 (FC 11.105–6; CCSL 35.87–88).
9. *Lord's Sermon on the Mount* 1.23.78 (FC 11.106; CCSL 35.88).

not simply the expression of one's faith; they are the means used by the Holy Spirit to bring us closer to God and make us what we are intended to be, made in the image of God, godlike.

In a later sermon Augustine cites Jesus's words "be ye perfect" as "be ye *like* your Father in heaven."[10] Jesus urges us to "imitate God," to "act in a Godlike way," or in the words of 1 John to become "like God." In other words, according to Augustine, Jesus is speaking about "theosis" or "divinization." It is often assumed that divinization is a distinctly Eastern notion, but it is thoroughly Augustinian, and one of the biblical texts he cites in support is the one he appeals to in the commentary on the Sermon on the Mount, John 1:12.

This insight is developed in later writings. Here, for example, is how Augustine puts it in another sermon. It is clear from the Scriptures, he says, that God calls human beings "gods" (Ps. 82:6–7) "in the sense that they were deified by his grace, not because they were born of his own substance. It is proper to God to justify us because he is just in himself and not by derivation from anyone else; and similarly he alone deifies who is God himself. . . . Moreover he who justifies is the same as he who deifies, because by justifying us he made us sons and daughters of God; 'he gave them power to become children of God'"[11] (John 1:12).

So the two statements in the Sermon—"do these things in order that you may *become* sons of God" and "be ye like your Father who is in heaven"—complement one another and provide a rationale for the Beatitudes as the gifts of the Holy Spirit. The Beatitudes direct our course toward God through the love that is shed abroad in our hearts by the Holy Spirit who has been given to us.

This gives us a feel for the exegetical and theological framework of an Augustinian interpretation of the Sermon on the Mount. From here on it is largely a matter of filling in the details from other pericopes in the Sermon.

First is the most startling beatitude, which reads: "Happy are the pure in heart for they shall see God." I say startling, because in 1 Timothy it is written that God dwells in unapproachable light

10. *Expositions of the Psalms* 100.1 (WSA III/19.29; CCSL 39.1405).
11. *Expositions of the Psalms* 49.2 (WSA III/16.381; CCSL 38.575–76).

and that "no man has ever seen or *can* see" God (1 Tim. 6:16). And there are the memorable words to Moses in Exodus: "No man shall see me and live" (Exod. 33:20). The church fathers puzzled over these passages (and others that seem to contradict them; for example, Isaiah's statement that he "saw God" [Isa. 6:1]). Augustine wrote a small treatise dealing with these texts, and he returns again and again to this beatitude in his writings.

It is cited four times in the opening book of his treatise *The Trinity*. The reason is that Augustine believed the goal of human life, the supreme good, the end toward which our lives are directed, is to behold the face of God in love. In fact, he wrote his great work on the Holy Trinity not so much to "understand" the Trinity as an exercise in learning to see God, citing the words of the psalmist—*quaerite faciem eius semper* ("seek his face always")—at key points in the treatise. So it is natural that at the beginning of a book about seeking the face of God Augustine would cite the words of Jesus: "Happy are the pure in heart for they shall see God."

The key to understanding what Augustine is after when he is expounding a text from the Scriptures is to look at those texts he cites to illuminate the passage under discussion. At this late date it is hardly necessary to say that the principle *Scriptura scripturam interpretat* ("Scripture interprets Scripture") is not a principle discovered in the sixteenth century by the Reformers. It is a foundational axiom of patristic exegesis. So let us see how Augustine interprets this beatitude by Scripture.

When he quotes the beatitude for the first time in *The Trinity*, he cites Acts 15:9: "Cleansing their hearts through faith."[12] His point is that seeing God—in Augustine's language, "contemplation"—is the reward of faith, and if we are to see God our hearts must be cleansed. Then he cites the psalm prayed in night prayer, Psalm 91, where God's blessing is an affair of seeing. Augustine puts it this way: the beatitude is speaking about "eternal life," and what the Scriptures mean by eternal life is seeing God, as is made clear in the psalm: "I will fill him with length of days and I will *show* him my salvation."

12. *Trinity* 1.17 (WSA I/5.77; CCSL 50.51–52).

In a particularly beautiful passage in *The Trinity* he explains the beatitude by citing four other biblical texts. The sight of God promised to the saints, says Augustine, Paul describes as seeing God "face to face" (1 Cor. 13:12). St. John says, "We shall be like him because we shall *see* him as he is" (1 John 3:2). The psalmist said, "One thing have I begged of the Lord, to *behold* the delight [*delectatio*] of the Lord" (Ps. 27:4). In the Gospel of John Jesus says, "I will love him and *show* myself to him" (John 14:21). And Augustine concludes with "blessed are the pure in heart for they shall *see* God." To which he comments: "Whatever else is said about this sight, which anyone who directs the eyes of love to seeking it may find scattered plentifully throughout the Scriptures; this sight alone is our supreme good, and it is to gain this that we are bidden to do whatever we do rightly."[13]

By citing a series of biblical texts Augustine has given us a lexicon of scriptural words: faith, eternal life, salvation, likeness to God, face to face, behold, love (and one nonbiblical phrase: *summum bonum* ["highest good"]) to interpret the beatitude. Of course, interpreted in this way this beatitude stands out from the others and is not so easily slotted in among the other seven as stages on the road to perfection. As Augustine has matured, the meaning of the beatitude has deepened.

For the fourth beatitude, "Happy are those who hunger and thirst for righteousness, because they shall be satisfied," Augustine draws on other biblical texts to give a christological reading. The key to this beatitude is found, says Augustine, not only in the meaning of the term *righteousness*, but also what is meant by *satisfy*. A common experience of satisfaction is eating and drinking. But, says Augustine, we all know that the satisfaction one receives from eating is short lived. Once the meal is digested you feel hungry again. There is, however, another kind of satisfaction that is not simply temporary. When one applies dressing to a wound, the dressing cures the wound and it no longer hurts. When the wound is healed, one no longer need apply the dressing.[14]

13. *Trinity* 1.31 (WSA I/5.90; CCSL 50.78).
14. Sermon 53.4 (WSA III/3.67).

This beatitude then is speaking about the kind of satisfaction that endures, that food for which our inner self hungers and thirsts. Augustine is thinking here—no, actually he is citing—Ephesians 3:16: "May he grant you to be strengthened with might through his spirit in the inner man [or inner self] and that Christ may dwell in your hearts through faith." In other words the hungering and thirsting of which the beatitude speaks is a hungering and thirsting for Christ, the food and drink that are proper to the soul. To drive home his point he cites the Gospel of John: "I am the bread who came down from heaven" (John 6:41)—the bread that satisfies this kind of hunger—and then the psalm: "With you is the fountain of life" (Ps. 36:9)—the drink of the thirsty soul.

The point then is this. If the beatitude is to be read in a genuinely Christian way, as the teaching of the divine Son of God, its meaning will have to be related to Christ, the bread of life and the water that comes down from heaven.

Augustine has gotten things right in his exposition of this beatitude, but he does stumble at one point and could have used the help of a friend. He has overlooked a key text that would have sealed his interpretation. And that is 1 Corinthians 1:30, where St. Paul writes that Christ was made "our wisdom, our righteousness and sanctification and redemption." Gregory of Nyssa did not miss this passage, and in his sermons on the Beatitudes he cites 1 Corinthians 1:30 to show that Christ is the righteousness for whom we hunger and thirst.

Finally the petition from the Lord's Prayer, "forgive us our debts as we forgive our debtors." In Augustine's first reading of the Sermon on the Mount his interpretation of this petition is quite straightforward. The petition has to do with wrongs that others have committed against us, including that of someone who has not paid back a financial debt.

But when he became involved in the controversy with Pelagius, Augustine came to quite a different interpretation of this petition. One of the propositions that Pelagius and his disciples held to was this: "Human beings can be without sin if they wish." This does not mean that it is possible for most humans or even for any human being to be without sin, but, given the nature of humans, namely, that human beings are created in the image of

God, Pelagius believed we have within ourselves the capacity to do what the law asks of us. He was willing to go even further to claim that "before the coming of Christ [i.e., in the Old Testament] some people lived holy and righteous lives."[15] The prime example was Job, because the Scripture said that Job was "blameless and upright [*or* righteous: *dikaios*], and godfearing."[16]

In response to Pelagius's claim that there were persons whose lives were wholly righteous, Augustine responded: "We should hope that this will be the case; we should strive to make it so; we should pray that it will be so. We should not, however, presume that it is already the case." As support for his critique of Pelagius, Augustine cites the petition from the Lord's Prayer: "Forgive us our debts as we also forgive our debtors." He explains: "Whoever claims that this prayer is not necessary in this life for anyone, even for a holy person who knows and does God's will (Deut. 9:24), is greatly mistaken and is utterly unable to please the very one whom he praises."[17] For good measure he adds the words of the psalmist: "No living person is found righteous in his sight" (Ps. 143:2).

Again and again Augustine cites the petition from the Lord's Prayer in his writings against Pelagius. And he surrounds the petition with other texts from the Scriptures. For example, "If we say we have no sin, we deceive ourselves, and the truth is not in us" (1 John 1:8). Or the statement from 1 Kings: "There is not a human being who will not sin" (1 Kings 8:46). Or Ecclesiastes: "There is not a righteous person on earth who will do good and will not sin" (Eccles. 7:21 [in Vulgate; 7:20 in modern editions]). To which Augustine comments: "No matter of what kind or how great may be the righteousness . . . found in this life, there is no human being in this life who has absolutely no sin." And that means that one "must still hunger and thirst" for the grace and righteousness that comes from God.[18]

---

15. Pelagius, *To Demetrias* 8.4 in B. R. Rees, *Pelagius: Life and Letters* (Woodbridge, Suffolk: Boydell, 1998), 2:44.

16. Job 1:1.

17. *Punishment and Forgiveness* 3.13.23 (WSA I/23.135 = Corpus scriptorum ecclesiasticorum latinorum 60 [Vienna: Tempsky, 1913], 150).

18. *Spirit and the Letter* 65 (WSA I/23.196 = Corpus scriptorum ecclesiasticorum latinorum 60.227).

The petition in the Lord's Prayer leads then to this theological conclusion: "Evil remains in our flesh, not by reason of the nature in which human beings were created by God, but by reason of the sinfulness into which they have fallen."[19]

So what is to be made of this momentary glance at the Sermon on the Mount through the eyes of St. Augustine? As I have already indicated, when one takes up for the first time his *Lord's Sermon on the Mount* and meets in the opening pages his proposal to interpret the eight beatitudes in light of the seven gifts of the Spirit, the temptation, at least for a modern reader, is to call his exegesis contrived or, in the modern put-down, an example of eisegesis rather than exegesis. And of course, to take another example, his interpretation of "forgive us our debts as we forgive our debtors" seems as much driven by the demands of his polemic against the theology of Pelagius as it is by the words of Jesus.

But if one looks a bit more closely at the way he works, it becomes clear that his interpretation is driven by a kind of interior guidance system powered by the Scriptures. A key to Augustine's exegesis is to be found, as I have already suggested, in the maxim *Scriptura scripturam interpretat*. He never proposes an interpretation of a biblical text without citing another biblical text. That means, of course, that by our standards Augustine is cavalier about historical setting, literary context, or social world—the topics that exercise contemporary biblical scholars. He reads the Bible as a single book and what one scriptural writer says, whether in the Old Testament or the New Testament, is fair game for interpreting what occurs in another part of the Scriptures.

Of course, one might say that if *Scriptura scripturam interpretat* simply means citing Bible passages it is a recipe for a very unbiblical stew, for the interpreter can play fast and loose with the Scriptures by citing texts at will. Which is to say that "Scripture interprets Scripture" does not imply *sola scriptura*, but Scripture interpreted within the context of the church's faith and life. In the Sermon on the Mount the focus is more on life than faith. That is, the Sermon speaks about holy living, the way of life that Christ sets before his disciples. But issues of faith come into play because

---

19. *Punishment and Forgiveness* 2.4.4 (WSA I/23.82).

Christians cannot speak about the moral life without setting forth the fullness of God's revelation in Christ and the sending of the Holy Spirit. The fulcrum on which Augustine's exegesis turns is the injunction "be ye perfect as your Father in heaven is perfect," a decidedly theological statement. The goal of our lives, our highest good, is to be like God and to cleave to God "whose spiritual embrace . . . makes [us] fertile with virtue."[20] To explain how it is that weak and sinful human beings are restless until they rest in God, Augustine sets forth the church's understanding of creation, fall, rebirth, and a life formed by the seven gifts of the Spirit oriented toward the final end, the vision of God.

In a final winsome conclusion to his commentary on the Sermon on the Mount Augustine says that such a life is possible only if it is built on Christ the "rock" (Matt. 7:24):

"And it came to pass when Jesus had fully ended these words, the people were in admiration of his teaching. For he was teaching them as one having power and not as their Scribes."

This [comments Augustine] is what I said earlier had been signified in the Psalms by the prophet when he said: "I will deal confidently in his regard. The words of the Lord are pure words, as silver tried by the fire, purged from the earth, refined *seven* times" [Ps. 12:6].

It was this number seven which suggested to me that these precepts also hark back to those seven maxims which he put at the head of this sermon when he spoke the Beatitudes, and to those seven operations of the Holy Spirit of which the Prophet Isaiah makes mention. But whether the order here given should be observed or some other, we must *do* what we have heard from the Lord if we wish to build on the rock.[21]

---

20. *City of God* 10.3, trans. Henry Bettenson, introduction by John J. O'Meara (Harmondsworth, Middlesex: Penguin, 1984), 376 (CCSL 47.275).

21. *Lord's Sermon on the Mount* 2.25.87 (FC 11.198–99; CCSL 35.188).

Hugh of St. Victor

4

Boyd Taylor Coolman

In a series of cantos devoted to the Sun in the *Paradiso*,[1] Dante celebrates the themes of harmony and reconciliation. The poet depicts two rings populated by various luminaries from the Christian tradition, including John Chrysostom, Boethius, Anselm, Thomas Aquinas, and Bonaventure. Also named among them is the twelfth-century Augustinian canon Hugh of St. Victor. Hugh's presence in this pantheon testifies to the esteem accorded him by later medieval generations. It also provides a fitting point of departure for a consideration of Hugh's theology, which consistently manifests a tendency to bring various, even disparate, elements into an overarching harmony. Nowhere is this more evident than in his treatment of the Sermon on the Mount.

Though not widely known today outside scholarly circles, Hugh of St. Victor is one of the most significant medieval European thinkers. Regarded by his contemporaries as an *alter Augustinus*, a "second Augustine," Hugh inaugurated a medieval theological tradition that built upon an Augustinian foundation, while also pioneering a distinctive approach to various aspects of Christian thought and life, including liturgy, Scholastic theology,[2] biblical

---

1. Dante Alighieri, *The Divine Comedy*, vol. 3: *Paradise*, trans. with introduction, notes, and commentary by Mark Musa (New York: Penguin, 1987), 12.133.
2. For Hugh's theology generally, see Roger Baron, *Science et sagesse chez Hugues de Saint-Victor* (Paris: Lethielleux, 1957); and the numerous articles by Grover A. Zinn Jr.,

exegesis,[3] and contemplative spirituality.[4] Largely due to Hugh's achievement, the abbey of Saint-Victor[5] in Paris, and the "Victorine school" associated with it, played an important role in the subsequent medieval Christian tradition. For some, the Victorine synthesis retains an enduring value.

The Victorine way of life itself brought together practices often segregated by their contemporaries. Living in community according to the so-called *Rule of St. Augustine*, these priests were not traditional monastics who fled the world to pursue holiness; rather, in distinctive fashion they wove together pioneering work in liturgy and in the emerging academic discipline of theology with life in community and active ministry of teaching and pastoral care to local student populations in the midst of the burgeoning urban society of twelfth-century Paris. In a phrase, the Victorines were urban scholar-monk-priests.[6]

---

including "Hugh of St. Victor and the Art of Memory," *Viator* 5 (1974): 211–34; "Hugh of St. Victor and the Ark of Noah: A New Look," *Church History* 40 (1971): 261–72; "*De gradibus ascensionum*: The Stages of Contemplative Ascent in Two Treatises on Noah's Ark by Hugh of St. Victor," *Studies in Medieval Culture* 5 (1975): 61–79; "*Historia fundamentum est*: The Role of History in the Contemplative Life according to Hugh of St. Victor," in *Contemporary Reflections on the Medieval Christian Tradition: Essays in Honor of Ray C. Petry*, ed. George H. Shriver (Durham: Duke University Press, 1974), 135–58; "Hugh of St. Victor's *De scripturis et scriptoribus sacris* as an *Accessus* Treatise for the Study of the Bible," *Traditio* 52 (1997): 111–34.

3. On Hugh's exegesis, the standard introduction remains Beryl Smalley, *The Study of the Bible in the Middle Ages* (Oxford: Blackwell, 1952; repr. Notre Dame: University of Notre Dame Press, 1964), 83–195. See also Jean Châtillon, "La bible dans les écoles du XIIe siécle," in *Le moyen âge et la bible*, ed. Pierre Riché and Guy Lobrichon (Paris: Beauchesne, 1984), 163–97 at 178–83. For a more recent discussion, see Boyd Taylor Coolman, "*Pulchrum esse*: The Beauty of Scripture, the Beauty of the Soul, and the Art of Exegesis in the Theology of Hugh of St. Victor," *Traditio* 58 (2003): 175–200.

4. See Steven Chase, *Contemplation and Compassion: The Victorine Tradition*, Traditions of Christian Spirituality Series (Maryknoll, NY: Orbis, 2003).

5. The abbey of Saint-Victor was founded in Paris by William of Champeaux in 1108 and housed an Augustinian order of regular canons. For the most recent study of the early history of the abbey, see Robert-Henri Bautier, "Les origines et les premiers développements de l'abbaye Saint-Victor de Paris," in *L'abbaye parisienne de Saint-Victor au moyen âge*, ed. Jean Longère, Bibliotheca victorina 1 (Turnhout: Brepols, 1991), 23–52.

6. For general discussions of various aspects of Victorine thought and life in the twelfth century, see Carolyn Walker Bynum, *Docere verbo et exemplo: An Aspect of Twelfth-Century Spirituality* (Missoula, MT: Scholars Press, 1979); idem, "The Spirituality of the Regular Canons in the Twelfth Century," in Bynum's *Jesus as Mother: Studies*

Hugh's reputation for masterful integration outlived him. Over a century after his death, the great Franciscan Scholastic theologian Bonaventure paid tribute to Hugh in this regard, as he surveyed the giants of the recent and remote Christian tradition. Augustine and Anselm excelled in speculative theology; Gregory the Great and Bernard of Clairvaux in practical morality; (Pseudo-)Dionysius and Richard of St. Victor in mystical contemplation. But Hugh, Bonaventure concludes, "excels in all three."[7]

De quinque septenis: A Medieval Schema for the Soul's Reformation

Hugh's most extensive treatment of the Sermon on the Mount occurs within a short treatise entitled *On the Five Sevens* (*De quinque septenis*),[8] which is concerned with the practical dimensions of the Christian life. Standing in a venerable patristic and medieval tradition that sees spiritual growth as proceeding through identifiable stages, Hugh finds five distinct series of such steps in Scripture. Given the symbolic significance that medieval thinkers attributed to certain numerical values, Hugh identifies seven such steps in each of these five series. Hence, the "five sevens." They are as follows (see appendix):

the seven vices[9]

---

in the Spirituality of the High Middle Ages (Berkeley: University of California Press, 1982), 22–58; Jean Châtillon, *Le mouvement canonial au moyen âge: réforme de l'église, spiritualité et culture*, Bibliotheca victorina 3 (Turnhout: Brepols, 1992); and Margot Fassler, *Gothic Song: Victorine Sequences and Augustinian Reform in Twelfth-Century Paris* (Cambridge: Cambridge University Press, 1993).

7. Bonaventure, *On Retracing the Arts to Theology*, trans. J. de Vinck, The Works of Bonaventure 3: Opuscula (Paterson, NJ: St. Anthony's Guild Press, 1966), 20 (chap. 5).

8. Hugh of St. Victor, *Six opuscules spirituels*, with introduction, critical text, French translation, and notes by Roger Baron, Sources chrétiennes 155 (Paris: Cerf, 1969), cited by line numbers. All English translations are mine, though I have benefited from the unpublished translation of Hugh Feiss.

9. *De quinque septenis* 6–8. On the history of the "seven deadly sins," covering such authors as Evagrius of Pontus, John Cassian, Gregory the Great, and Thomas Aquinas, see David L. Jeffery, ed., *A Dictionary of Biblical Tradition in English Literature* (Grand Rapids: Eerdmans, 1992), 698–701. Though Hugh claims to have found the seven vices

the seven petitions in the Lord's Prayer[10]

the seven gifts of the Holy Spirit as traditionally found in Isaiah[11]

the seven virtues found in the Beatitudes[12]

the seven beatitudes found in the Beatitudes[13]

Of these five sevens, then, three are drawn from the Sermon on the Mount.

In a general way, Hugh is continuing a long-standing Christian tradition of linking various sets of biblical sevens.[14] Both Augustine before him and Thomas Aquinas after him, to give just two well-known examples, did the same.[15] Hugh is here engaging in a

there, "the Bible is not the direct source of the traditional list of vices. The individual sins that compose the catalog of seven all occur in the Bible, however, and medieval exegetes found it relatively easy to provide scriptural warrant for the list" (698).

10. *De quinque septenis* 9–19. See Jeffrey, *Dictionary of Biblical Tradition*, 587: "The seven petitions of the Lord's Prayer were regarded from patristic times as a compendium of the things for which the Christian should pray; to these petitions a good deal else in Christian doctrine could be and was related, frequently in parallel heptemerologies. St. Augustine associated the seven petitions with the seven gifts of the Holy Ghost and with seven of the eight Beatitudes. Later writers added the association with the seven deadly sins, seven virtues, seven works of mercy, etc."

11. *De quinque septenis* 19–23. See Jeffrey, *Dictionary of Biblical Tradition*, 307: "Isaiah prophesied that the Spirit of God would bestow upon the coming messiah 'the spirit of wisdom and understanding, the spirit of counsel and might, the spirit of knowledge and of the fear of the Lord' (Isaiah 11:2); to these 'six gifts,' the Vulgate adds a seventh (i.e., piety) from the opening phrase of 11:3. These gifts, often represented in early art by seven doves, lamps, or flames, are listed in medieval commentaries as *Sapientia, Intellectus, Consilium, Fortitudo, Scientia, Pietas*, and *Timor Domini*. They represent a scala of the good life in St. Augustine and St. Ambrose, and are attached by Augustine to two similar lists, the seven petitions of the Lord's Prayer and seven Beatitudes."

12. *De quinque septenis* 24–28. These seven virtues are not the traditional three theological virtues added to the four cardinal virtues, but rather the seven conditions found in the first part of each of the Beatitudes.

13. *De quinque septenis* 29–32.

14. Jeffrey, *Dictionary of Biblical Tradition*, 79: "In Roman Catholic exegesis, which follows St. Augustine and St. Thomas Aquinas, the Beatitudes are sequential stages in temporal spiritual growth ending with the person's becoming perfected in the divine image; they are also adjunct to the gifts of the Holy Spirit and to the vices and virtues."

15. See Augustine, *De sermone domini in monte* (Patrologia latina 34.1229–1308); and Thomas Aquinas, *Summa theologiae* I-II Q. 69 (24.43–63), as noted in Jeffrey, *Dictionary of Biblical Tradition*, 79.

quintessentially medieval mode of thought. Yet his arrangement and treatment of the five sevens is a distinctive and influential contribution to this venerable tradition.

At first glance, such a scheme—apparently artificial, even arbitrary in the extreme—will not likely compel and may even repel the modern reader. Such a reader may be dismayed to find that Hugh has abstracted the Sermon on the Mount from its original biblical context. He does not dwell on the preacher of the Sermon or on his audience; he does not consider the Sermon in the larger context of Matthew's Gospel; he does not consider the Lord's Prayer or the Beatitudes individually as literary or rhetorical units. Despite its off-putting appearance, however, Hugh's strategy facilitates insights regarding the theological significance and practical application of the Sermon. In this work, he offers a highly integrated and progressive account of the spiritual life, and the rubric of the five sevens provides him an overarching framework within which to do so. Within this framework, material from the Sermon on the Mount, in particular, the Lord's Prayer and the Beatitudes, occupies a central place. At the same time, by setting these within the five sevens framework, Hugh is able to link them with other aspects of his theology, namely, Christology, pneumatology, and his general conception of sin and grace in the economy of salvation. If, then, Hugh has lifted the Sermon out of its original Matthean context, he has done so in order to place it within the larger context, no less biblical, of a distinctively medieval, even uniquely Hugonian, theological conception of the Christian life.

More precisely, employing this framework of the five sevens, Hugh prescribes a process that gradually reestablishes the integrity of human nature and thereby reforms it in the image of God. From beginning to end, Hugh gauges this process in relationship to interior affectivity. In Hugh's terms, deformed human nature has lost its capacity for "spiritual taste," and its gradual, step-wise reformation is measured by a restored affective disposition toward God. In the end, the rubric of the five sevens is not just an analytical description of psychological states; rather it is a prescribed practice of prayer and theological meditation designed to remedy the fallen human situation.

"Disintegration"—The Nature and Consequence of Vice

While Hugh sees the five sevens as a unified framework, his presentation assumes a basic subdivision that pits the seven "capital or principal" vices against the remaining petitions, gifts, virtues, and beatitudes. The former describe the malady in human nature; the latter present the remedy.

Hugh's treatment of the seven vices lays the foundation for the remainder of the treatise. His analysis is in many ways traditional. Yet he offers a subtle, discerning analysis of the nature of sin that on at least two counts bears his original stamping. Traditional is his view of sin as deeply rooted, as growing organically from one vice to the next, and as eventually blooming in full, yet devastating flower. In his words, the vices are the "seeds of all evil,"[16] from which "all evils originate."[17] Distinctive is Hugh's depiction of the relationship between the vices. The metaphors and images he employs suggest that "disintegration" best characterizes the cumulative effects of vice: "We will speak," he says, "concerning these seven vices, devastators which corrupt the whole integrity of nature."[18] For the Victorine, vice entails the progressive forfeiture of the goods of creation generally and of the good of human nature in particular. It is the loss of creaturely integrity. Also original is Hugh's construal of the effect of this creaturely disintegration. Put simply, Hugh casts this loss of creaturely integrity in terms of psychology not ontology. For him, vice results in a perverted and therefore lost affectivity or capacity for interior feeling.

As he begins his treatment of the vices, Hugh previews the entire process and its outcome: "There are seven [vices]," he says, and the first three "despoil [*expoliant*] humanity," for "pride carries man away from God; envy carries him away from his neighbor; anger carries him away from himself." Then, having been despoiled, "sadness lashes him." Finally, "greed expels the beaten one, gluttony seduces the outcast, and lust enslaves the one seduced."[19] In

16. *De quinque septenis* 47.
17. *De quinque septenis* 38–39.
18. *De quinque septenis* 45–49.
19. *De quinque septenis* 50–56.

effect, Hugh divides the vices into two groups of three, the fourth vice acting as a hinge between them.

The "Despoiling" Triad: Pride, Envy, and Anger

Following Cassian, Gregory the Great, and especially Augustine, Hugh sees pride as the root vice. He defines pride as "the love of one's own excellence when the mind loves only the good which it possesses, that is, without Him from whom it receives the good."[20] In the simplest terms, pride loves the good which it has received from God *as if* it had not received it from God, *as if* it were *its own*. Such a one loves "the gift apart from the giver," and thus "perversely claims for himself the part of the good which is given to him from [God]."[21] The problem of pride is not that it loves its own excellence, but rather, the way it does so—*as if* it were its own. Adopting an Augustinian intuition, Hugh sees pride as born in a refusal to acknowledge creaturely dependency and the resulting willful divorce of gift from giver, of creaturely possession from gratuitous reception. Thus, pride manifests itself as a perverse affection funded by a false intellection: that is, a misconstrual of the gift nature of creaturely existence leads to a perverse love for one's own excellence, as if it were one's own. Rejecting the inexorable link between created gift and divine giver, pride issues in the love of the latter apart from the former. Piling up illustrative images, Hugh says that pride urges man "to the rivulet, so that he separates himself from the fountain," and to the sun's ray as if it was separable from the sun itself.[22]

The effect of pride's perverse affection is the loss of that very good which the creature had already received. When man "ceases to be filled," says Hugh, he "dries up," and when man "turns away from the one who illuminates," he "becomes darkness."[23] Hugh implies here that all creaturely good is always having-to-be-given (a *dandum*) and never given as an autonomous possession (never a *datum*). Accordingly, when the proud "cease to receive that which

20. *De quinque septenis* 58–62.
21. *De quinque septenis* 66–69.
22. *De quinque septenis* 61–63.
23. *De quinque septenis* 63–65.

they do not yet possess, immediately they lose what they already possess," forfeiting "all the good" that is in them.[24]

What precisely does Hugh mean by this forfeiture of all good? In a word, this loss is psychological not ontological. The proud person does not, of course, literally cease to exist; rather, he or she loses the capacity to relate with proper affectivity to that which he or she has received from God, and this also entails a lost affectivity in relation to God himself:

> He is not able to possess *usefully* that which he has, as long as he does not love it in Him from Whom he has [received] it. For just as every good is truly from God, so no good can be possessed *usefully* apart from God. But rather that very thing which man has is lost through this: that what he has is not loved in God, and with God, and from God.[25]

The essential character of this loss of creaturely good is that it ceases to be a cause of the soul's delight in God. This loss of useful possession of creaturely excellence refers to the lost capacity for delighting in God on the basis of what one has received from God and what one truly possesses only in and with God. For the proud, creaturely excellence ceases to be God-referential and becomes self-referential, and such a one thereby becomes a kind of viciously circular, self-enclosed contradiction. The immediate fruit of pride, therefore, is the loss of God: "Pride carries man away from God."[26]

For Hugh, pride naturally gives birth to envy, for, as soon as one's own excellence is loved *as one's own* and not as wholly from God and therefore necessarily in and with God, then all the goods of others become rival excellences.[27] Hugh's underlying intuition here is that when human goods are loved as from God, and thus in and with God, then such delight is possible regardless of who possesses such goods. Loved in this way, another's excellence is

24. *De quinque septenis* 65–66.
25. *De quinque septenis* 70–75 (emphasis added).
26. *De quinque septenis* 58.
27. *De quinque septenis* 80–83: "Hence, envy always follows pride. For whenever someone does not attach his love where all good is, then, the more perversely he extols himself, the more gravely he is tormented by the good of another."

no less a source of my delight in God than my own excellence. By contrast, the one who "does not wish to love the good common to all, is now rightly consumed with envy regarding another's good."[28] The success of another "burns" the envious one, says Hugh, because he does not possess through love "him in whom is every good." The envious one considers "another's good to be foreign from himself," when he does not through love "possess his own good and another's good together" in God.[29] Thus, the lost affectivity of pride with respect to God gives birth to a lost affectivity with respect to the neighbor, "since [the soul] is not delighted at the good of another through charity."[30] Rather than loving the neighbor as corecipient of gratuitous goods, envy burns and pines for the goods of the neighbor as a rival competitor. And, just as the perverse affection of pride resulted in loss of God, so envy's perverse affection loses the neighbor as well.[31]

Envy, however, is not only the offspring of pride. Together with pride, envy engenders anger. Anger (which captures Hugh's meaning better than "wrath") is but the corollary of envy. To desire another's excellence for oneself implies, of course, that one lacks such goods. And for the person both proud and envious, the awareness of such deficiency produces anger at himself or self-hatred "in light of his own imperfection."[32] So, even that which he already possesses now "begins to displease," "since he recognizes in another that which he is not able to possess."[33] Here again, perverse affectivity yields a severed relationship, for the perversity of anger directed at the self for lacking another's excellences results now in self-alienation.

The cumulative effect of this vicious triad is the "despoiling" of human nature. The root problem is perverse affectivity funded

28. *De quinque septenis* 84–86.
29. *De quinque septenis* 86–90.
30. *De quinque septenis* 97–98.
31. *De quinque septenis* 90–93: "Now, therefore, the more he extols himself through pride against the Creator, the more he falls under his neighbor through envy; the more he falsely rises up in one place, the more he is truly brought low in another."
32. *De quinque septenis* 94–97: "This corruption, once begun, cannot stop here: for as soon as envy has been born of pride, anger is born from envy, since the wretched soul is now angered at itself because of its own imperfection."
33. *De quinque septenis* 98–100.

by a false construal of the nature of creaturely excellence. The failure to recognize God as the supremely good source of all creaturely goods results in the failure to delight both in God as the source of such goods and in the goods themselves as from God. This primal affective failure manifests itself in a twofold affective perversity: envy and anger. The result of perverse affectivity is the psychological forfeiture of all goods, created and uncreated. Hugh sums up the resulting situation thus:

> He who could have everything in God through charity loses through envy and anger what he attempted to have through pride. After he loses God through pride, he loses his neighbor through envy and himself through anger.[34]

Perverse affectivity results in the loss of basic creaturely integrity—loss of God through love of one's own excellence apart from God; loss of neighbor through love of one's own excellence in opposition to the neighbor; loss of self through hatred of one's own lack of excellence.

Tristitia: A Punishing Sadness

Hugh's unhappy tale now reaches a transition point with the fourth vice: "Since, therefore, everything has been lost . . . the soul is cast down within itself by sadness."[35] Perhaps reflecting his distinctive interest in affectivity, Hugh (following Gregory the Great) prefers *tristitia* ("sadness") over the more traditional *acedia* ("sloth"). Having now lost God, neighbor, and self, "nothing remains," says Hugh, "in which the unhappy conscience can delight." Cut off from God, neighbor, and self, the soul is "confined within itself" in its disaffected state. For Hugh, moreover, this is a punishing sadness, illustrated by a graphic image: "After pride, envy, and anger . . . sadness follows immediately, which lashes the one now stripped."[36] Yet this punishment is not inflicted from without, but rather is the natural outcome of the preceding vices. "He who

34. *De quinque septenis* 100–104.
35. *De quinque septenis* 105–6.
36. *De quinque septenis* 108–10.

would not rejoice lovingly over another's good," he says, is "justly tortured [*cruciatur*]."[37]

The "Exiling" Triad: Greed/Avarice, Gluttony, Lust/Luxury

Hugh now turns to the final triad of vices: greed, gluttony, and lust. Here his analysis is surprisingly brief: after sadness comes avarice or greed, which, "once interior joy has been lost," compels the soul "to seek consolation in external things."[38] Greed then propels the soul outside of itself. Next, gluttony seduces the one thus "externalized."[39] And, finally, "lust arrives, which violently subjects to servitude the one thus seduced." As Hugh explains: gluttony's inebriating excess has inflamed the flesh such that "its resolution has been softened and weakened," and it can no longer resist "the supervening ardor of lust." The mind, now "unseemly subjugated, serves this domination most cruelly."[40]

This is Hugh's overall conception of vice. Welling up internally out of pride, envy, and anger, the spring of vice carries humankind away from God, neighbor, and self and, pausing momentarily to lash humankind with sadness, then gushes forth externally into greed, gluttony, and lust, which expel, seduce, and reduce humans to slavery. This progressive despoliation, dissipation, and bondage is a movement from interiority to exteriority, as Hugh indulges a deeply Augustinian priority on the integrity of the former and a corresponding horror at the dissipation of the latter. Vice for Hugh is centrifugal: it flees the centeredness of the soul.

After completing his analysis of vice, Hugh pauses to emphasize its destructive effects by offering another "similitude," which adopts an equally graphic metaphor:

> Through pride, then, the heart is puffed up, through envy it is dried out, through anger it is shattered, through sadness it is pounded and

37. *De quinque septenis* 107–8.
38. *De quinque septenis* 111–13.
39. *De quinque septenis* 114.
40. *De quinque septenis* 118–21.

as it were reduced to dust, through avarice it is scattered, through gluttony it is infected and as it were moistened, through lust it is trampled under foot and reduced to mud.[41]

Here, Hugh graphically depicts the overall effect of vice as the loss of integral creaturely form, whereby the person is reduced to a state of inchoate, unformed matter reminiscent of the state in Genesis prior to God's imposition of creaturely form upon the slime of the earth. In short, vice disintegrates and deforms.

With these graphic images, Hugh depicts a progressive psychological disintegration, whose primary manifestation is a lost interior capacity for feeling with respect to God, neighbor, and self and thus a corresponding perverse affective extroversion toward riches, dishes, and sex.

The Christological Source of Pneumatological Grace

Having established the sevenfold malady besetting human nature, Hugh turns to the remedy, which as noted will entail the remaining four sevens: the seven petitions from the Lord's Prayer, the seven gifts of the Spirit, the seven virtues, and their seven rewards found in the Beatitudes. As noted, excepting the gifts of the Spirit, Hugh's conception of the restoration of human nature is drawn from the Sermon on the Mount. Before exploring these sevens in detail, three general observations are warranted in light of Hugh's own introductory remarks.

First, at this juncture Hugh observes that "when the soul has become stuck fast in the mire of the deep . . . it can never be extracted, unless it calls out to Jesus and implores his assistance."[42] Though prime facie a pious platitude, Hugh's remark here is telling. In one sense, it could merely be a matter of course, for he is about to introduce the seven petitions of the Lord's Prayer, which will collectively constitute just such a request for divine assistance. Further consideration, however, suggests that Hugh is making a specific christological point, for he proceeds to present the Lord's

41. *De quinque septenis* 135–39.
42. *De quinque septenis* 141–44.

Prayer to his readers, not merely as given *by* Jesus to his disciples, but also as prayed *to* Jesus by them: "There follows then the seven petitions against the seven vices: with these petitions, he who taught us to pray [namely, Jesus], *is prayed to* that he might assist us."[43] Hugh proceeds to underscore the point. Jesus "promised," he says, "that to us who pray these [petitions] *he* would give the good Spirit so that our wounds might be healed and the bonds of our captivity would be loosed."[44] Hugh depicts Jesus here as both source of the prayer and the one to whom it is prayed. But the reference here to receiving the "good spirit" (*spiritum bonum*) cinches the point, for it is a clear allusion to the parallel passage in Luke 11:13. There, after giving his disciples the Lord's Prayer, Jesus tells them, in the Vulgate version: "If you then, being evil, know how to give good gifts to your children, how much more will *your Father* from heaven give the good Spirit [*spiritum bonum*] to them that ask him!" (emphasis added). In these statements, Hugh has shifted the petitionary valence of the Lord's Prayer so that it is directed, not to the Father, but to Jesus himself. Though subtle, these shifts indicate a distinct christological emphasis: Hugh's remedy for vice has its source in Jesus: "For this reason," Hugh concludes, "[Jesus] taught us to pray, so that our every good may come from him."[45]

Having situated Jesus, not merely as the giver of the Lord's Prayer, but also as the one to whom it is prayed and the source of what is received by praying it, a second point emerges regarding the remedy. Recognizing that our every good comes from Jesus, we come to understand both "that we ask" and "that, asking, we receive" to be "his gift and not our merit."[46] Hugh thus asserts the deeply gratuitous nature of the remedy. Recalling that the root of all human vice entails a misconstrual of the source of creaturely excellence, the remedy begins by reducing the sinner to a posture of radical receptivity. By situating the Lord's Prayer as the foundation of the remedy, Hugh foregrounds the dependence of the creature upon the grace of the creator. The posture of petitionary prayer

43. *De quinque septenis* 126–27 (emphasis added).
44. *De quinque septenis* 127–30 (emphasis added).
45. *De quinque septenis* 147–48.
46. *De quinque septenis* 148–50.

is, moreover, never transcended. Every step in the seven stages of reform begins with a prayerful petition. At every point, then, the remedy begins not with human striving for virtue but with prayerful petition for divine assistance. And, moreover, the very possibility and vehicle of prayer are themselves not meritorious initiatives, but rather gratuitous gifts.

The third observation regarding Hugh's conception of the remedy underscores its gratuitous nature, while also highlighting an important pneumatological feature of the four sevens. As noted, three of the four sevens constituting the remedy are drawn from the Sermon on the Mount. The remaining set is the sevenfold gift of the Holy Spirit. Hugh's choice of where to insert these gifts is noteworthy. Significantly, he locates them immediately after the seven petitions of the Lord's Prayer and thus before the sevenfold virtues and beatitudes. In effect, each petition is a request for a gift.[47] At the heart of the remedy, accordingly, Hugh locates a christologically grounded act of prayer that requests a set of pneumatological gifts, which, in turn, lead to virtue and beatitude. In sum, the gifts of the Spirit given by Jesus in response to the Lord's Prayer are the foundation of the remedy. Linking these in this way, Hugh erects an integrated christological and pneumatological structure for the remedial process.

The Five x Seven Schema

Turning now to the remedy in greater detail, it is surprising at first glance that, having treated the first three vices at length but the remaining four vices in a perfunctory way, Hugh now reverses the pattern. He discusses the remedies for pride and envy with little elaboration. In these, nonetheless, the basic relationship among the remaining four sevens is apparent. When we "who through pride are rebellious and insolent" pray "may your name be sanctified," we are requesting to learn how "to fear and to venerate his name."

---

47. The patristic and medieval tendency to derive the gifts of the Spirit from Isaiah 11 (which Jesus quotes with reference to himself at the beginning of his ministry) rather than from Paul's list in 1 Cor. 12–14 encourages this connection between Christology and pneumatology in relation to the gifts of the Spirit.

Accordingly, the gift of the fear of the Lord is given, so that "upon entering the heart this gift creates the virtue of humility, which heals the disease of pride, so that the humble man may arrive at the kingdom of heaven."[48] And, he who prays "let your kingdom come" "asks for the common salvation of all." He receives, accordingly, "the spirit of piety," which "enkindles generous kindness in him," so that he himself arrives at the same possession of eternal inheritance which he desires his neighbor to achieve."[49] These first two rungs illustrate the pattern: each petition is for a gift; each gift produces in the soul a virtue that supplants the corresponding vice and so paves the way for the accompanying beatitude.

Already in these first two rungs the difficulty, as well as the ingenuity, of Hugh's septenary scheme is visible. In order to make poverty of spirit the remedy for pride, for instance, Hugh glosses it with the notion of humility; in order to counteract envy he defines gentleness (*mansuetudo*) as generous kindness (*benignitas*). Again, the beatific reward at the first rung is the "kingdom of heaven," even though the petition "may your kingdom come" is in the second level. Yet, remarkably, despite an occasional inapposite coordination, a logic, or at least a fittingness, frequently emerges in the alignment of the sevens.[50] In opposition to pride, the gift of fear does seem an apt source of humility. To pray that the kingdom of God should come does seem to overcome the narrow egocentrism of envy so as to encompass the whole earth as an eternal inheritance. Perhaps the third rung works best: to pray that God's will "be done, on earth as in heaven" is to find pleasing "whatever the will of God dispenses . . . either in oneself or in others." To this request is given a certain kind of knowledge (*scientia*) by which one comes to "know that the evil that he suffers comes from his own fault, but that the good that he possesses proceeds

48. *De quinque septenis* 151–59.
49. *De quinque septenis* 160–71.
50. In his introduction to Augustine's exegesis of the Sermon on the Mount (in *The Preaching of Augustine; "Our Lord's Sermon on the Mount,"* trans. Francine Cardman, ed. Jaroslav Pelikan, Preacher's Paperback Library 13 [Philadelphia: Fortress, 1973], xvii), Jaroslav Pelikan notes that at points Augustine's interpretations seem to be "superimposed on the text, but it is a tribute to the power of his rhetoric that one often begins to wonder whether perhaps they have really been there all along." A similar sentiment seems appropriate at times with Hugh's arrangement.

from divine mercy." In this way, continues Hugh, the soul "learns, either in the evil which he sustains or in the good that he does not possess, not to become angry," but rather in "all things to exhibit patience." Such knowledge produces compunction (*compunctio*), that is, sorrow for sin, which is rewarded ultimately with comfort (*consolatio*), "so that he who willingly afflicts himself in this life before the face of God through lamentation, will merit to find true joy and gladness in the next life."[51] Despite the artificiality of the five x seven schema, then, a certain harmonization of the various elements does seem to occur.

"Wisdom according to Its Name": Recovering Lost Affectivity

It is in his analysis of the latter part of the septenaries that Hugh's overriding interest in affectivity reemerges, as he explores the psychological dynamics at hand in the remedies that he finds in the Sermon on the Mount for sadness, greed, and lust.

The fourth vice, *tristitia* ("sadness"), discussed above, entails the transition from a perverse interior affectivity to its exterior manifestation. Fittingly, this stage of the remedy begins with the fourth petition: "Give us today our daily bread." Hugh will now capitalize on the metaphor of eating and tasting food. Expanding on his initial description of sadness, Hugh notes that it "is weariness of the soul from grief, when the mind, in a certain manner dissolved and embittered by its vice, no longer has an appetite for internal goods." More forcefully than before, Hugh stresses here how this vice entails the suppression of interior affectivity construed as spiritual appetite: "with all its vigor deadened," he says, "the soul is no longer cheered with the desire for spiritual refreshment." Such a soul is admonished to invoke "the mercy of the Lord" and his "habitual tender pity," that Jesus "may nourish the languishing soul with spiritual food." Then, observes Hugh, "what the soul does not know how to seek when it is absent, it may begin to love by being aroused by a taste of its presence." To

---

51. *De quinque septenis* 172–92.

the one who prays for this spiritual daily bread is given the Spirit-gift of fortitude, which "creates in the heart the hunger for righteousness." Such a hunger, if consistently "enkindled" in this life, will be rewarded with "the full satiety of beatitude" in the next. The remedy for sadness's loss of spiritual appetite, then, is this "hunger for righteousness," to which Hugh gives his characteristic affective twist. The effect of the gift of fortitude is to restore to the "fainting soul" the "strength of its pristine vigor" and thereby its "desire of interior savor." In this way, concludes Hugh, "admonished by the taste of what is made present to it, it begins to love that which, when it was absent, it did not even know to desire."[52]

Finding little in the fifth rung[53] pertaining to affectivity, Hugh moves quickly to the final two rungs, which pertain to the fully exteriorized state of vice manifest in gluttony and lust. Here, he simply builds upon the foundation laid in the discussion of sadness, for the now-reinvigorated interior appetite begins to counteract the exteriorizing valence of vice. Hugh's analysis here reflects an emerging twelfth-century interest in the relative autonomy and integrity of the natural world, including human nature.[54] Accordingly, Hugh considers gluttony and lust to be excessive, disordered expressions of valid natural appetites. Gluttony, says Hugh, "is the temptation by which the enticement of the flesh, often through the natural appetite, strives to drag us to excess and unwittingly subject us to pleasure, while it flatters us that these things are obviously necessities."[55] Its remedy begins, therefore, with an attempt to discern the point at which these natural appetites exceed "the measure of necessity."[56] Without supernatural aid, however, this is impossible. And so, the soul prays, with apparent appositeness, "do not permit us to be lead into temptation," to which request is given the spirit of understanding. This gift "cleanses and purifies the heart" and "brings about in the interior eye luminosity and serenity by the cognition of the word of God, healing it like

52. *De quinque septenis* 193–209.
53. *De quinque septenis* 210–20.
54. See M.-D. Chenu, *Nature, Man, and Society in the Twelfth Century*, trans. Jerome Taylor and L. K. Little (Chicago: University of Chicago Press, 1968), 1–48.
55. *De quinque septenis* 222–26.
56. *De quinque septenis* 226–29.

a liquid eye-salve, so that it may also be made perspicacious for the contemplation of divine beauty." In this way, "purity of heart is born," which merits the vision of God.[57]

Though "understanding" typically lends itself to the metaphor of seeing, and the biblical text here invokes the language of interior sight, it is a measure of Hugh's predilection for affectivity that he weaves into this discussion too, somewhat awkwardly, the metaphor of interior eating. Through the gift of understanding, "the interior nourishment of the word of God restrains the exterior appetite, and the need of the body cannot break a mind nourished by spiritual food, nor can the pleasure of the flesh overcome it." As an example, Hugh recalls Jesus's temptation in the wilderness. When tempted by "bodily bread," Jesus had recourse to the word of God, "every word that proceeds from the mouth of God" (Matt. 4:4). In this way, claims Hugh, Jesus "clearly showed that when the mind is fed inwardly by that bread, it does not care much if it suffers bodily hunger for a time. Thus the spirit of understanding is given against gluttony."[58]

The remedy for gluttony here entails reestablishing an inward "center of spiritual gravity," as it were, and this occurs through interior affectivity. Hugh seems to envision the reinvigorated interior appetite for the word of God as providing a counterweight to exterior appetites, thus reining them in. Having begun in relation to sadness, where lost interior affectivity was reintroduced into the soul, here in relation to gluttony, as interior taste acquires sufficient vigor to bring the soul back into balance, it counteracts the excessive exterior orientation of vice with an emerging interior taste for the word of God. At the same time, such interior affectivity counteracts the dissipating fragmentation of vice, and the implication, though not yet stated explicitly, is that such interior refection accomplishes the opposite of fragmentation, namely, integration. Hugh's conception of the remedy here is that of a restored integrity and order to the soul through affectivity. For him, the cognition of the word of God through the Spirit's gift of understanding, encountered by the soul as a kind of spiritual food, effects its healing.

57. *De quinque septenis* 240–50.
58. *De quinque septenis* 231–40.

This reintegration born of restored affectivity finds its experiential consummation in the seventh and last rung of the five septenaries. Here, the soul prays: "Deliver us from evil," as a remedy for lust. Hugh understands this call for deliverance as a cry for freedom. "Fittingly," he says, "the healed servant asks for freedom." In return, he receives the gift of wisdom, "which gift restores lost liberty to the captive," so that "now, through the help of grace, he escapes the bonds of unjust domination that he was powerless in his own strength [to escape]."[59] Evangelical liberty, then, is the result of the gift of wisdom. But how precisely does wisdom restore liberty? Predictably, Hugh's answer is that freedom is a function of the soul's affectivity. He notes that the Latin *sapientia* ("wisdom") is derived from *sapor* ("savor"). Accordingly, he argues, "when the mind is touched by a taste of interior sweetness, desire gathers the whole self within. It is thus no longer weakly dissipated into fleshly pleasure, because that in which it delights is totally within it."[60] For Hugh, the affective experience of interior tasting has the effect of restoring order and integrity to the soul. With the centrifugal force of vice and its fragmenting, dissipating, dissolving effects now overcome, the centripetal energy of desire, infused by the gift of wisdom, forges a gathered concentration on God deep within the soul. And this state of affairs constitutes freedom, "so that the more the mind savors and enjoys the interior, the more freely and the more gladly it disdains exterior pleasure." Interior integration establishes liberty in relation to exterior desires. The end result is a tranquil composedness within the soul, which Hugh, following Augustine, calls rest and peace: "Finally, the soul, at peace within itself and desiring nothing externally, rests wholly within through love."[61] Hugh describes this final state in a lapidary summary:

> Therefore, the spirit of wisdom, when it touches the heart through its sweetness, both tempers the ardor of external desire and . . . creates peace within, so that when the mind is wholly concentrated on interior delight, a person is fully and perfectly reformed in the

59. *De quinque septenis* 251–56.
60. *De quinque septenis* 256–60.
61. *De quinque septenis* 260–65.

image of God: as it is written: *Blessed are the peacemakers for they shall be called the sons of God* (Matt. 5:9).[62]

The entire process of the four x seven remedy for vice comes to fruition in this sapiential state of interior affectivity. A composed integration, wrought by a concentrated affective intensity, whose center is the soul's interior love for and delight in God as the highest good, emerges as a temper, a tranquil, liberating peace within the soul. This notion of complete concentration suggests that everything is summed up and experienced here, in the soul's delight in God as the *summum bonum*. The fragmenting, dissipating quest for exterior goods is not so much wrong, as wrongheaded and unnecessary, for what was sought in them is found, possessed, and enjoyed to the full within, from, with, and in God. This is the soul's reformation in the image of God, and when it has occurred the servant has now become a son, who enjoys the liberty befitting his status.

Conclusion: Practices of Prayer and Meditation

These then are the five sevens. By way of conclusion, two observations are warranted. On the one hand, the five sevens rubric *describes* both the predicament and the remedy for fallen human nature. The predicament is perverse affectivity. The remedy is christologically grounded prayer for pneumatologically facilitated grace. It involves the reformation of human nature through a process that gradually, step by step, reintegrates and reorders human affectivity, that is, the disposition of the soul's desires and delights, recentering them on God, the *summum bonum*, the continual source of all created goods and excellences. By so doing, it establishes in the soul the virtuous conditions that lead to beatitude.[63] As noted above, the Sermon on the Mount thus stands at the center of the remedy.

On the other hand, it should not go unnoticed that this rubric *prescribes* a set of practices. First, there can be little doubt that

62. *De quinque septenis* 265–68.
63. It is worth noting that Hugh consistently treats the Beatitudes as eschatological realities—never realized fully here, but only in the next life.

the five sevens framework was meant to be a memory device. Hugh ends the treatise by addressing the recipient directly in the second person: "Accept this little gift concerning the five sevens . . . and when you think about it, remember me."[64] This reference to memory is not likely casual. For the medievals, and for Hugh of St. Victor in particular (as Mary Carruthers demonstrates),[65] memory was a central moral faculty and intellectual act. Much more than simply a means of information storage and retrieval, memory in the medieval context was, in a word, soul-forming. Like a seal on wax, the soul was deeply shaped by what it stored in memory. For the medievals, furthermore, what was stored in memory was not simply tucked away. Rather, it thereby was to be always readily retrievable, so as to be an object of thoughtful reflection and analysis, that is, to be an object of meditation. The act of meditation facilitated this formation of the soul. Yet again, meditation was not an end in itself, but issued forth in virtuous action. One can assume, then, that the five sevens served all these practical purposes. Their arrangement made them easily memorizable. This, in turn, allowed them all, in various ways—their individual elements as well as their relation to other elements—to be the object of meditative reflection. Finally, with the Lord's Prayer standing at the heart of the remedy, the five sevens offered a practice of prayer that was enriched by being situated thus in relation to the other sevens. Once committed to memory it would be impossible to pray the *Pater Noster* without "seeing" its connections to the vices, gifts, virtues, and Beatitudes and in so doing to be drawn further into the reforming process found in the five sevens.

With this rubric, Hugh attempts to sum up in a unified, comprehensive fashion much of the lived Christian life as conceived of in his time. For our Victorine, as presumably for his contemporaries, the five sevens framework, with the Sermon on the Mount as its center, reveals that "fitting correspondences" (*convenientia*)[66] truly

64. *De quinque septenis* 272–74.
65. See Mary J. Carruthers, *The Book of Memory: A Study of Memory in Medieval Culture*, Cambridge Studies in Medieval Literature (Cambridge: Cambridge University Press, 1990).
66. *De quinque septenis* 4.

existing among and between the various elements of the sevens. From that perspective, Dante was right to see Hugh of St. Victor as a symbol of overarching harmonies.

Appendix: Hugh of St. Victor's Five Sevens

Vices	Petitions	Gifts	Virtues	Beatitudes
1. pride (*superbia*)	hallowed by your name (*sanctificetur nomen tuum*)	fear of the Lord (*timor Domini*)	poverty of spirit/ humility (*paupertas spiritus/ humilitas*)	kingdom of heaven (*regnum coelorum*)
2. envy (*invidia*)	your kingdom come (*adveniat regnum tuum*)	piety (*pietas*)	meekness/generous kindness (*mansuetudo/ benignitas*)	inherit the earth (*possessio terrae viventium*)
3. anger (*ira*)	your will be done on earth as in heaven (*fiat voluntas tua . . . in coelo/ in terra*)	knowledge (*scientia*)	mourning/sorrow (*compunctio/dolor*)	comfort (*consolatio*)
4. sadness (*tristitia*)	give us today our daily bread (*da nobis hodie panem nostrum*)	fortitude (*fortitudino*)	hunger for righteousness/ desire for the good (*esuries justitiae/ desiderium bonum*)	satiety (*justitiae satietas*)
5. greed (*avaritia*)	forgive us our trespasses (*dimitte nobis debita nostra*)	counsel (*consilium*)	merciful (*misericordia*)	mercy (*misericordia*)
6. gluttony (*gula*)	lead us not into temptation (*ne nos inducas in tentationem*)	understanding (*intellectus*)	purity of heart (*cordis munditia*)	vision of God (*visio Dei*)
7. lust (*luxuria*)	deliver us from evil (*libera nos a malo*)	wisdom (*sapientia*)	peacemakers (*pax*)	sons of God (*filiatio Dei*)

Dante and Chaucer

David Lyle Jeffrey

5

To compare Dante and Chaucer as readers of the Sermon on the Mount is to sample perhaps the most overt sensibility shift, with regard to the place of Scripture in Christian pedagogy, to occur between late antiquity and the Reformation. If this seems too immodest a claim, I pray you bear with me, as we strive to catch up with Dante and Virgil, mid-*Purgatorio*, canto 12, on the first cornice:

> As we turned thither, voices in our ear
> Sang out *Beati pauperes spiritu*;
> No tongue could tell how sweet they were to hear.
>
> What different passes these from those we knew
> In Hell! For there with hideous howl of pain,
> But here with singing, we are ushered through.[1]

So Dante, still with Virgil, "step by step, like oxen in the yoke" (12.1), remembers where he has but lately been. Now his feet are gliding over mosaics on the floor, like funerary *memento mori* in

1. Dante's text is cited here from *Dante Aligheri: The Divine Comedy*, trans. with commentary by Charles S. Singleton, 6 vols., Bolingen Series 30 (Princeton: Princeton University Press, 1973), 3.128; the translation is by Dorothy Sayers, *The Comedy of Dante Alighieri the Florentine*, 3 vols. (New York: Basic Books, 1962), 2.

a mausoleum. He looks down on fleeting images of those who, since Lucifer, have fallen prey to Pride and fallen far, then up to see by contrast a "beauteous creature, clothed in white . . . a star of dawn all tremulous with light" (12.88–90). It is the Angel of Humility, mentor of the first cornice. As Dante mounts the proffered stair, his burden seems suddenly lighter, and as from cornice to cornice he climbs, the weight and the stain of sin lifts slowly, stage by stage, through six of the Matthean Beatitudes. At the summit of Mount Purgatory a mediate *summum bonum* will be his, to become "blessed as those whose sins are covered" (Ps. 32:1; *Purgatorio* 29.3); correspondingly he will have here at last a renewed vision of beatitude in the person of Beatrice.

Beata/Beatitudo/Beatrice

That Dante thus employs the Matthean Beatitudes in his pilgrim's purgatorial education is widely known. Although this rich text contains but a small fraction of his allegedly 570 allusions to Holy Scripture (principally in the *Commedia*) it is for many moderns easily the best-known instance of Dante's use of the Bible. Perhaps partly as a consequence, much has been made of the mere fact of it. Yet with but two exceptions these are the only portions of the Sermon on the Mount to be integrated into his poetic theology.

It will be apparent to readers of the *Commedia* that Dante's primary intellectual sources are classical poetry and philosophy on the one hand, Scholastic theology and the liturgy of the church on the other. It may be the case, as Peter Hawkins seems to suggest, that Dante more or less habitually read the Bible directly.[2] But if so, it was surely in a context laden with exegetical and theological reflection, perhaps as in the glossed Bible or in a compendium commentary such as the *Catena aurea* of Thomas Aquinas. Further,

2. Peter S. Hawkins, *Dante's Testaments: Essays in Scriptural Imagination* (Stanford: Stanford University Press, 1999), 14, 37–38, passim. Elsewhere, Hawkins says that the "absorption of the Vulgate into the poet's vernacular shows on a minutely linguistic level the larger effort of the *Commedia* to rewrite the Bible"; see his "Dante and the Bible," in *The Cambridge Companion to Dante*, ed. Rachel Jacoff (Cambridge: Cambridge University Press, 1993), 128.

since his biblical allusions are cryptic, disconnected, and even in the case of the Beatitudes textured with associated liturgical psalms and hymns and allusions to poetry and the visual arts, it seems wiser to me to be cautious about attributing to Dante any sustained textual reflection on the Sermon on the Mount in and for itself. John Freccero rightly observes, I think, that "major revelations come to the pilgrim subjectively . . . in a landscape suffused with mist," fragments in a cortex of nostalgic reminiscence or reverie.[3]

Analysis of Dante's biblical allusions suggests that liturgy provides the dominant formation: biblical quotations thus come chiefly from the Psalms, Song of Songs, Isaiah, Jeremiah, the Gospels, Pauline Epistles, and Revelation in more or less that order of frequency. Unsurprisingly the *Inferno* offers least. It may surprise us that the *Purgatorio* alludes to the Bible most profusely in the *Commedia*, with thirty direct citations and about forty allusions.[4]

What makes Dante's citations from the Beatitudes in the *Purgatorio* somewhat unusual is that they are quoted in a sequence at least evocative of their biblical context and are systematically integrated into an ordered spiritual pilgrimage, even a kind of Bonaventuran *itinerarium mentis in deum*. Thus, they can be said to contribute to structure or form in the poem itself.[5] The structure, however, remains more Bonaventuran than biblical. Bonaventure's work begins as a mediation upon the vision that St. Francis experienced on Mount Alverna; in Bonaventure there are not, as in Dante, seven angels to symbolize stages and elements of the required *askēsis*, but the one seraph with six wings, which Francis saw and whose bibli-

---

3. John Freccero, *Dante: The Poetics of Conversion*, ed. Rachel Jacoff (Cambridge: Harvard University Press, 1986), 210.

4. John A. Scott, *Understanding Dante* (Notre Dame: University of Notre Dame Press, 2004), 299; cf. Hawkins, *Dante's Testaments*, 36, 42–43.

5. See Anne Maria Chiavacci Leonardi, "Le beatitudini e la struttura poetica del 'Purgatorio,'" *Giiornale storico della letteratura italiana* 141/fasc. 513 (1984): 1–29, esp. 7–8, 24. Also Christopher Kleinhenz, "Dante and the Bible: Biblical Citation in the Divine Comedy," in *Dante: Contemporary Perspectives*, ed. Amilcare A. Iannucci (Toronto: University of Toronto Press, 1997), 74–93; and, though less usefully for present purposes, Giovanni Barblan, ed., *Dante e la bibbia: atti del convegno internazionale promosso da "Biblia": Firenze, 26-27-28 settembre 1986* (Florence: Olshki, 1988).

cal source was the vision of Isaiah (Isaiah 6). Yet in Bonaventure, quite precisely as in Dante,

> he who wishes to ascend to God must, avoiding sin which deforms nature, exercise [knowledge of the truth according to the symbolic, literal, and mystical modes of theology] . . . strive toward the reflection of truth [so that] . . . by striving he mounts step by step to the summit of that high mountain where we shall see the God of gods in Zion [Ps. 84:7]. (*Itinerarium* 1.7–8)

Bonaventure's goal, like Dante's, is a state of beatific vision. It is to be obtained by an experience of grace that follows upon a practice of the virtues (both four cardinal and three theological) and marked by the addition, *gratia gratis data*, of seven gifts of the Holy Spirit, which had been thought of as their analogues at least since the time of St. Augustine (*Breviloquium* 5.5). Here, if not also from the "five senses" of Hugh of St. Victor, is a prototype for Dante's *scala* of seven pedagogical ministrations.[6] But their ordering is not parallel to the order, *in situ*, of the Matthean Beatitudes, and it is difficult thus to construe Dante's handling of the Beatitudes as, in any normative sense, either a commentary or a direct engagement with the biblical text.

From Dante this is, quite precisely, what we should expect. Here, as usually for him, his response is far more to *sacra doctrina* than to the Scriptures themselves, and he is in this respect typically Scholastic (cf. Thomas Aquinas, *Summa theologiae* 1.1). For example, in Thomas, as with Bonaventure, treatment of the Beatitudes is also situated in a formative discussion of the habits and virtues. It follows immediately upon the distinction Thomas makes between moral and intellectual virtues and on the cardinal

6. *Breviloquium*, trans. Erwin Esser Nemmers (London: Herder, 1946), chap. 6. Hugh of St. Victor's *De quinque septenis* relates five sets of seven topoi in a pattern of doctrinal correspondence. In this work the Beatitudes are prescribed as antidotes to the seven deadly sins. For a good discussion, see Erich Loos, "Die Ordnung der Seligspreisungen der Berpredigt in Dantes Purgatorio," in *Literatur und Spiritualität: Hans Sckommodau zum siebzigsten Geburstag*, ed. Hans Rheinfelder, Pierre Christophorov, and Eberhard Müller-Bochat (Munich: Fink, 1978), 153–64. Hugh's system is generated from Isa. 11:1–3 and New Testament passages on the sevenfold gifts of the Holy Spirit. See also Etienne Gilson, *Dante and Philosophy* (New York: Harper, 1949), 2–16.

and theological virtues as a subset of these. (Immediately precedent to the four articles on the Beatitudes is Thomas's account of the gifts of the Holy Spirit.)[7] But lest we who are focused primarily on an interpretative history of the Sermon on the Mount should become too quickly dismissive, this type of virtue "schematic" actually arises quite early in the exegetical literature itself. Dante would have been familiar with some of it, perhaps even from such an encyclopedic compendium of biblical commentary as the *Catena aurea* of Thomas Aquinas. He could hardly have escaped, if so, connecting Augustine's remarks in his *The City of God* (19.1) relating the supreme good of philosophical enquiry and biblical "blessedness" or noting that John Chrysostom allegorized the mount from which Jesus addressed his followers as signifying that "he who teaches, as he who hears the righteousness of God should stand on a high ground of spiritual virtues"[8] or that Augustine in his commentary on the text in Matthew connected the "seven degrees of blessedness" to the "seven-form Holy Spirit" as he finds it proleptically present in Isaiah (*De sermo domine in monte*). But it may be that Augustine's teacher Ambrose and Lactantius are those most formative in framing evaluations of the Beatitudes in this way. In these early-fourth-century writers the virtue ethics of Jesus are seen not so much as a perfection, but rather a contrary of Roman, especially Stoic, accounts of virtue—not least because the Christian virtues of the Beatitudes can be practiced, as Lactantius famously insisted, by women and children.[9]

7. This relates to the work of Hugh of St. Victor just cited. See Thomas Aquinas, *Summa theologiae* I-II Q. 69. For the Latin text, I used the Dominican edition by Nicolai, Sylvii, Billuart, and C.-J. Drioux, *S. thomae aquinaatis summa theologica*, 7th ed., 8 vols. (Rome, 1856–73), but supplemented by the Blackfriars edition (London: Eyre & Spottiswoode, 1964–81). (Translations were checked against this edition.)

8. As cited in Thomas Aquinas, *Catena aurea: Commentary on the Four Gospels, Collected out of the Works of the Fathers*, ed. John Henry Newman, 4 vols. (London: Parker, 1841; repr. London: Saint Austin Press, 1997), 1.1146; regarding Augustine on Isaiah, see 157 (on Matt. 5:10).

9. This point contrasting the Beatitudes with Roman accounts of virtue has been made frequently: e.g., Lactantius, *Divine Institutes* 5.9.1; 5.15.1 (see the translation by Sister Mary Francis McDonald [Washington, DC: Catholic University of America Press, 1964], 347–48, 365–66). It was then taken up by Ambrose in *Exposition of the Holy Gospel according to St. Luke*, trans. Theodosia Tomkinson (Etna, CA: Center for Traditionalist Orthodox Studies, 2003), 174–82 §5.49–63, 76. The point about women

None of this genealogy need in itself detain us. Yet we should acknowledge Dante's debt to the patristic and medieval tendency to situate the Beatitudes (and the Sermon on the Mount more generally) in a context of a comparative study of virtue ethics whose purpose was generally Christian apologetic. Such a contextualization had become formative for medieval readings of both Matthew's and Luke's accounts of Jesus's discourse. In such accounts the Beatitudes are the farthest things from "Be Happy Attitudes"; rather, they are disciplines, cultivated habits of the heart, at their most rigorous an *askēsis* or purgation essential to the process of Christian perfection. Five of the Beatitudes from Matthew's Sermon are employed so as to provoke a practice of the virtue they embody in redressing a dominant vice. Thus, "blessed are the poor in spirit" counters pride, as the Angel of Humility makes clear. So also the "merciful" oppose envy (*Purgatorio* 15.38), the "peacemakers" anger (17.68–9), the "pure in heart" lust (27.8), and so on. Yet in Dante the commandment ultimately enjoined is evidently (though tacitly) the most intimidating of all: "Therefore you shall be perfect, just as your Father in heaven is perfect" (Matt. 5:48). He does not undertake to show how such perfection should be possible in this mortal life.[10] Though the doctrine of purgatory that Dante inherited draws little from the Sermon on the Mount (Matt. 5:25–26 is marginal, even extrinsic to the main tradition), it had long been established in relation to a forensic understanding of the Pauline doctrine of grace (e.g., 1 Cor. 3:11–15) and certain other sayings of Jesus (notably Matt. 12:32).[11] Moreover, the doctrine about purgatory developed in such a way that the Beatitudes, understood in terms of the expurgation

and children receives modern attention in Leonardi, "Le beatitudini," 7–8; and Patrick Boyde, *Human Vices and Human Work in Dante's Comedy* (Cambridge: Cambridge University Press, 2000), 110, though Boyde comments on the Matthew text directly.

10. Thomas Aquinas offers no comment on Matt. 5:48.

11. Among the sources typically adduced were Isidore of Seville, *De ordine creaturae* 14.6; Augustine, *City of God* 21.24; Gregory the Great, *Dialogues* 4.39—all on Matt. 12:32. First Cor. 3:11–15 attracts similar connections to the idea of purgation in the afterlife, e.g., by Ambrose, *Commentarium in Amos* 4; Augustine (on Ps. 37); Gregory again (as cited); and Thomas Aquinas in his *Contra gentes* 4.91. For a modern overview see Jacques Le Goff, *The Birth of Purgatory*, trans. Arthur Goldhammer (Chicago: University of Chicago Press, 1984).

of contrary vices, could be seen as anagogy, a meditatively internalized process of completion in ultimate virtue. When infused by sacramental grace their practice becomes mystically propedeutic to an absolute fulfillment of beatitude possible only in the world to come. That the one beatitude Dante omits (the second in the Vulgate: "Blessed are the meek, for they shall inherit the earth" [Matt. 5:5]) has unambiguously to do with this world rather than eternal reward may well explain his omission of it and, for his purpose, his dividing the fourth ("blessed are they who hunger and thirst for righteousness" [5:6]) into two parts (*Purgatorio* 22.6; 24.151–54).

Accordingly, it is important to stress at this point the subordination of biblical allusion to Dante's elaboration of an *anagogicus mos*. As every reader has seen, his focus, as in all mystical literature, is intensely (even if representatively) personal.[12] It is in his own individual consciousness, Dante the poet suggests, that the great poetic and theological synthesis both occurs and is rendered explicit. As with much mystical literature, we who are readers are overhearers and bear witness not so much to a repentance and conversion as to a word of prophecy. In Dante this is a powerful word, and the *Purgatorio* in particular is, as Dorothy Sayers insists, for theologically attuned readers the most powerful of the *Commedia's* three books. But it makes little or no contribution of substance to our understanding of the Sermon on the Mount. Indeed, even though it may be regarded as Dante's most extended meditation on a pericope in Scripture, the comment of Karl Vossler applies: "Whoever runs through the biblical references, reminiscences and allusions in Dante's writings will be amazed to see how great are the poet's debts in number, and how small in artistic importance."[13] Yet perhaps that does not so much matter in a realm where it is poetic imagination itself that makes us *puro e disposito a salire a le stelle* ("pure and prepared to leap up to the stars") (*Purgatorio* 33.145).

---

12. Cf. Sayers, who describes the *Commedia* as "at the same time intensely personal and magnificently public" (*Comedy of Dante Alighieri*, 2.42). My point is that in a comparison with Chaucer, there is overwhelmingly a greater sense of the poet's/persona's personal consciousness.

13. Karl Vossler, *Medieval Culture: An Introduction to Dante and His Times*, 2 vols. (New York: Ungar, 1929; repr. 1966), 2.100.

Blessedness and Social Virtue

Geoffrey Chaucer admired Dante but had a lower view of poetry. Chaucer's pilgrim guide in *The Canterbury Tales* is not Virgil or any other of the honorable classic Roman poets, but a rather boisterous, inept, ale-mongering innkeeper with a tin ear for poetry as well as theology. The voice of Chaucer's narrative persona, meanwhile, though as with Dante deliberately identified with the actual author, appears far less univocal, much more tentative, willing to let a wide array of fictive narrators speak as if for themselves, even obtrusively so, to the point of disruption. "Diverse folk diversely they seyde" (e.g., Reeve's Prologue, 3587; Man of Law's Tale, 211; Merchant's Tale, 1469; cf. Tale of Melibee Prologue, 2131, etc.) is a recurrent motif, often appearing precisely at those moments in which—were it Dante's *Commedia*—Dante, Virgil, Beatrice, or St. Bernard would be speaking somberly and authoritatively about a lesson to be drawn, so that the pilgrims' progress could move forward in something like tranquility and good order.

Structurally, several features invite comparison rather than contrast between the two great works. Both poems are presented as Lenten or Eastertide exercises; each is overtly penitential in presupposition and thematic development.[14] The basic linear structure of medieval pilgrimage narrative, figuratively from a *civitas terrena* to the *civitas aeterna*, is drawn from scriptural commentary and in such conceptual terms as famously formalized by Augustine in his *City of God*. There is a profound sense, moreover, in which it might be said that the goal of each work is "communion," not merely as a matter of theme but as aspiration in the poet himself.

Yet even as we consider these plausible analogies, at each point we are confronted with a deliberated *différence* in Chaucer that

14. The overt Eastertide setting in Dante is much discussed. See Hawkins, *Dante's Testaments*, 247–64; Guiseppe Mazotta, *Dante: Poet of the Desert* (Princeton: Princeton University Press, 1979); Dunstan J. Turner, "'In exitu, Israel' . . . the Divine Comedy in the Light of the Easter Liturgy," *American Benedictine Review* 11 (1960): 43–61; and Charles Singleton, "*In exitu Israel de Aegypto*," in *Dante: A Collection of Critical Essays*, ed. John Freccero (Englewood Cliffs, NJ: Prentice-Hall, 1965), 102–21. Comparatively less notice has been made of the Lenten setting for *The Canterbury Tales*, but see Chauncey Wood, "The April Date as Structuring Device in *The Canterbury Tales*," *Modern Language Quarterly* 25 (1964): 259–71.

bears directly on his considerably more prominent use of biblical text. Space here permits noting only a few of the most obvious points. First, Chaucer's more explicit invocation of the two-cities motif (London/Southwark as a point of worldly departure is succeeded by Canterbury as a "City of God" symbolically)[15] is plainly in evidence at the "literal" level of his fiction. Dante's spectral pilgrimage is from shadow (albeit the shadow of Rome) to light (that of the Celestial City), and his poetic form evokes a distinctive genre, namely individual dream-vision allegory and its topos of mystical ascent. Chaucer's pilgrims by contrast travel in a much more workaday world as in "a compagne of folke . . . and pilgrims were they all." They ride on to a place of evident temporal as well as spiritual reconciliation—with each other as well as with God— and toward an Eastertide celebration of Holy Communion at a literal English Cathedral in Canterbury. That is to say, Chaucer's pilgrimage foregrounds a more mundane realism textured with allegory and tropology in contrast to Dante's mysteries of dream vision, transfigured by anagogy.[16] In elaborating by means of fictive narrators a wide diversity of voices and potential perspectives— shaped (or distorted) as these must be by divergent motives in the human heart—Chaucer's poem becomes notoriously polyvocal. Though much of it was presented in person orally in the court as a species of court counsel (something Dante's work could not be), the poem as a seriatim social performance conveys, inter alia, a sense of practical political urgency for the active life, a feature that contrasts sharply with the studied inwardness of Dante's imaginative *via contemplative*.[17]

15. Much is made in the General Prologue of the pilgrimage origin and destination, yet only in the Parson's Prologue does the analogy of the English Eastertide pilgrimage to Canterbury with the voyage of the *civitas aeterna* become explicit (Parson's Prologue 48–51). See Russell A. Peck, "Number Symbolism in the Prologue to Chaucer's *Parson's Tale*," *English Studies* 48 (1967): 205–15.

16. Dante, as is evident from both the *Letter to Can Grande della Scala* and his *Convivio*, was intimately familiar with the typical four-level schemata of medieval exegesis. So was Chaucer, and not only because it was included in, e.g., the preface to the Wycliffite Bible. But in *The Canterbury Tales* little anagogy is suggested, and certainly nothing to support readings on that level of the sort proposed by Dante's son Pietro and later commentators for the *Commedia*.

17. See Gilson, *Dante and Philosophy*, 129–42.

Perhaps it is Chaucer's choice of polyvocity, rather than reliance on polysemeity alone,[18] which makes his appeal to Scripture itself as authority so apparently inevitable. Though riskier, there are certain advantages in such a strategy: when a diversity of voices eventually converges in meaning, their "collective witness" gains in strength. But one can discern something more: Chaucer's characters, adroit or inept, effective or (for our ironic instruction) most laughably misguided, seem natively far more naturally engaged in a conversation with the texts of Scripture directly. There is little Scholastic context or embedding, nor, for Chaucer's purposes, does there need to be. Indeed, one can easily trace in *The Canterbury Tales* a deep hermeneutic of suspicion of commentary, which often is dismissed as a "gloss" meant to gild the lily or even, when assigned to more malign characters, revealed as a deception concerning the actual teaching of Holy Scripture. (Chaucer's sensibility, when compared with Dante's, seems almost Protestant.)

The Summoner's false friar offers a representative example of Chaucer's rhetorical strategy, arousing suspicion because he preaches "after his symple wit, / Nat al [entirely] after the text of hooly writ"—offering as his reason that he reckons the text of Scripture would be too difficult for his hearers. Therefore he will teach rather the "glose" (ostensibly scholia on the text), since, after all,

> Glosying is a glorious thyng, certayn,
> For lettre sleeth, so as we clerkes seyn. (Summoner's Tale,
>   1789–94)

The implication here is plainly that, in the friar's eyes, commentary is in some sense both more appealing and of more spiritual value than the text itself. Similar views—always from characters of dubious integrity—are sprinkled through *The Canterbury Tales*.[19] Scrip-

18. Dante's seminal discussion of the polysemous character of poetic language is found in the *Letter to Can Grande* 7, in Robert S. Haller, trans., *Literary Criticism of Dante Alighieri* (Lincoln: Nebraska University Press, 1973), 99.

19. For a full account, see Lawrence Besserman, "Glosynge Is a Glorious Thyng: Chaucer's Biblical Exegesis," in *Chaucer and Scriptural Tradition*, ed. David Lyle Jeffrey

ture and its institutional apparatus of interpretation are thus set in tension in Chaucer, and the cumulative effect of many "stagey" misreadings by his fictive narrators early on heightens the actual reader's suspicions about slanted and repackaged citation of the Bible in such a way as to create a desire for a clarifying, more direct encounter with the Holy Scriptures in and for themselves.[20]

Nowhere is this tactic of *sensus interruptus* more evident than in Chaucer's extensive use of the Sermon on the Mount. The Sermon first makes obvious entrance into Chaucer's text in the Prologue to the Reeve's Tale. The Reeve, as a carpenter, is angered by the Miller's Tale just ended, which he perceives as a slight to his guild if not outright slander, and so he sets out to get even through a pillory of the Miller's Tale in the same low terms he sees have been used by his enemy:

> I pray to God his nekke mote to-breke [might break];
> He kan wel in myn eye seen a stalke,
> But in his owene he kan nat seen a balke [big board].
> (Reeve's Tale, 3918–20)

Two characteristic features of Chaucer's use of the Sermon are here immediately apparent. First, the text of Matthew 7:3–4 (cf. Luke 6:41–42) is transliterated fully enough that the reader sees it as evidence that the Reeve, so to speak, thinks he "knows" and has to some degree appropriated a familiar biblical text to his purpose. But the Reeve's selfish purpose is here actually to replicate the *fault* to which the biblical text is diagnostic, whereas the intent of our actual author, Chaucer, in control of the wider context of this verse in Matthew, is to allow the Reeve's perverse reading of Scripture to function as a kind of dramatic irony that prepares us for a better resolution to come from another quarter. Presently, the actual "readers" or "hearers" of Chaucer's text are able, whether such dullards as the Miller or Harry Bailey can manage it or not, to refer the "spirit" of the Reeve's use of the text back to that legalistic dis-

(Ottawa: University of Ottawa Press, 1984), 65–73.

20. I have discussed this matter at length in a chapter entitled "Authorial Intent and the Willful Reader," in my *People of the Book: Christian Identity and Literary Culture* (Grand Rapids: Eerdmans, 1996), 167–207.

position that Jesus has already condemned earlier in his mountain discourse. Thus, when the agent of the Reeve's revenge, the carnal Cambridge divinity student Aleyn, gets to planning a comeuppance for the mischief done him and his fellow student by the Miller's thievery (their plot is to cuckold the Miller), Aleyn says:

> For, John, there is a lawe that says thus,
> That gif [if] a man in a point be agreved,
> That in another he shall be releved. (Reeve's Tale, 4180–82)

The biblically literate reader, remembering Chaucer's initial direct evocation of the Sermon on the Mount, will be on guard at this point or, to put it in our terms, will be inclined to a hermeneutic of suspicion where these Cambridge divinity students' sense of "the law" is concerned.

There were actually many biblically literate readers in the court of Richard II, not only the so-called Lollard Knights but also the Bohemian courtiers of Queen Anne, many of whom were simultaneously students of John Wyclif at Oxford. Nor should we forget the Queen herself, who kept a copy of the Wycliffite translation by her bedside and read from it daily.[21] Such readers would readily remember here Matthew 5:38, the evocation by Jesus of the familiar lex talionis. But what follows from that verse in Jesus's Sermon, and famously so, of course, is a corrective: rather than take revenge in the manner of the old law, the disciple of Jesus is admonished to turn the other cheek (Matt. 5:39–44). One might expect a divinity student to know that (though perhaps not a Cambridge divinity student, Chaucer seems to suggest!). But the force of the allusion is to reinforce the first citation from Matthew 7:3–4 in the Reeve's Prologue, so highlighting the Reeve, with his well-advertised tale-telling motives, as a "measure for measure" judge of the stamp we meet later on in Shakespeare's play of that title—in which play, of course, the Sermon on the Mount likewise prominently figures.[22]

---

21. David Lyle Jeffrey, *The Law of Love: English Spirituality in the Age of Wyclif* (Grand Rapids: Eerdmans, 1988), 40–43 and notes; repr. as *English Spirituality in the Age of Wyclif* (Vancouver: Regent Publishing, 2000).

22. See Paul A. Olson, "The *Reeve's Tale*: Chaucer's *Measure for Measure*," *Studies in Philology* 59 (1962): 1–17; and G. Wilson Knight, "*Measure for Measure* and the Gospels,"

Chaucer seldom introduces a text from the Bible without subsequent allusion or citation of such a fashion as to make of the
quotation a motif or theme. Thus, it is characteristic of him that
in the Prologue of the next full tale (in the normative sequence),
that of the Man of Law, Matthew 5:38 returns again via the lips
of this officious yet obtuse lawyer as he announces the theme of
his own tale as he imagines it:

> For swiche [such] a lawe as a man yeveth [gives] another
>   wight [person]
> He sholde hymselven usen it, by right;
> Thus wole [this is the intention of] oure text. (Man of Law's
>   Tale, 43–46)

But we soon learn that we have been misled: this is not at all the
Man of Law's actual text. Rather, the tale he remembers turns out
to be about a saintly woman (Custance, whose name suggests "perseverance" or "constancy") who seems the very embodiment of the
Beatitudes, one who never descends to the letter of the law or seeks
revenge, but takes in patience all the harm done to her. By creating
such deliberate frisson between actual intention ("entente") in a
work itself and that which may be merely strategic for one who
uses that work, Chaucer shows us that the intention-driving use of
any text, in any tale, requires almost as much interpretation as the
text itself. Further, he frames and corrects his fictive storytellers in
such a way as to show that when a governing authorial intention
is independently declared, it can correct misunderstandings or,
indeed, legalistic precisionism authoritatively.[23] That, of course,
would seem to be what Jesus himself was doing in his Sermon
on the Mount, and it is apparent that both Wyclif and his favorite
predecessor Nicholas of Lyra understood the Sermon on the Mount
in this way—that is, a divine declaration of authorial intent.[24]

---

in his *Wheel of Fire* (London: Oxford University Press, 1930), 80–106. This play is still
referred to conventionally in such terms: a *Guardian* review (May 3, 2003) of the pro-
duction in London's West End by the Royal Shakespeare Theatre Company of that year
refers to the "complexity of Shakespeare's version of the Sermon on the Mount."

23. Jeffrey, *People of the Book*, 194–204. See Chauncey Wood, "Chaucer's Man of
Law as Interpreter," *Traditio* 23 (1967): 149–90.

24. Nicholas Lyra, *Postilla super totam bibliam* (Strassburg, 1492; repr. Frankfort
am Mainz: Minerva, 1971), is followed closely by Wyclif in his own *postilla* on Matthew

Chaucer, like Wyclif his contemporary, worked simultaneously under the patronage of John of Gaunt. It may safely be said that they shared at least one concern: each was almost as preoccupied with drawing attention to a plague of faulty or perverted interpretation of Scripture as with presenting a "right reading" correctively. Even before he gets to the antifraternal satire of the Friar's and Summoner's tales, Chaucer offers, in the Wife of Bath's supersized Prologue, an unmistakable burlesque of biblical exegesis par excellence. By it we are prepared in ways we do not yet realize for more conclusive satisfactions to come. For instance, the Wife of Bath cites the Bible more than any other pilgrim except the Parson, yet every text she adduces she chops out of context, radically misconstrues, or knowingly deconstructs to hilarious effect in a fashion transparent to the medieval audience. But her overt misreading—of New Testament as well as Old Testament texts—has about it a more insidious character. When her ardent ecclesiastical suitors (especially the Friar and the Summoner) appear no more reliably acquainted with Scripture than she is, we begin to see just how self-serving "glossing" (rather than taking the text on its own terms) can become a problem for reliable religious authority. Here is the friar's ploy:

> But herkne [listen] now, Thomas, what I shal seyn.
> I ne have no text of it, as I suppose,
> But I shall fynde it in a manner glose,
> That specially oure sweete Lord Jhesus
> Spak this by freres, when he seyde thus:
> *"Blessed be they that povre in spirit been."* (Summoner's Tale,
>   1918–23)

After this apparently accurate citation of the first beatitude, the Summoner's false friar makes a claim regarding the divine *intentio auctoris*, namely that his "profession" or order (doubtless, he insists, the friars are those to whom Jesus was referring) live more in conformity with the gospel than people who, like his next

---

5–7. See Douglas Wurtele, "Chaucer's Canterbury Tales and Nicholas of Lyre's *Postillae litteralis et moralis super totam bibliam*," in *Chaucer and Scriptural Tradition*, ed. David Lyle Jeffrey (Ottawa: University of Ottawa Press, 1984), 89–107.

victim, Thomas, are reluctant to cough up money to support their increasingly opulent lifestyle (cf. Summoner's Tale, 1836–53). Perforce, his argument goes, Thomas must yield to the shameless religious fraud that supports the friar, whether he can afford to or not (Summoner's Tale, 1854–84). No Angel of Humility appears on this "cornice," then, but rather a chubby little bundle of greed and prideful vices, entirely alien to the first condition of beatitude (cf. 1935–36). Fittingly, when, in the friar's groping attempt to recover gold from the breeches of his host, he gets instead a gargantuan *bumbulum* (fart) in the face, everyone feels he has had his just deserts. Even the lord to whom he is confessor (and who is likely his biggest donor) cannot resist a humorous allusion to the Sermon on the Mount in precisely such terms as the Friar has been misappropriating it:

> Distempre yow noghte, ye be me confessour;
> Ye been the salt of the earth and the savour. (Summoner's
>   Tale, 2195–96)

Now, lest any reader think this allusion to Matthew 5:13 to be approbatory, Chaucer has this same lord, completely doubled up in laughter, take up the literal-minded friar's "problem," namely finding an "ars-metrike" by which to divide the odious booty in twelve parts, so that each member of his conventicle gets an equal share: "Who shoulde make a demonstracioun," he asks in his hilarity, "That every man sholde have ylicke his part / as of the sound and the savour of a fart?" (2224–26). Both audiences for this ribaldry have more than enough occasion at this point to recall the *rest* of the sentence in Matthew's text—"but if the salt have lost his savour, wherewith shall it be salted?" (Matt. 5:13)—and to realize that this point is the precedent and, for the friar's lost spiritual authority, really the determinative question. The repeated use of one word, "savour," performs the necessary mnemonic trick. Of these sorry interpreters it may be concluded that their "savour" is thoroughly degraded. Here again, like Wyclif, Chaucer regards the friars as destructive of the authority of Scripture and betrayers of their own rule.[25]

25. Antifraternal literature abounds in the fourteenth century, and texts from the Sermon on the Mount figure prominently. Thus, in Dante's ringing denunciation of

There are far more allusions to the Sermon on the Mount in Chaucer than are possible to discuss here.[26] It is right, however, that we give special attention to those that occur in the homiletic Tale of Melibee, the tale that Chaucer allots to himself, so to speak, in his fictive pilgrim persona, as well as to the Parson's Tale, which concludes *The Canterbury Tales* and is, after all, itself a sermon calling for repentance.

The theme of the Tale of Melibee is drawn from Matthew 5:9: "Blessed are the peacemakers." This was a theme of some importance to Chaucer. There is evidence that he, like at least two of the knights close to Wyclif, belonged to a confraternal association that called itself the "Order of the Passion of our Lord." The objectives of this group included ending warfare between Christian nations (especially England and France), ending the papal schism, and reestablishing European courtly values.[27] By 1391, in the political contretemps at court over these issues, Chaucer and his colleagues had come out on the short end, and for his part Chaucer lost his job as Clerk of the King's Works.[28] (Would-be peacemakers are not always well regarded by those of a more bellicose nature. John of Gaunt was bellicose.) In addition, by this time Wyclif had lost his teaching chair at Oxford and been sent down to Lutterworth parish, where in 1384 he died of a stroke during Holy Communion. By the 1390s storm clouds were swiftly gathering for Wyclif's sympathizers.

---

friar preachers (in the *Paradiso* 29.85–126, no less), it follows upon St. Peter's invective (in 27.55–56) against corrupt clergy of all kinds as "rapacious wolves clothed in the garb of shepherds" (cf. Matt. 7:15), Dante's only other significant use of our text (also occurring in his *Convivio* 4.16). Chaucer's antifraternal attack is, if anything, more intense (and certainly more sustained) than Dante's, especially in his treatment of the Friar, the friar in the Summoner's Tale, and the Pardoner.

26. See Lawrence Besserman, *Chaucer and the Bible: A Critical Review of Research, Indexes, and Bibliography* (New York: Garland, 1988), 352–53, for a basic list.

27. Still useful here is W. T. Waugh, "The Lollard Knights," *Scottish Historical Review* 11 (1914): 55–92. Cf. N. Jorgu, "Phillippe de Mezières et la Croisade au XIVième siècle," *Bibliotheque de l'ecole des hautes études* 110 (1896) (repr. London, 1973).

28. *Chaucer Life-Records*, ed. Martin M. Crow and Clair C. Olson (Oxford: Oxford University Press, 1966), 402–76. When one of his Wyclif sympathizing friends, Phillipe de la Vache, suffered a similar fate, he took it rather badly, prompting Chaucer to send him as exhortation his well-known short poem "Truth."

We generally date Chaucer's version of the Tale of Melibee to just after the death of Wyclif and before the death of Queen Anne in 1394.[29]

Beatitude and Political Wisdom

As a kind of intensifying frame for the tale he gives to himself, Chaucer the pilgrim commences his turn at bat with an abortive swing at low-grade, soap-opera-like romance in hideous doggerel rhyme. This lame effort is cut off by the Host's exasperated roar in midsentence, who demands something in which there is either "murthe" or "doctrine." Chaucer the pilgrim then agrees to tell a "moral tale vertuous . . . Al be it told sometyme in sondry wise / Of sondry folk [in various times in various ways by various people]," invoking again the principle of polyvocity, yet which he surprisingly illustrates not by indulging the perverse and ribald misuse of Scripture to which his hearers have been much exposed, but by sober reference to the example of the four gospels. While of Matthew, Mark, Luke, and John, he says, "al be ther in hir telling difference," "natheless hir sentence is al sooth [entirely true]," and there is evident concord as to meaning: "Douteless, hir sentence [meaning] is al oon [in agreement]" (Tale of Melibee, 2130–42). So also with my tale here, he says. Though he intends to recount somewhat more "proverbs" than his audience has yet heard, we are to understand that the meaning of his own signature story diverges as to meaning *not at all* from the overall meaning of *The Canterbury Tales*.[30]

Once again the issue in Melibee is injury and revenge. But here a solution is not to be found except through the offices of a wisdom personified as Dame Prudence, who patiently reviews both biblical and classical authorities to argue that the restoration of health in such circumstances can come only by forgiveness and a practice

29. The Tale of Melibee is a free translation of a French *Le livre de melibee et de dame prudence*, in turn based on the thirteenth-century *Liber consolationis et consilii* by Albertanus of Brescia, most probably reworked by Chaucer and inserted in its present position in the final stages of assembly for *The Canterbury Tales*.

30. For a fuller discussion, see Jeffrey, *People of the Book*, 198–202.

of justice tempered with mercy. In this critical part of the overall poem Chaucer alludes to the Sermon on the Mount intermittently (e.g., to Matt. 7:1–2, "judge not that ye be not judged," in Tale of Melibee, 1458, 1865ff.), but more significantly the whole narrative is built in such a way that a concordance of both biblical and classical texts is made to revolve on two key *themes* from the Sermon on the Mount, namely the blessedness of peacemaking and the necessity of forgiveness rather than lex talionis judgment. "Ye knowen wel," says Prudence to her vengefully minded husband Melibee,

> that oon of the grettest and moost souereyn
> thing [stabilizing forces] that is in the world is unytee and
> pees.
> And therefore seyde our Lord Jesu Christ to
> his apostles in this wyse: *Well happy and*
> *blessed been they that loven and purchacen*
> *pees, for they be called children of God.* (Tale of Melibee,
> 2867–70)

As Chaucer's exemplary peacemaker, Dame Prudence here takes on a quality of beatitude at once more dialogic and, in its extensive development, of greater political immediacy than is the case even for Dante's Beatrice. The direct citation of Matthew 5:9 here recapitulates the discourse of Prudence to this point; it declares "authoritatively" her intent as a narrator within Chaucer's tale and, as we know from the *incipit* and see again at the conclusion of the tale, it signals Chaucer's authorial intention representatively as well. The "entente" of Prudence is made explicit in her last speech:

> Wherefore I pray you, let mercy been
> in your herte, to th' effect and entente [purpose]
> that God almighty have mercy on yow
> in his laste juggement.

She then adds, as often in this tale, confirmation from the earliest canonical commentary on the Sermon on the Mount:

98

For Seint Jame seith in his Epistle:
Juggement withouten mercy shal be
doon to hym that hath no mercy of another
wight [person]. (Tale of Melibee, 3055–58)

Chaucer's narrative voice then comments that in light of her faithful teaching, "the herte" of Melibee "gan enclyne to the wyl of his wif, considering her trewe entente [purpose]"—that is, her intention to be faithful to Christ's teaching—and he "conformed hym anon," forgiving his enemies and reconciling them to himself. The last words of the tale still more deliberately recall the conditional clause of the Lord's Prayer (Matt. 6:14–15) as application:

For douteless, if we be sory and repentant
of the synnes and giltes [faults] which we han trespassed
in the sighte of oure Lord God, he is so free
and so merciable that he wole foryeven us
our giltes, and bryngen us to the blisse that
never hath ende. Amen. (Tale of Melibee, 1883–86)

We see, then, that Chaucer has put in the mouth of his own "pilgrim" persona a sermon—indeed, a sermon whose thesis and key texts come openly from the Sermon on the Mount. The form of his exposition of the text in this tale is not by means of a "gloss" in the conventional sense moreover, but rather by a concordance of many related Scriptures, supplemented in Augustinian fashion by a few apt citations from Cicero and Seneca, yet in such a way that the Matthean text provides not merely the theme but authoritative closure to a reflection on the wisdom of peacemaking. In this concordance of wisdom authorities, internal commentary on the Matthean text from elsewhere in Scripture (e.g., the letter of James) is granted the next highest level of authority after the words of Jesus. James's apostolic emphasis on enactment of virtue—here the highlighted virtue of peacemaking—gets correlative and dramatic embodiment in the Knight's counterintuitive, genuinely shocking insistence that the sexually ambiguous, loathsome Pardoner and his enraged would-be victim, Harry Bailey, literally kiss and make up so that the fellowship of pilgrims en route to communion be not destroyed (Pardoner's Tale, 946–68).

It may to some degree reflect a modernist bias that available translations of Chaucer typically omit the Tale of Melibee and likewise the tale with which Chaucer concludes his great work, the Parson's Sermon.[31] For similar reasons, perhaps, these two texts are seldom taught now, however incongruous that must appear for any structural consideration of *The Canterbury Tales*. In respect of structure, however, to some degree analogously with Dante's *Purgatorio*, Chaucer's Parson's Sermon is not merely a "knitting up," as the Host on the outskirts of Canterbury asks that it be, of all the "greet mateere" (28–29) of the collected tales. It is a prompt to examination of conscience in both fictive and actual readers (or hearers) of the *Tales* and a catechism in respect of true repentance. Chaucer's Parson is highly conscious of the social nature of sin and the healing social function of repentance. After all, the pilgrims are about to end their voyage by being restored to Holy Communion. Because repentance is notoriously easier to talk about than to perform (whatever the original intention, a pilgrimage to Canterbury could be about as unpenitential as the average Cook's tour to the Holy Land), the Parson is appropriately concerned at this point to distinguish between true and feigned repentance. Hence, he takes up the matter of genuine contrition at the outset. "And therfore our Lord Jhesu Crist seith thus," he quotes Matthew 7:20, *"By the fruyt of hem [them] shall ye knowen hem"* (Parson's Tale, 116).

As is typical of late medieval penitential manuals,[32] the requisite examination of conscience follows a diagnostic schema ordered

31. For example, the following statement about the Parson's Tale: "This is the longest of the tales, and it is not a tale at all but a sermon. Like 'The Tale of Melibeus' it is written in prose, and I have also omitted it as being unlikely to interest the general reader"; David Wright, *The Canterbury Tales: A Prose Version in Modern English* (New York: Random House, 1965), 333.

32. One such frequently but unconvincingly associated with the Parson's Tale is the *Summa virtutum de remediis anime*, ed. Siegfried Wenzel (Athens: University of Georgia Press, 1984); another is the *Summa de vitiis* of Raymond Pennaforte. I agree with Wenzel that Chaucer worked quite independently with the biblical sources—probably from both the Vulgate and a French translation. Wycliffite work came late and, given Chaucer's situation, was possibly too politically charged after 1384 for him to quote overtly. At least since Dudley R. Johnson's 1941 Yale dissertation "Chaucer and the

by the seven "chieftaynes of synnes," as Chaucer's Parson calls the "seven deadly sins" (Parson's Tale, 385). In respect of the second of these, envy (*invidia*), in particular as to its remedy, the Gospel of Matthew becomes critical to the Parson's purpose. He begins with the Great Commandment or Law of Love, from Matthew 22:37–40, translating it and elaborating in such a way that the hearer is given to understand that by the term *neighbor* we are to understand not only "brother" but "enemy":

> Certes, man shal louen [love] his enemy, by the commandement of God; and smoothly [truly] thy freend shaltow love in God.

He then moves seamlessly into exposition dependent on citations from the Sermon on the Mount, each carefully paraphrased and expounded. One citation must suffice:

> Agayns hate and rancour of herte, he shal love hymn in herte. Agayns chidyng and wikkede wordes, he shal preye for his enemy. Agayns the wikked dede of his enemy, he shal doon hym bountee [be generous toward him]. For Crist seith: *Loveth your enemys, and preyeth for hem that speke yow harm, and eek for hem that yow chacen and pursewen, and dooth bountee to hem that yow haten* [hate you]. Loo, thus comaundeth us oure Lord Jhesu Crist to do to oure enemys. . . . For right as the devel is disconfited by humylitee, right so is he wounded to the deeth by love of our enemy. Certes, thanne is love the medicine that casteth out the venym of Envye fro mannes herte. (Parson's Tale, 520–30)

Curiously enough then, for those who like Chaucer himself are apparently familiar with Dante,[33] the counterbalance to envy in this equivalent to Dante's second cornice of the *Purgatorio* is neither the Angel of Mercy nor the fifth beatitude, "Blessed are the merci-

Bible," there has been consensus that Chaucer seems to have been using an unglossed version of the Bible in most instances of citation.

33. Chaucer names Dante specifically in many places, and in *House of Fame* 1.499ff. may be borrowing directly from *Purgatorio* 9.19–20 and 2.17–24. Chaucer spent time in Italy between 1372 and 1376. The Wife of Bath's old loathly lady also quotes extensively from the *Convivio* in her account of *gentilesse* ("true nobility of character"), beginning at 3.d.1125–65.

ful" (Matt. 5:7). Rather, it is the *last* of the Beatitudes, "Blessed are you when they revile and persecute you" (5:10–11). This was (no surprise) a portion of the Matthew text dear to the heart of many who sympathized with John Wyclif.[34] They knew about having evil said of them falsely and that much of it was borne of *invidia*. A good deal of it of it took the form of a hair-trigger prejudice against what might appear to some as excessive piety. That is, serious piety itself could seem to be Wycliffite. In the first abortive attempt by the Host to get the Parson to address the pilgrims, following the Man of Law's Tale, Harry Bailey, dismissively refers to him twice as a "Lollere" (Lollard). He does this simply because the Parson has expressed concern about Harry's penchant for profanity (Man of Law's Tale, 1170–83). The Shipman, notably one of the most profane of the pilgrims, then angrily intervenes to prevent the Parson from accepting the Host's invitation.

Under *ira*, anger, in the Parson's Sermon, comes the problem of spiritual "homicide" or "spiritual manslaughtere," which on the Parson's account is akin to profanity. The text recollected here, Matthew 5:21–22, has analogues in John's Gospel also, and the resulting analysis is synthetic. Nevertheless, as Chaucer's Parson develops the point, our Matthew text is central:

> Also oure Lord Jhesu Crist seith, by the word of Seint Mathew, *"Ne wol ye nat swere in alle manere [you ought not to swear in any fashion]; neither by hevene, for it is Goddes trone; ne by erthe, for it is the bench of his feet; ne by Jerusalem, for it is the citee of a greet kyng; ne by thyn heed, for thou mayst nat make an heer [hair] whit ne blak. But seyeth by youre word 'ye, ye,' and 'nay, nay'; and what that is moore, it is of yvel [evil],"*—thus seith Crist. (Parson's Tale, 587–90)

The development through Matthew 5:33–37 is here again by way of direct quotation: the Parson is determined to adduce irrefragable

---

34. Wycliffite writings and others conventionally refer to the Lollard preachers as "povre men," and the language of the Beatitudes permeates their work. Thus, in the Wyclifitte exposition of the Lord's Prayer, this language figures richly in respect of the holiness that those who pray "halwid be thi name" ought to pray. See F. D. Matthew, *The English Works of Wyclif*, Early English Text Society, old series 74 (1880; repr. Millwood, NY: Krauss, 1975), 197–202.

authority, namely the words of Jesus himself, "for Crist is verray trouthe [true truth]" (592). Because "true Truth" is a matter of Christ's example, not his words only, the remedy for ire is not then, as with Dante, *beati pacifici* (Matt. 5:9) imagined as a verbal intervention; rather, it is the virtue of patience "that maketh a man lyk to God, and makyth hym Goddes owene deere child, as seith Crist" (Parson's Tale, 600–601). Here Matthew 5:9 is clearly conflated with James 1:2–4 in such a way as to let us see how Chaucer regards the letter of James as the best of commentaries on the Sermon on the Mount.[35] Scripture upon Scripture is the Parson's general *regula*: though Ambrose, Augustine, Jerome, Gregory, Isidore of Seville, and Bernard of Clairvaux all are adduced at some point in the Parson's Sermon, the place of the magisterial tradition is distinctly secondary to that of the text of Scripture itself, and the concordance of Scripture as *lex Dei, lex Christi* invariably forms the main channel of his exposition.

Always in the background, as in Wycliffite sermons, are "wolves in sheep's clothing" (here in Chaucer, e.g., the Friar, Summoner, and Pardoner) and those secular authorities who, like the Man of Law and Reeve, "devouren the possessiouns or the catel of povre folk wrongfully, withouten mercy or mesure." Yet part of what enables patience in the face of such adversaries is confidence in the ultimate sovereignty of God and knowledge that "they shul receyven [receive], by the same measure than they han mesured to povre folk [Matt. 7:2], the mercy of Jhesu Crist, but if it be amended" (Parson's Tale, 774–75).

The Parson's Sermon systematically (in a fullness that can only be hinted at here) provides Chaucer's audience a measure by which the full range of sinful miscreance exhibited in the intentions and actions of the pilgrims, as well as of the overt high jinx of the characters in their tales, can be instructively assessed. And that sinful deeds need not actually be performed to occasion real sin—even in a reader of inordinate affections—is made clear in the Parson's treatment of *luxuria*, lechery. What Dante thought of

---

35. This has been noticed in respect of other of the tales. See especially here John McNamara, "Chaucer's Use of the Epistle of St. James in the *Clerk's Tale*," *Chaucer Review* 7 (1972–73): 184–93.

as "l'adulterio del cuore" (cf. Matt. 5:28) can rather easily become a reader's problem too: witness Paolo and Francesca, it can also lead to a damnable performance (*Inferno* 5). Augustine from his *De sermo domine in monte* is cited by the Parson in support:

> "In this heeste [commandment]," seith Seint Augustyn, "is forboden [forbidden] alle manere coveitise [imaginative desire] to doon lecherie." Lo, what seith Seint Mathew in the gospel, that *"whoso seeth a womman to coveitise of his lust, he hath doon lecherie with hire in his herte."* Heere may ye seen that nat oonly the dede of this synne is forboden, but eek the desir to doon that synne. (Parson's Tale, 844–46)

Already we can anticipate in the self-deprecating Chaucer, actual author of this entire work, an acknowledgement that in an attempt to deal candidly with sin a poet—or poetic confessor—can occasion by his narrative that form of voyeurism that may lead its practitioner along a path to perdition. Indeed, once the *Tales* are ended, he confesses as much, in his very last words, by way of his Retractions.[36]

But these are not his last words as to meaning, or to *intentio autoris*, in his concluding tale, the Parson's Sermon. These words have to do no longer with contrition (he is most brief about this) or even with auricular confession, but rather with the traditional third part of the traditional process of repentance, what the apostle Paul calls "works meet for repentance" (Acts 26:20), or "satisfaction" as the traditional doctrine refers to it. For Chaucer's Parson these works are to be done, if possible, unostentatiously—or, if not out of view, then in a spirit of self-displacement and gratitude to Christ for the grace that is our means of redemption. But the portion of the Sermon on the Mount adduced here, as we draw toward the conclusion of the Sermon and, thus, the *Tales*, is explicitly such as to cause us to think of the corporate character of our accountability to bear a faithful witness to our salvation:

---

36. "Wherefore I beseke yow mekely, for the mercy of God, that ye preye for me that Crist have mercy on me and foryeve me my giltes; and namely of my translecions and enditynges of wordly vanitees, the which I revoke in my retracciouns. . . . And many a song, and many a leccherous lay; that Crist for his grete mercy foryeve me the synne" (*Retractions* 10.1084–86).

For, as witnesseth Seint Mathew, *capitulo quinto* [chapter five], *"A citee may nat been hyd that is set on a montayne, ne men lighte nat a lanterne and put it under a busshel, but men sette it on a candle-stikke to yeve light to the men in the hous. Right so shal youre light lighten before men, that they may seen youre goode werkes, and glorifie your fader that is in hevene."* (Parson's Tale, 1035–38)

Among these good works in Matthew 5:14–16, is prayer, which the Parson defines as a "pitous wyl of herte, that redresseth it in God [a self-effacing desire of the heart that seeks its completion in God]." In the exemplar,

the orison [prayer] of the *Pater noster* hath Jhesu Crist enclosed moost thynges. Certes, it is privyleged of thre thynges in his dignytee, for which it is moore digne [more worthy] than any oother preyere; for that Jhesu Crist hymself maked it; and it is short, for it sholde be koud [memorized] the moore lightly [easily], and for to withholden [retained] it the moore esily in herte, and helpen hymself the ofter [more often] with the orisoun; and for a man sholde be the lasse wery [less weary] to seyen it, and for a man may nat excusen hym to lerne it, it is so short and so esy; and for it comprehendeth in it self alle goode preyers. (Parson's Tale, 1039–43)

As he expounds the significance of the Lord's Prayer (Matt. 6:7–15) as a model for all prayer in the Christian life, the Parson acknowledges that deeper exposition is to be had from "this maistres [masters] of theologie," but that for him (as for Augustine) a key point is

that whan thow prayest that God sholde foryeve [forgive] thee thy giltes [wrongdoings] as thou foryevest hem that agilten to thee, be ful wel war that thow ne be nat out of charitee. (Parson's Tale, 1043–44)

It is crucial, he says, that this prayer and all prayer should be prayed "ordinately, discreetly, and devoutly" and that "alwey a man shal putten his wyl to be subget to the wille of God" (1045). Yet prayer is to be continued not with mere words, but "with the werkes of charitee."

105

This summarizes the entire force—as penitential doctrine and social criticism both—of Chaucer's *Canterbury Tales*. It shows us how the Sermon on the Mount has not only been present all along the pilgrim ride from London to Canterbury, but in a crafted, deliberate way has served to declare the intention of "oure Auctor," as Chaucer calls him, the ultimate Author, making plain his will for those who would seek to align their will with it.

Accordingly, the goal of Chaucer's journey is not, as in Dante's ethereal voyage, a mystical vision. Rather, it is a moment in the pilgrimage of this ordinary life where, in the glad recognition of sins forgiven, we are prepared once again to become "one with the Body of Christ" even as, by means of that host more real, we become one with his body in an act of obedience, participation in the eucharistic meal. That this state of grace, this experience of communion, is a foretaste of divine glory (or *paradiso*) the Parson grants. But in Chaucer it is the experience not of solitary mystical vision, but the worship of a gathered church that occasions our understanding of future hope:

> Thanne shal men understonde what is the fruyt of penaunce [repentance]; and, afer the word of Jhesu Crist, it is the endelees blisse of hevene, ther joye hath no contrarioustee of wo [sorrow] ne grevaunce [nor aggravation]; ther alle harmes been passed of this present lyf; ther as is the sikernesse [preservation] fro the peyne of helle; ther as is the bisful compaignye that rejoysen hem everemo, everich [each person] of otheres joye; there as the body of man, that whilom [beforehand] was foul and derk, is moore cleer than the sonne; ther as the body, that whilom was syk, freele, and fieble, and mortal, is inmortal, and so strong and so hool that ther may no thyng apeyren [injure] it; ther as ne is neither hunger, thurst, ne coold, but every soule replenyssed [restored to wholeness] with the sighte of the parfit knowynge of God. (Parson's Tale, 1076–79)

And the *very* last word in *The Canterbury Tales*? Well that, most fittingly, alludes to the first words of the Sermon on the Mount and, indeed, of the Beatitudes:

> This blisful regne may mene purchace by poverte espiritueel, and the glorie by lowenesse, the plentee of joye by hunger and thurst,

106

and the reste by travaille [disciplined labor], and the lyf by deeth and mortificacion of synne.

Following Chaucer the poet's confession to the reader concerning his own inevitable failure to realize his better intentions, he appeals for the prayers of his readers and hearers that he shall be granted the "grace of verray [true] repentance, confessioun and satisfaccioun to doon in this present lyf." Chaucer's focus is not on a prospect of purgatory. It is on repentance and perseverance—grace for obedience in the here and now.

Conclusion

Dante makes minimal use of the Sermon on the Mount, more narrowly the Beatitudes, as the traditions of *sacra doctrina* make it possible for him to incorporate them into a mystical *askēsis* in which the purgation of sins for which penitential satisfaction is incomplete in the world may be imagined as being satisfied postmortem. Chaucer by contrast finds in the Sermon on the Mount primarily a key to the moral appropriation of Scripture for personal and social action—to works meet for repentance in this present life. This key portion of Jesus's teaching is for him a kind of exegetical cornerstone in terms of which all of Scripture finds its focus, and its resolution, in Christ. In the words of Jesus he finds an irrefragable declaration of the divine author's authorial intent—gathering in and ordering to meaning all those divergent, unruly narratives from Genesis, Judges, and Job as well as the occasional befuddlement of his disciples, so declaring the finally unified meaning of "oure Auctor" for us. *Lex dei, lex Christi.* But in the law as Jesus lives and teaches it, the question of "our author's" intention, the alignment of our diverse wills with his own singular will, in purity of heart, is distilled for the sake of action—what is to be done *now.* For Chaucer that obedience must begin in true contrition, proceed through confession of mouth, then move toward restorative deeds done in gratitude, works meet for repentance, which in their grateful doing can just possibly transform the world.

107

Martin Luther

6

Susan E. Schreiner

When we think of the Sermon on the Mount we commonly recall themes of meekness, mercy, love, and peace. Matthew 5–7 is the section best known for the Lord's Prayer, turning the other cheek, and the lilies of the field. It may come as a surprise, therefore, that Martin Luther's interpretation of the Sermon on the Mount was a polemical call for battle against all enemies, particularly Satan. Luther's interpretation originated in a series of sermons delivered between 1530 and 1532. They were published as a commentary in 1532, in 1533, and again in 1534. These dates will help to explain the polemical context of his interpretation. As usual, when commenting on a biblical text, Luther operated on several different levels and against various fronts. For Luther, the Sermon on the Mount was fundamentally about the difficulty of living the Christian life within the world. Luther expressed that difficulty in terms of an attack on his opponents.

Before identifying these enemies, however, the polemical nature of this commentary requires a brief comment about Luther's exegetical method. It is often the case that when reading Luther's biblical exegesis, students cannot understand how he could find references to the pope, the monks, the radicals, and other sixteenth-century people within this ancient text. Was this a naïve precritical attitude toward the Bible, or was there another reason? Luther's exegetical method depended on one underlying theological proposition, namely, that the human condition before God has never changed over time. The forms, styles, conventions, and outward circumstances of human life have varied, but the basic stance of the human race remained unchanged. In his eyes, therefore, the Bible spoke immediately to his own time, without having to apply the fourfold sense of Scripture. Thus Luther repeatedly used the phrase *the same is true today*. In short, this theological presupposition allowed Luther to collapse time without denying the historical context of Scripture. The enemies Luther addressed, therefore, existed both in the past and the present.

We should, however, begin with Luther's own starting point. The Sermon on the Mount presented Luther with a potentially troubling issue. This passage in Matthew seemed to name certain works that God would reward. For example, "Blessed are the merciful for they shall obtain mercy" seemed to promise a reward for being merciful. Luther warded off any allowance for merit by insisting that Christ was talking only about the conduct of life and not about the doctrine upon which that life was based. As Luther stated, Christ was saying nothing in this sermon "about how we become Christians, but only about the works and fruit that no one can do unless he is already a Christian and in a state of grace."[1] For Luther, we cannot understand the Sermon on the

---

1. Luther, "Sermon on the Mount," in Luther's Works 21, ed. Jaroslav Pelikan (St. Louis: Concordia, 1956), 291 (hereafter LW). The German edition is found in *D. Martin Luthers Werke: Kritische Gesamtausgabe: Abteilung Schriften* (Weimar, 1883–1990), 32.541.14–17 (hereafter WA). Luther made clear that the Sermon on the Mount referred to the second table of the law. Explaining the nature of the Scriptures in terms of the Law and Prophets, Luther said, "'They contain the doctrine of faith and promises, which are not mentioned here.' The answer is that here Christ names the Law and the Prophets in direct contrast to the Gospel of the promise. He is not preaching here about the sublime doctrine of faith in Christ but only about good works. These are two distinctive proclamations, both must be preached, but each at its appropriate time. You can tell that plainly from the words in the text where He says: 'Whatever you wish that men would do to you, do so to them.' By this He indicates that His preaching here does not go beyond the relation that people have with us and we with them and that it is not talking about the grace of Christ which we receive from God. What he intends to say now is this: 'When the time comes to preach about the good life and about the works which we should perform in our relations with our neighbor, you will find nothing in all the Law and the Prophets except what this saying teaches.'

Mount unless we are first grounded in the doctrine of justification by faith alone. Having been justified, the believer should *then* turn to the Sermon in order to find ethical instructions about living the life of faith. The Sermon, therefore, is not law, nor is it exactly the gospel; the moral injunctions of the Sermon are the fruits of justification by faith.

Luther knew, however, that the Sermon had been interpreted in terms of meritorious works. He believed that he was rescuing the Sermon on the Mount from centuries of misinterpretation. He vehemently disagreed with the traditional belief that the moral teachings of the Sermon, especially the Beatitudes, were only counsels for the spiritual elite and not commands for the common Christian. Luther was referring to the view that the evangelical counsels were only for those "who wished to live a more perfect life than that of other Christians."[2] In the exegetical tradition, the Sermon gradually had become "counsels" for those living the cloistered life.[3] Therefore, Luther's opponent in his commentary on the Sermon was the monk or, as he called it, all the forms of "monkery" in the world.[4] The monk, he explained, thought that by leaving the world behind and secluding himself in the desert or in a monastery he could achieve a higher perfection. Thus, the Sermon was thought to belong to those who had withdrawn from

He uses the words 'men' and 'do so to them' to specify that He is discussing only the commandments of the Second Table" (LW 21.240; WA 32.498.7–21).

2. LW 21.4; WA 32.300. Luther characterized this position in his comments on Matt. 5:21: "That is the kind of holiness our papists have. They have become past masters at this business. To keep their holiness from being condemned and themselves from being bound by Christ's Word, they have generously helped Him by deducing twelve counsels from His Word. These Christ did not command as necessary, but left them up to the free choice of each individual, to observe them as good advice if he wants to merit something more special than other people. It is a completely superfluous and dispensable bit of instruction." The University of Paris condemned Luther's denial of this position in 1521. See LW 21.4, 74; WA 32.300.12–28; 32.361.5–13. The condemnations are in WA 8.267–312 and 9.717–61.

3. The distinction between precept and counsel dates back to Ambrose.

4. LW 21.258–59; WA 32.514.3–8: "Until recently they were called monks, now they are the Anabaptists, the new monks. In previous ages it was the Pelagians, Ishmaelites, Esauites, and Cainites. This faith has lasted since the beginning of the world, and though these Anabaptists may be on the way out, others are on their way in. In other words, monkery must remain as long as the world stands, although it may assume other names and new activities."

the world in the attempt to live the life of purity. But this "delusion" was not unique to the Catholic monasticism. In his own day, Luther warned, "new monks" had sprouted up and were making the same mistakes. As we will see, these "new monks" were the Anabaptists who had revived the error of monasticism by teaching that the Christian had to renounce society and live a life separated from the world. Consequently, they refused any governmental office, would not take oaths, and generally were pacifists.

Luther was determined to reclaim the Sermon on the Mount for the world. The Beatitudes and the other moral teachings, he insisted, were commands to all Christians in every walk of life. It is a commonplace in Reformation scholarship that Luther and the other Reformers enhanced secular life. In Luther's case, this enhancement centered on the idea of one's calling. He maintained that God ordained all stations of life and that believers did not need to retreat from their place in the world in order to live according to Christ's teachings. The monk, Luther argued, believed that a man had "to run away from human society into a corner, a monastery, or a desert, neither thinking about the world nor concerning himself with worldly affairs and business, but amusing himself only with heavenly thoughts."[5] They "beguiled" everyone by calling "profane" the acts and stations that the world required and that God himself had ordained. As Luther said, "We are not made for fleeing human company, but for living in society and sharing good and evil."[6] Luther explained, "Scripture speaks of this pure heart and mind in a manner that is completely consistent with being a husband, loving wife, and children, thinking about them and caring for them, paying attention to other matters involved in such a relationship. For God has commanded all of this. Whatever God has commanded cannot be profane."[7] Against the "new monks" Luther argued:

> Reason decries this and thinks to itself, "Why that is an ordinary thing that anyone can do in his own home!" It yearns for something

5. LW 21.32; WA 32.324.15–18. See also LW 21.36–37, 85–86; WA 32.327.31–36; 32.370.33–371.2.
6. LW 21.86; WA 32.371.3–4.
7. LW 21.32; WA 32.324.21–25.

else that is strange and special, stares at it, and lets itself be led by all the clatter. This is all just a pretense. They come along and rebuke us with their worthless way of life, in order to make every other way, though it may be God's ordinance and station, seem contemptible and worthless. Our inadequacy comes from our failure to hold onto the Word of God seriously enough; otherwise we would soon say: "Bring on the Carthusians, the Anabaptists, the devil himself, or his mother."[8]

Luther's point was that the humble ordinary life in the world was not at all easy and, in fact, was much *more* difficult than the strictest monastic rule or the most severe life lived separated from society. The Sermon on the Mount demonstrated the difficulty, and indeed danger, faced by the Christian living within the world. But can a Christian member of society really live according to the following commands: "make friends quickly with your accuser while you are going with him to court"; "if anyone would sue you and take your coat, let him have your cloak as well"; "do not resist the one who is evil, but if anyone should strike you on the right cheek, turn to him the other also"; "do not be concerned about your life, what you shall eat or what you shall drink, nor about your body, what you shall put on"? Can one really achieve this while remaining in society? Perhaps the University of Paris had a point in 1521 when it condemned Luther's view of the Beatitudes. Are not these "counsels" possible only outside the difficulties of living in society? This advice would put too many burdens on the ordinary Christian. To take the Sermon of the Mount out of the monastery and bring it into society made Luther address the nature of "the world." As he recognized all too well, the present world was fallen. The Sermon on the Mount, moreover, referred not to a future kingdom but to life within this fallen and sinful world. This world in which Christians were to obey the Sermon on the Mount was one that Luther described as "one big whorehouse, completely submerged in greed." If that was not clear enough, he added, "What is the world but a big, wide, and turbulent ocean of inexhaustible wickedness and villainy, all made to look beautiful and good?"[9]

8. LW 21.256–57; WA 32.512.16–24.
9. LW 21.180, 184; WA 32.451.21–22.

When applying the Sermon on the Mount to human society, Luther never mitigated the difficulty posed by the world. He argued that in this Sermon, Christ was telling his followers that they were not to institute a new realm. Rather, Christ taught that every Christian had the duty to participate in the existing earthly regime, administer its laws and punishments, maintain order and distinctions, distribute property, and help the neighbor. And, Luther insisted, they were to do all these things on the basis of Christ's words in the Sermon on the Mount.[10]

Luther's explanation of how the Sermon was to be lived within the world depends on a series of distinctions. According to Luther Christians always had to distinguish the two kingdoms and the two governments ordained by God.[11] The two kingdoms correspond to the two relationships in which the Christian stands: the spiritual kingdom involves the Christian *coram Deo* or before God; the earthly kingdom involves the Christian *coram hominibus* or before the neighbor. *Coram Deo*, the Christian stands in a passive or receptive relationship. Here the Christian receives only faith and justification by that faith. The Christian must put all his or her trust in the promise of God and never in any works, no matter how "dazzling" those works might be. *Coram hominibus*, the Christian is always active in works of love. The two governments refer to the two ways in which God governs the world: God governs the church through his word, and in this government there is no coercion; God governs the world, however, by means of laws that exact punishment, and in the earthly realm, human reason is competent to create and preserve society. As Luther observed in his comments on the Sermon on the Mount, the gospel does not "trouble itself" about the administration of laws, government, and property. That, he says, "is what lawyers are for." He noted further "that Christ has no intention here of interfering in the

10. LW 21.108–9; WA 32.388.34–39; 32.389.1–390.18.
11. LW 21.108–9; WA 32.389.10–390.32. On Luther's view of the two kingdoms and the two governments, see David C. Steinmetz, *Luther in Context* (Bloomington: Indiana University Press, 1986), 112–25; Heinrich Bornkamm, *Luther's Doctrine of the Two Kingdoms* (Philadelphia: Fortress, 1966); and F. Edward Cranz, *An Essay on the Development of Luther's Thought on Justice, Law, and Society*, Harvard Theological Studies 19 (Cambridge: Harvard University Press, 1964).

order of the secular realm, nor of depriving the government of anything. All he is preaching about is how individual Christians should behave in their everyday lives." As he explained, "The Word of God is not here to teach a maid or a servant how to work in the household and to earn his bread, nor a burgomaster how to rule, nor a farmer how to plow and make hay. In brief, it neither gives nor shows temporal goods for the preservation of this life, for reason has already taught all this to everyone." The word of God, Luther insisted, "is intended to teach how we are to come to that other life. It tells you how to make use of this life and to feed your belly here as long as it lasts, knowing all the while where you will remain and live when this life has ended."[12]

For Luther, the Sermon on the Mount was about how to live in all these realms simultaneously; that is, how to live spiritually before God and how to participate in the world. In order to live in both realms at the same time, Luther made a further distinction. The Christian, he said, consisted of two persons. The Christian was both a spiritual person and a secular person at the same time. In order to understand how he applied these distinctions to the Sermon on the Mount it is best to go back to his earlier treatise, *On the Freedom of the Christian*. In this work, Luther argued two seemingly contradictory theses: "A Christian is a perfectly free lord of all, subject to none," and "a Christian is a perfectly dutiful servant of all, subject to everyone."[13] Both, he insisted, are equally true. From the standpoint of one's spiritual nature, the Christian is free from all laws, duties, and works. Most importantly, Christians are free from having to earn their own salvation. However, Luther reminded the reader, the Christian "remains in this mortal life on earth." From the standpoint of the flesh, the Christian must discipline the body, obey the government, and do good works for the neighbor. Luther's Sermon on the Mount is the ethic for the theology expressed in *On the Freedom of the Christian*. In his

12. LW 21.9, 13, 93, 99, 102, 108–9; WA 32.304, 308, 377, 384, 389–90. In LW 21.13 Luther states: "All this is intended to say that while we live here, we should use all temporal goods and physical necessities, the way a guest does in a strange place, where he stays overnight and leaves in the morning. He needs no more than bed and board and dare not say: 'This is mine, here I will stay'" (WA 32.308.5–7).

13. LW 31.344.

commentary on the Sermon, Luther wrote, "There is no getting around it, a Christian has to be a secular person of some sort. As regards his own person, according to his life as a Christian, he is in subjection to no one but Christ, without any obligation either to the emperor or to any other man. But at least outwardly, according to his body and property, he is related by subjection and obligation to the emperor, inasmuch as he occupies some office or station in life."[14]

Luther explained that the Sermon on the Mount demonstrated how God regarded the "conscience," "heart," and "motivation" of the Christian.[15] The Christian, he said, should use temporal goods and make use of the means of the world. But he will not do so *as a Christian*." The believer will oppose every evil within the limits of his office and may go to court to remedy some violence or injustice. The Christian may go to war, be a governor or a lawyer, or work in any other occupation. Christians may maintain their households, swear oaths, and engage in secular affairs. Nonetheless, they never do these things *as Christians*."[16] The Christian is acting in these positions as a secular person. The two persons in each Christian must move in their own proper sphere. As Luther explained, "The Christian lives simultaneously as a Christian toward everyone, personally suffering all things in the world, and as a secular person, maintaining, using, and performing all the functions required by the law of his territory or city, by civil law and by domestic law." Living according to the Sermon on the Mount means that the Christian "does not live for the things that are visible and pertain to the outward life."[17] *As a Christian*, the believer should not sue anyone, but as a secular person he can go to court and seek redress. However, he must do so without greed, anger, envy, hatred, or attachment to the things of this world. We can hear the echo of Augustine in Luther's commentary: the Christian only "uses" the things of the world but without trusting and loving them. The true home of the Christian lies elsewhere; he is only a pilgrim as he travels through this earthly kingdom.

14. LW 21.109; WA 32.390.19–24.
15. LW 21.90, 135; WA 32.374.29; 32.411.38–412.3.
16. LW 21.113–14, 119; WA 32.393.14–395.10.
17. LW 21.113; WA 32.393.27–29.

Luther's interpretation means that the Christian has to live in constant tension with the world. More so than Augustine, Luther emphasized the aggressive nature of the world in which the Christian must live. Luther knew that the way of life dictated by the Sermon always seems absurd to human reason. Its teachings contradict and overturn the normal, rational conduct of the world. When the text says, "Blessed are they that mourn," human reason balks and rebels. As Luther writes, "Thus, all these statements are aimed and directed against the world's way of thinking, the way the world would like to have things."[18] In Luther's interpretation, the Christian lives both in the world and against the world. Commenting on the passage "you are the light of the world," Luther explained that the true preaching of the word, including the Sermon on the Mount, would inevitably meet the "universal opposition" of the world because the intention of Scripture was "to step forward and to show up the worthlessness of the world's light and teaching."[19] Because the life of faith seems absurd and worthless, Luther depicted it as hidden. He explained that "the whole of the Christian life has to be hidden and remain hidden this way. It cannot achieve great fame or put on much of a display or show before the world. So let it go at that. Do not worry about the way it is hidden, covered up, and buried, and the way no one sees it or notices it. Be content with the fact that your Father up there in heaven sees it. . . . The life of all Christians is intended for the eyes of God alone, and that is how it all comes out."[20] The hiddenness of the Christian life and of the church is a theme that permeated all of Luther's writings. The world seeks the visible, the apparent, the clear, and the obvious. Human reason admires a visible display of piety. In short, the world seeks what Luther called the "theology of glory." But the Sermon on the Mount belongs to what he called the "theology of the cross" because it involves suffering, teaches a life aimed at the invisible, and always stands in opposition to human reason.

18. LW 21.17; WA 32.311.25–26.
19. LW 21.64; WA 32.352.12–14.
20. LW 21.163–64; WA 32.435.11–14.

It would be tempting to stop here and present Luther's understanding of the Sermon on the Mount only as an exposition of the two-kingdoms theory. This theory alone does account for a large part of his interpretation and does present us with a coherent and very familiar aspect of Luther's thought. However, this is not what the text is ultimately about for Luther. To be true to Luther's interpretation, we must go further and delve into a part of Luther's thought that has, at times, made Luther scholars uneasy. We have to talk about the devil. Heiko Oberman's book *Luther: Man between God and the Devil* taught us that the frequent references to the devil were not some kind of medieval remnant in Luther's thought.[21] They were, in fact, an essential part of his worldview. Luther had an extensive demonology and only by fully appreciating this aspect of his thought can we understand his reading of the Sermon on the Mount.

As he moved through the various sections of Matthew 5–7, Luther introduced an additional element into his understanding of the world. In so doing, he added a deeper dimension to the difficulty involved in the life of faith. As we have seen, the Sermon on the Mount gave expression to the theory of the two kingdoms, both of which God ordained. Nevertheless, Luther never forgot that the world was fallen so deeply into sin that danger now lurked everywhere. Consequently, Luther never relinquished his Augustinian view of government. Worldly ranks, laws, and tasks of the government are ordained by God, but their purpose was the restraint of sin. Human association is now so corrupted by sin that the government must hold back the forces of evil. As Luther repeatedly observed, the great majority of people were not true Christians and were not members of the true church. The church, which is ruled by love, must exist in a world where sin, injustice, violence, and wickedness thrive. This conviction about the nature of the fallen world led Luther beyond the two-kingdom theory and to the demonic. The earthly kingdom, ordained by God, has its own prince; namely, the devil. Moreover, Christians are expected to live "as Christians" precisely

21. Heiko Oberman, *Luther: Man between God and the Devil*, trans. Eileen Walliser-Schwarzbart (New Haven: Yale University Press, 1989).

according to the commands of the Sermon on the Mount in the midst of the demonic.

It was not only Luther's theological presuppositions that led him to the theme of the demonic. Certain verses in the Sermon elicited this subject, including Matthew 5:11–12: "Blessed are you when men revile you and utter all kinds of evil against you falsely on my account. Rejoice and be glad, for your reward is great in heaven, for so men persecuted the prophets who were before you." In these statements Luther focused on the fact that Christ spoke about a particular kind of suffering and persecution. These verses referred to not just any form of suffering; they spoke only about being persecuted "for righteousness' sake." It was inevitable that Luther immediately read such verses as descriptions of the persecution inflicted on the Reformation church. But it was Matthew 7:15 that gave these verses their meaning. Luther interpreted earlier references to persecution in terms of Christ's words: "Beware of false prophets, who come to you in sheep's clothing but inwardly are ravenous wolves."

Luther's historical situation in the 1530s helps us understand why these verses gained such prominence in his interpretation of the Sermon on the Mount. By 1530 Luther had, of course, experienced excommunication from the Catholic Church. But he had also experienced the splitting apart of the Protestant movement. The sacramental controversies had erupted, giving rise to the Anabaptists as well as to those whom Luther referred to as the "fanatics." The controversies over the interpretation of the Bible had created major disputes about the claim to the Spirit.[22] The iconoclastic controversy had divided Luther from Carlstadt. Thomas Müntzer had deserted him and become a supporter of the hated Peasants' War. Luther perceived himself as embattled on all sides. He was surrounded by what he called the "enemies from within" and the "enemies from without," all of whom Satan inspired. By now, Luther's apocalyptic worldview had profoundly affected his theology. The devil was everywhere; he inspired the Catholics, or "enemies from without," whose church the antichrist now governed. The devil also inspired the "enemies from within,"

22. LW 21.127, 211–12, 243; WA 32.405, 474, 500.

119

or the schismatic Anabaptists. As Mark Edwards shows, by the 1530s Luther had come to identify himself with St. Paul.[23] Like Paul, Luther saw himself as surrounded by "false brethren" such as Carlstadt, Müntzer, the Anabaptists, and others who had broken away from him and had been urged by the devil to form their own little sects. In Luther's mind the "false brethren" of 2 Corinthians 11:26 became the "false prophets" of Matthew 7:15. Keeping this historical context in mind, we can more fully understand why the Sermon on the Mount, which talks so much about mercy and peace, became for Luther a description of the great battle between the gospel and Satan. This situation also explains why he so frequently read this text as a portrayal of how the minister of the gospel had to suffer and bear the demonic persecution of the world.

In this context, therefore, the world becomes more than the secular realm. Now it is not sufficient to "render to Caesar what is Caesar's" and then continue on one's way to "a higher existence, a divine and an eternal kingdom, where the things that belong to the world are unnecessary and where in Christ everyone is a lord for himself over both the devil and the world."[24] The world becomes even more that "great whorehouse" of greed and envy. Now the world is a great darkness and in the grip of an evil and dangerous power. Luther went beyond Augustine's descriptions of the pilgrim who merely uses the world on his way to the heavenly Jerusalem. For Luther, the world takes on a hostile and intimidating nature that attacks believers and endangers their very existence and salvation.

To appreciate this important element in Luther's reading of the Sermon on the Mount, we must understand his view of how the gospel interacts with the world. For Luther, it was inevitable that the gospel will always create strife and uproar. In his treatise *On the Bondage of the Will*, he had mocked what he called Erasmus's "precious external peace." He told Erasmus that "it is the most unvarying fate of the Word of God to have the world in a state of tumult because of it. . . . The world and its god cannot and will

---

23. Mark U. Edwards Jr., *Luther and the False Brethren* (Stanford: Stanford University Press, 1974). See also idem, *Luther's Last Battles: Politics and Polemics, 1531–46* (Ithaca: Cornell University Press, 1983).
24. LW 21.180; WA 32.448.22.

not endure the Word of the true God, and the true God neither will nor can keep silence; so when these two Gods are at war with one another, what can there be but tumult in the world? . . . Stop your complaining, stop your doctoring: this tumult has arisen and is directed from above and it will not cease till it makes all the adversaries of the Word like the mud on the streets."[25] Luther reiterated this belief in his comments on the Sermon on the Mount. The preaching of the gospel, he said, never brings peace. This is because the gospel arouses Satan to battle. As long as a false gospel is preached, Satan allows the world to slumber in peace. But the true gospel brings tumult. Commenting on Matthew 5:12, Luther warned, "So do not hope for any peace and quiet so long as Christ and his gospel are in the midst of the devil's kingdom. And woe upon the peaceful and smooth situation that used to exist and upon those who want to have it back! This is a sure sign that the devil is ruling with all his might and that no Christ is there."[26] The Christian, Luther said, must always be "armed against the world, the devil, the sects, and whatever else may be lined up against him."[27] In Matthew 5:43–48 Christ tells his followers to love their neighbor, to love their enemies, and to be perfect as their heavenly Father is perfect. However, in these verses Luther found the following meaning: "But that is the way God's Word proceeds. It hammers the great and mighty mountains with its thunder and lightening and storms, so that they smoke. It shatters everything that is great, and proud, and disobedient."[28] Preaching on Matthew 7:6, where we are told not to throw pearls before swine, Luther insisted, "Well there is nothing we can do about it. We have to put up with these snakes, dogs, and swine surrounding us and corrupting the gospel both in doctrine and in life. Wherever there are faithful preachers, they always have to take this. Such is the fortune of the gospel in the world."[29]

---

25. *Luther and Erasmus on the Bondage of the Will*, trans. E. Gordon Rupp and Philip S. Watson, Library of Christian Classics 17 (Philadelphia: Westminster, 1969), 129–30.
26. LW 21.52; WA 32.341.13–18.
27. LW 21.53; WA 32.342.33–34.
28. LW 21.120; WA 32.399.6–8.
29. LW 21.224; WA 32.485.6–9.

The devil, of course, is behind the resistance of the world. Satan, Luther explained, "is a wicked and angry spirit. He will not and cannot stand seeing a man enter the kingdom of God. And if the man undertakes to do so, he blocks the way himself, arousing and attempting every kind of opposition he can summon. If you want to be God's child, therefore, prepare yourself for persecution."[30] Luther not only identified the devil with the blind captivity of the world, but he also explained the *way* in which the devil worked. The method of the devil was one of Luther's favorite themes. He was fascinated with how human evil justifies and rationalizes itself. He emphasized that evil always appears to be noble and respectable. The biblical passage that governed Luther's view of the demonic was 2 Corinthians 11:13–14, where Paul spoke about Satan and the false apostles: "For such men are false apostles, deceitful workmen, disguising themselves as apostles of Christ. And no wonder, for even Satan disguises himself as an angel of light." The idea of the devil disguising himself as an angel of light captivated Luther.[31]

Reformation scholars have long known that Luther's theology is permeated by the theme of hiddenness. But that scholarly discussion has focused on the hiddenness of God, particularly God's hiddenness within revelation.[32] According to Luther, God reveals himself under a contrary; that is, in a way that completely contradicts human reason and expectation. The revelation of God is never obvious in the sense that reason expects. However, Luther's interest in hiddenness extended also to Satan. Satan, too, comes hidden under a contrary, in a disguise, or wearing a mask. Coming under a contrary, Satan appears under the guise of that

30. LW 21.45; WA 32.335.29–33.
31. For the role of 2 Cor. 11:13–14 and the hiddenness of Satan in Luther's thought, see Susan E. Schreiner, "Unmasking the Angel of Light: The Problem of Deception in Martin Luther and Teresa of Avila," in *Mystics, Presence, and Aporia*, ed. Michael Kessler and Christian Sheppard (Chicago: University of Chicago Press, 2003), 118–37.
32. Steinmetz, *Luther in Context*, 23–31; B. A. Gerrish, *The Old Protestantism and the New* (Chicago: University of Chicago Press, 1982), 131–49; Hellmut Bandt, *Luthers Lehre vom verborgenen Gott: Eine Untersuchung zu dem offenbarungsgeschichtlichen Ansatz seiner Theologie*, Theologische Arbeiten 8 (Berlin: Evangelische Verlaganstalt, 1958); and Heinrich Bornkamm, "Der verborgene und der offenbare Gott," *Theologische Rundschau* 16 (1944): 38–52.

which is good, pious, devout, and religious. The evil of Satan is no more obvious than is the goodness of God. In Luther's thought, Satan's primary disguise was idolatry. In order to make sense out of Luther's polemical reading of the Sermon on the Mount, it is critical to recall the centrality and meaning of idolatry in his thought. For Luther, idolatry was the overriding and all-pervasive condition of the fallen world.[33] He explained that idolatry had a twofold nature: it was supremely religious and it was completely rational. Luther was keenly aware that no one ever wanted to be an idolater. But idolaters cannot discern that their god is an idol. The reason idolatry is undetectable is that it conforms perfectly to human reason. Idolatry meets our needs, particularly our spiritual needs, in such a complete and rational way that it never occurs to us that our world is false. Idolatry simply is now what we call reality. Moreover, idolatry is all-embracing: it forms a total and self-enclosed world that satisfies every desire. In his commentary on the third chapter of Genesis, Luther described the fall. He delighted in showing the step-by-step way in which Satan deceived Eve and then Adam. Satan did not insult or directly despise God. He did not deny God. Under the guise of praising God, Satan slowly convinced Eve that she must have misunderstood God; surely he would not deny them anything and would not make them die for eating of the tree. Satan appeared to praise the goodness of God and convinced Eve that her understanding of God's command was irrational.[34]

For Luther, this is the way the devil always acts. He always comes under the cover of the good, the true, the rational, and the divine. The devil, Luther warned, always speaks about God, Christ, the church, prayer, and salvation. In his comments on the Sermon on the Mount, Luther repeated his favorite German proverb in order to express the religiously seductive way that Satan mimics God: "Wherever God builds a church, Satan builds a chapel right next door."[35] Thus, in the fall, Satan seduced Adam and Eve by gradually

---

33. On the theme of idolatry in Luther's thought see my "Appearances and Reality in Luther, Montaigne, and Shakespeare," *Journal of Religion* 83, no. 3 (2003): 345–80.

34. LW 1.146–49; WA 32.110–13.

35. LW 21.212; WA 32.474.36–38; cf. LW 21.282. In LW 4.237 Luther wrote: "For wherever Christ builds a temple and gathers a church, Satan invariably has the habit

insinuating himself into their minds and making them distrust the word of God. When they fell, they fell into a world of indiscernible idolatry. In a very telling statement, Luther wrote, "Satan created a new god for them without their even being aware of it."[36] Luther understood that the power of idolatry depends precisely on its invisibility or the human inability to recognize it.

Luther assumed this reality of idolatry throughout his reading of the Matthew 5–7. In these chapters, Luther represented the grip of idolatry in terms of the Catholics and the "false prophets" or Anabaptists. Like all idolaters, they were intensely religious and truly believed what they taught. They could not detect the very delusions they created. The devil, Luther said, had "bewitched" them so that they were just like a man who was sleeping and dreaming: "He is so enthralled that he cannot see that he is dreaming. As far as he thinks or knows, all this is really happening. He feels nothing as certainly as he feels this, so sure is he of it. And yet it is all just a dream, which vanishes quickly and is all gone when he wakes up."[37]

In the Sermon on the Mount, Luther explained idolatry as the creation of a form of worship that corresponded to one's own ideas.[38] The Sermon had been stolen by the monks and Anabaptists

---

of imitating him like an ape and inventing idolatrous forms of worship and idolatrous traditions similar to the true doctrine and the true forms of worship. . . . For it is the devil's rule to build a chapel next to a church and temple of Christ, that is, to appropriate the works and examples of the fathers, disfigure them, and turn them into a work that is performed without regard to faith."

36. LW 1.148; WA 32.112.3. In this same section Luther argued, "This slyness and villainy of Satan is imitated by all the heretics. Under the appearance of something good they rob men of God and of His Word before their very eyes; and they fabricate for them another, new god, who exists nowhere. If you look at their words, there is nothing holier, nothing more devout. They call upon God as a witness that with all their heart they are seeking the welfare of the church . . . and they avow that it is their desire to spread the name and glory of God with great zeal. . . . It is useful to know these snares. If Satan were to teach that people ought to kill, commit fornication, and disobey their parents, who would not realize that he is suggesting something that is forbidden by the Lord? Therefore it would be easy to be on one's guard against him. But here, where he propounds another word, when he discourses about the will of God, when he uses the names: God, 'the church,' and 'the people of God,' as a pretext, then people cannot so readily be on guard against him. But we need the keenest judgment of spirit to distinguish between the true God and the new god."

37. LW 21.178; WA 32.446.32–38.

38. LW 21.36, 38, 46, 50, 204, 205, 265, 270, 275, 281; WA 32.327, 329, 336, 339, 468, 508, 519, 533.

and interpreted according to the figments of their imagination. Being supremely religious, such people always try to fashion a religious life of perfection. They imagine that this perfect life pleases God and earns rewards or merits. They became what Luther called "counterfeit saints."[39] They acted on their own authority, according to their own ideas, and set up a false god and a false devotion to that god. Luther admitted that they were sincere; they honestly believed in the truth of their own delusions; they were filled with religious zeal.[40] There was nothing that Luther distrusted more than zeal; religious zeal manifested itself in the striving to offer pure, perfect, and meritorious works to God. The life of counterfeit saints, he said, is always visible; they insist on displaying their righteousness. As Luther remarked, they "fill the world with worship," they have a "beautiful appearance" and the "highest kind of sanctity." While the Christian's life is hidden, they have "dazzling" and "showy" works. They display, Luther said, "big beautiful works of love."[41] They wear the "mask" of purity and righteousness.[42] They always seem to be doing so much more than the ordinary Christian. Thus Luther remarked, "No one is deeper in hell than the great servants of God, the most saintly monks."[43]

However, the Sermon on the Mount does speak of perfection and the purity of heart. Matthew 5:48 states: "You, therefore, must be perfect, as your Father in heaven is perfect." This did not deter Luther. He took on these verses by saying, "Here our sophists have spun out many dreams about perfection and have applied them to all their orders and classes—as if only priests and monks were in a state of perfection."[44] But Christ did not mean this kind of perfection. Commenting on the phrase *purity of heart*, Luther explained:

> What is meant by a pure heart is this: one that is watching and pondering what God says and replacing its own ideas with the

39. LW 21.29, 30, 31, 105; WA 32.322.17; cf. 32.387.14.
40. LW 21.79; WA 32.365.21.
41. LW 21.166, 257, 271, 281; WA 32.507, 512, 524, 533.
42. LW 21.33, 266; WA 32.511.15; see also 32.533.19.
43. LW 21.268; WA 32.522.10–11.
44. LW 21.128; WA 32.406.7–10.

Word of God. This alone is pure before God. . . . Therefore, though a common laborer, a shoemaker, or a blacksmith may be dirty and sooty or may smell because he is covered with dirt and pitch, still he may sit at home and think: "My God has made me a man. He has given me my house, wife, and child, and has commanded me to love them and support them with my work." Note that he is pondering the Word of God in his heart. . . . But if he attains the highest purity, so that he takes hold of the Gospel and believes in Christ . . . then he is pure completely, inwardly in his heart toward God, and then outwardly toward everything under him on earth.[45]

We must not allow this homey picture of the shoemaker to lure us into thinking that living according to the word is easy. The shoemaker is always surrounded by false prophets who are trying to deceive him into thinking he must do something to "scramble up to heaven."[46] These people are the wolves who come in sheep's clothing. They always come in sheep's clothing because, like Satan, they can deceive only under a "beautiful impression and appearance."[47] Moreover, "they claim to teach nothing but the Word and use grand words like 'the glory of God,' 'truth,' 'eternal salvation' . . . they give the impression of being strict ascetics with their fasts, chastisements, hard beds and the like . . . this, too, is very impressive and really bewitches people so that whole crowds fall into line."[48] Then, recalling the fall in Genesis, Luther said, "The same thing happens to them that happened to Adam and Eve when they were seduced by the serpent, who made them open up their eyes to see the forbidden tree and who insinuated such beautiful thoughts as these, contrary to the Word of God, 'Why should we not eat of this tree too?'"[49]

These wolves in sheep's clothing are a demonic threat to one's soul. Consequently, Luther saw the whole Sermon on the Mount not merely as an ethic but a call to battle against Satan's delusions. Matthew 7:15 says, "Beware of false prophets." It is the term *beware* that captures Luther's imagination. Against the false

45. LW 21.34; WA 32.325.33–326.7.
46. LW 21.37; WA 32.328.28.
47. LW 21.251; WA 32.507.24.
48. LW 21.253; WA 32.509.31.
49. LW 21.252; WA 32.508.37–40.

brethren, the Christian had to be on guard and vigilant at all times. No one, Luther warned, should think he is secure. He emphasized that Christ said, "'Beware.' The outward appearance and the name are so beautiful that no one can recognize it . . . unless he has the correct understanding of the Word of God."[50]

There is a terrible sense of urgency in Luther's interpretation of the Sermon on the Mount. The seductive nature of idolatry is so powerful that it constantly threatens to destroy the Lord's "little flock."[51] The believer must unmask the ravenous wolves and counterfeit saints. This requires a keen "spiritual vision" or "spiritual understanding" that comes only from faith.[52] Luther cautioned, "Beneath us in the world is the devil, who is continually snapping at us with his jaws in order to bring on impatience, despair, and murmuring against God." For Luther, the main message of the Sermon on the Mount is that the wolves have hemmed in the church on all sides. All Christians can do is "cling," "hold on," or "hold tight" to the word lest they be swept away.[53] Believers are, Luther explained, on the field of battle where there was "no rest."[54] Their weapon is the power of prayer.[55] Believers must pray that God helps them "endure" and will "protect and preserve us against all the power of the devil and his kingdom."[56] Only by this clinging to the word and praying that God will sustain them in the midst of danger can they keep on that "narrow way." The Christian, Luther believed, must live in hiding, walk in darkness, follow the invisible, beware of the devil, and trust God.

---

50. LW 21.250; WA 32.506.39–507.4.
51. LW 21.246; WA 32.503.31.
52. LW 21.260, 264; WA 32.515.2; 32.518.29.
53. LW 21.191, 235, 242, 257, 263, 274, 282, 283; WA 32.457, 493, 500, 512, 517, 526, 533, 535.
54. LW 21.138; WA 32.414.18.
55. LW 21.232–33; WA 32.491.36; 32.420.31–32.
56. LW 21.146.

John Calvin   7

Stephen R. Spencer

In July 1536 the French humanist scholar John Calvin (1509–64) detoured into Geneva overnight on his way to Strasbourg.[1] He stayed for nearly thirty years (interrupted only by a brief Strasbourg exile in 1538–41). He served fervently and faithfully, if often controversially, as teacher and pastor to the newly reformed city.[2] Calvin is popularly known as a theologian, but he has been highly praised as a biblical expositor as well.[3] Throughout his ministry in Geneva, he preached or taught several times a week to a variety of audiences lay, clerical, and academic, in Latin or French, primarily by exposition of Scripture. From 1559 he served as professor of Old Testament (not theology!) in the newly founded Genevan Academy. He wrote commentaries on every New Testament book (except 2 John, 3 John, and Revelation) and on much of the Old Testament, including the Pentateuch, Joshua, Psalms, and all of the Prophets. He preached sermon series that sometimes presaged

1. See Bernard Cottret, *Calvin: A Biography*, trans. M. Wallace McDonald (Grand Rapids: Eerdmans, 2000), 118–20.
2. See William G. Naphy, *Calvin and the Consolidation of the Genevan Reformation* (Manchester: Manchester University Press, 1994; repr. with a new preface, Louisville: Westminster John Knox, 2003).
3. See John L. Thompson, "Calvin's Exegetical Legacy: His Reception and Transmission of Text and Tradition," in *The Legacy of John Calvin: Calvin Studies Society Papers, 1999*, ed. David Foxgrover (Grand Rapids: CRC, 2000), 41–56.

his commentaries but also included books on which he never published commentaries, such as 2 Samuel and Job.[4]

His first commentary, on Romans (1540), states his ideals for commentators in the "Dedicatory Epistle" to his friend Simon Grynaeus. Recalling their conversation three years earlier, he said: "We both thought that the chief excellency of an expounder consists in *lucid brevity*." Second, "almost his only work is to lay open the mind of the writer whom he undertakes to explain," and thus an expounder strays from his purpose and transgresses the boundaries of his responsibilities if he leads readers from the writer's mind.[5] They also agreed that commentators should strive for concise expositions in clear, plain language. Accordingly, Calvin distributed his work among several genres, in particular, commentaries and the *Institutes of the Christian Religion*. In the *Institutes'* prefatory "Address to the Reader" (1539, revised 1559), Calvin stated that he would "condense" the discussions in his commentaries, reserving "long doctrinal discussions" for the *Institutes*.[6]

Calvin and the Sermon on the Mount

Calvin provided his most extensive exposition of the Sermon on the Mount in his *Commentary on a Harmony of the Evangelists: Matthew, Mark, and Luke*.[7] Published in 1555 (first in Latin and

4. The best recent introduction to Calvin's biblical interpretation is John L. Thompson, "Calvin as a Biblical Interpreter," in *The Cambridge Companion to John Calvin*, ed. Donald K. McKim (Cambridge: Cambridge University Press, 2004), 58–73 and 331–32 (bibliography); also see Donald K. McKim, ed., *Calvin and the Bible* (Cambridge: Cambridge University Press, 2006).

5. "Epistle Dedicatory, John Calvin to Simon Grynaeus," in *Commentary on the Epistle of Paul the Apostle to the Romans*, trans. and ed. John Owen (Edinburgh: Calvin Translation Society, 1849), xxiii. See also W. Ian P. Hazlett, "Calvin's Latin Preface to His Proposed French Edition of Chrysostom's Homilies: Translation and Commentary," in *Humanism and Reform: The Church in Europe, England, and Scotland, 1400–1643: Essays in Honor of James K. Cameron*, ed. James Kirk (Oxford: Blackwell, 1991), 129–50.

6. See his "John Calvin to the Reader," in *Institutes of the Christian Religion*, ed. John McNeill, trans. Ford Lewis Battles, Library of Christian Classics 20 (Philadelphia: Westminster, 1960), 5.

7. John Calvin, *Commentary on a Harmony of the Evangelists: Matthew, Mark, and Luke*, trans. William Pringle (Edinburgh: Calvin Translation Society, 1845; repr. Grand Rapids: Baker, 1993), xxxvii–xxxviii. Unless otherwise noted, subsequent citations will

then in his own slightly revised French translation), the *Harmony* completed his New Testament commentaries.[8] From 1549, following the example of Zurich's "prophesyings" for pastors and upper-level students, the pastors from Geneva and its vicinity gathered Friday mornings in their *congrégation* to expound the New Testament books (including the Synoptics, beginning in 1553) and for mutual exhortation and admonition.[9] Calvin participated in this series of expositions and later published at least two of his New Testament expositions.[10] Though this earlier work presumably provided some background for his commentary, Calvin's Synoptic commentary is not a transcription of these expositions.[11]

In addition, following Luther's Small Catechism and a long-established catechetical tradition, every edition of the *Institutes* included an exposition of the Lord's Prayer as part of a larger treatment of prayer.[12] The *Institutes'* treatment of the Lord's Prayer is significantly longer than that in the *Harmony*, in keeping with Calvin's policy. In the final Latin edition (1559) of the *Institutes* (and thus subsequent to the 1555 *Harmony*), this treatment is frequently enlarged or revised, though I did not find any substantive

---

be from this edition. In quoting from this translation, I have sometimes modified spelling and punctuation. See also *A Harmony of the Gospels: Matthew, Mark, and Luke*, vol. 1, trans. A. W. Morrison, ed. David W. Torrance and Thomas F. Torrance (Grand Rapids: Eerdmans, 1972). The Latin text is available in the *Calvini opera* of the *Corpus Reformatorum* 73.159–229. See W. De Greef, *The Writings of John Calvin: An Introductory Guide*, trans. Lyle D. Bierma (Grand Rapids: Baker, 1993), 100n28.

8. De Greef, *Writings of John Calvin*, 101. For a condensation of Calvin's exposition, see Z. N. Holler, "Calvin's Exegesis of the Sermon on the Mount," in *Calvin Studies III: Presented at a Colloquium on Calvin Studies at Davidson College and Davidson College Presbyterian Church*, ed. John H. Leith ([Richmond]: Union Theological Seminary in Virginia, 1986), 5–20. For a brief analysis, see Hermann Schlingensiepen, *Die Auslegung der Bergpredigt bei Calvin*, inaugural dissertation (Berlin, 1927).

9. See De Greef, *Writings of John Calvin*, 117–20; and T. H. L. Parker, *Calvin's Old Testament Commentaries* (Edinburgh: Clark, 1986), 14–15. See also Cottret, *Calvin*, 296–97.

10. T. H. L. Parker, *Calvin's New Testament Commentaries*, 2nd ed. (Louisville: Westminster John Knox, 1993), 28–29. See also De Greef, *Writings of John Calvin*, 118–20.

11. Parker, *Calvin's New Testament Commentaries*, 29.

12. In the 1536 edition, this exposition is 3.14–30; in the 1559 edition it is 3.20.34–49. For an outline of the contents of the various editions, see the chart in Ford Lewis Battles and John Walchenbach, *Analysis of the Institutes of Christian Religion of John Calvin* (Grand Rapids: Baker, 1980), 15.

changes in his interpretation from the *Harmony*. My analysis of Calvin's exposition of the Sermon on the Mount principally attends to the *Harmony*, with only occasional references to his treatment of the Lord's Prayer in the *Institutes*.[13]

Calvin first commented on the Fourth Gospel (1553) and then, two years later, the Synoptic Gospels. The significance of John's Gospel warranted this reversal of order, he explains. Though the last to be written, John's Gospel is "a key to open the door to the understanding of the others."[14] He observes that John "differs widely" from the Synoptic Gospels, "almost wholly occupied in explaining the power of Christ, and the advantages which we derive from him." The other three Gospels "insist more fully on one point, that our Christ is that Son of God who had been promised to be the Redeemer of the world." The Synoptics do not neglect Christ's teaching, however. "They interweave, no doubt, the doctrine which relates to the office of Christ, and inform us what is the nature of his grace and for what purpose he has been given to us." Nonetheless, they are "principally employed . . . in showing that in the person of Jesus Christ has been fulfilled what God had promised from the beginning."[15] As we will see, the Synoptic Gospels' relatively minor doctrinal emphasis includes the Sermon on the Mount, a singularly concentrated account of Jesus's teaching.

Calvin notes that it is "beyond dispute" that expounding one Synoptic Gospel requires constant comparison with the other two.[16] "Persons of ordinary ability," however, find it difficult to "pass at every turn from the one to the other." Calvin's *Harmony* seeks to spare readers the effort of turning back and forth between the three gospels and the confusion over their proper relationship. "I thought it might prove to be a seasonable and useful abridgment of

13. See Elsie Anne McKee, "John Calvin's Teaching on the Lord's Prayer," in *The Lord's Prayer: Perspectives for Reclaiming Christian Prayer*, ed. Daniel Migliore (Grand Rapids: Eerdmans, 1993), 88–106, who provides helpful comparisons to other contemporary treatments of the Lord's Prayer, including those by Erasmus, Luther, and Bucer.

14. John Calvin, "The Argument of the Gospel of John," in *Commentary on the Gospel according to John*, trans. William Pringle (Edinburgh: Calvin Translation Society, 1847; repr. Grand Rapids: Baker, 1993), 1.22.

15. "Argument," *Harmony*, xxxviii–xxxix.

16. Ibid., xxxix.

their labor, if I were to arrange the three histories in one unbroken chain, or in a single picture, in which the reader may perceive at a glance the resemblance or diversity that exists."[17] His exposition of the Sermon of the Mount is part of this harmony approach, of course, and so he addresses the historical and literary relationship between the accounts in Matthew and Luke.

Calvin treats the Sermon in twenty-seven units. After Matthew 5:1–12, only one other unit has as many as six verses. Several units are five verses long, most are three or four verses long, a few contain only two verses, and one unit is a single verse (Matt. 7:6). Though Calvin often moves through a scriptural book by small steps, this exposition involves unusually small steps. In general, this pace reflects the detailed exposition that Calvin practices. Here, however, it may also reflect Calvin's judgment that the Sermon is not a unity, but a collection, as we will see.

The Gospel Accounts of the Sermon: Calvin as Redaction Critic

Calvin begins his exposition by describing the literary character of these three chapters. The "design" of both Matthew and Luke was "to collect into one place the leading points of the doctrine of Christ, which related to a devout and holy life."[18] Fewer than ten lines later, he concludes his brief introduction: "Pious and modest readers ought to be satisfied with having a brief summary of the doctrine of Christ placed before their eyes, collected out of his many and various discourses."[19]

He frequently reiterates this point, either noting that Matthew's or Luke's account comes from a variety of Jesus's discourses on a variety of occasions or emphasizing that Matthew and Luke gathered them together in literary collections or both.[20] This en-

17. Ibid., xxxix.
18. Matt. 5:1 (258). From here on out, references to Calvin's *Harmony* take the form of verse number plus page number in parentheses.
19. Matt. 5:1 (259).
20. See, e.g., Matt. 6:9 and Luke 11:1 (315); Matt. 6:22 (335); Matt. 7:6 (349); Matt. 7:12 (355); Matt. 7:13 and Luke 6:31 (357); Luke 6:43 (366). Note also the apparent

tails another point Calvin frequently makes—that the Sermon is "not a continuous discourse," but that portions of it are "detached sentences" that are "entirely separate" and "not at all connected with what came immediately after" or what preceded.[21] Matthew's purpose in collecting Jesus's teaching, according to Calvin, was "that he might bring more fully under our view the manner in which Christ taught his disciples" and "that the whole amount of them may be more clearly perceived by the readers when they are placed in close succession."[22]

Calvin warns readers not to be overscrupulous in these matters. "As the Evangelists frequently introduce, as opportunity offers, passages of our Lord's discourses out of their proper order, we ought to entertain no scruple as to the arrangement of them."[23] Accordingly he rearranges the other gospels, matching them to Matthew's sequence. Elsewhere he hopes that readers will forgive him "for not being more exact than Matthew in the arrangement of the doctrine."[24]

The point of the gospels' accounts, on Calvin's reading, is not the historical chronology and settings, but Jesus's teaching. In his *Harmony*, Calvin, following the evangelists' precedent, chose "to pay more regard to the doctrine than to the time," connecting "those passages which are closely related in meaning" though Jesus spoke them "on a different and later occasion."[25]

Sometimes Calvin is unsure of the historical and literary aspects of a passage. Regarding the Lord's Prayer, he observes: "It is uncertain whether this form was once only or twice delivered by Christ to his disciples. Some think that the latter is more probable, because Luke says that he was requested to do so, while Matthew represents him as teaching it of his own accord. But as we have said that Matthew collects all the leading points of doctrine in order that the whole amount of them may be more clearly per-

---

suggestion of literary interdependence: "It is also possible that [Luke] may have briefly glanced at what is more fully explained by Matthew" (Luke 6:43 [366]).

21. See Matt. 6:22 (335); Matt. 7:6 (349); Matt. 7:12 (355).
22. Matt. 7:13 and Luke 6:31 (357); Matt. 6:9 and Luke 11:1 (315).
23. Matt. 6:24 and Luke 16:13 (337).
24. Matt. 7:13 and Luke 6:31 (357).
25. Luke 13:25 (359).

ceived by the readers when they are placed in close succession, it is possible that Matthew may have omitted the occasion which is related by Luke."[26] Though elsewhere he is critical, even dismissive, of other interpreters and interpretations, here he concludes irenically: "On this subject, however, I am unwilling to debate with any person."

Though both Matthew and Luke compile their accounts of the Sermon on the Mount, Calvin insists that the Sermon contained in Matthew and Luke is the same. More precisely, judging from his introductory remarks, Matthew and Luke begin from an account of a single discourse and add to those remarks other principal teachings of Christ:

> Those who think that Christ's sermon, which is here related, is different from the sermon contained in the sixth chapter of Luke's Gospel, rest their opinion on a very light and frivolous argument. Matthew states that Christ spoke to his disciples on a mountain, while Luke seems to say that the discourse was delivered on a plain. But it is a mistake to read the words of Luke, *he went down with them, and stood in the plain* (Luke 6:17), as immediately connected with the statement that, *lifting up his eyes on the disciples*, he spoke thus. For the design of the Evangelists was to collect into one place the leading points of the doctrine of Christ which related to a devout and holy life. Although Luke had previously mentioned a *plain*, he does not observe the immediate succession of events in the history, but passes from miracles to doctrine without pointing out either time or place, just as Matthew takes no notice of the time but only mentions the place. It is probable that this discourse was not delivered until Christ had chosen the twelve, but in attending to the order of time, which I saw that the Spirit of God had disregarded, I do not wish to be too precise. Pious and modest readers ought to be satisfied with having a brief summary of the doctrine of Christ placed before their eyes, collected out of his many and various discourses.[27]

Correspondingly, Calvin clarifies Matthew's observation that, when Jesus had finished these sayings, the people marveled at Jesus's teach-

26. Matt. 6:9 and Luke 11:1 (315).
27. Matt. 5:1 (258–59).

ing: "By *these sayings* I understand not only the discourse which he delivered when he came down from the mountain, but the rest of the doctrine which had already been made known to the people."[28] That is, this account of the people's response to Jesus's teaching is generalized, or at least cumulative, from more than one occasion, just as the account of his teaching was.

Throughout his exposition, Calvin compares the gospel accounts, carefully notes the variations, and assesses their significance. Some of these he finds to be inconsequential, some he finds more significant. For example, he notes, "Matthew expresses more clearly the intention of Christ."[29] Sometimes, on the other hand, he concludes that Luke "explains the whole matter more fully" or that "this appears more clearly from the words of Luke" or that "this is more clearly expressed by Luke."[30]

Sometimes Calvin regards the different wordings as altering the scope of the statements. For example, "Instead of *good things* [*agatha*] in the last clause, Luke says *the Holy Spirit*. This does not exclude other benefits, but points out what we ought chiefly to ask."[31]

More often, Calvin notes the differences in wording between the Synoptics but finds in them no appreciable interpretive significance: "Luke expresses it a little differently, but to the same import."[32] "The different modes of expression . . . employed by Matthew and Luke do not alter the meaning."[33] Likewise, the variation between "sins" (Luke) and "debtors" (Matthew) does not change the request for God to remove our condemnation.[34]

Variations between the Synoptic Gospels frequently evoke from Calvin reminders that the Sermon accounts do not record a single, unified discourse given on one occasion. Regarding Jesus's warning against hiding a light, Calvin comments: "Mark and Luke appear to apply the comparison in a different manner,

28. Matt. 7:28 (370).
29. Matt. 5:3 (260).
30. Matt. 5:42 and Luke 6:34 (301–2); Matt. 5:48 and Luke 6:36 (308); Matt. 6:29 and Luke 12:26 (342).
31. Matt. 7:11 and Luke 11:13 (354).
32. Matt. 5:18 and Luke 6:17 (278).
33. Matt. 5:40 and Luke 6:29 (300).
34. Matt. 6:12 and Luke 11:4 (327).

for there Christ gives a general admonition that they ought to take particular care lest any one, trusting to the darkness, indulge freely in sin, because what is hidden for a time will afterwards be revealed. But perhaps the discourses related by both of them are detached from the present context."[35]

Hermeneutics

Interpretive judgments, of course, occur throughout Calvin's exposition. Sometimes he argues for his reading on the basis of the immediate context. The Anabaptists' prohibition of all swearing of oaths, for example, is refuted by the phrase *neither by heaven nor by earth*, added "by way of exposition," specifying the "circuitous or indirect ways of swearing" that Christ forbade.[36] Conversely, he argues *against* reading "detached sentences" on the basis of the immediate context. He judges that the admonition against giving what is holy to the dogs is "not at all connected with what came immediately before, but is entirely separate from it."[37]

He admonishes his readers: "It is not the business of the good and judicious commentator to seize eagerly on syllables, but to attend to the design of the speaker," a theme he reiterates at least ten times in these chapters.[38] He warns that we should not interpret literally the exhortations to retire to our "closet" for prayer or not to be anxious.[39] In addition, "Nothing is more unbecoming the disciples of Christ, than to spend time in caviling about words, where it is easy to see what the Master means." Yet this does not prohibit disputing other interpretations, for, when Jesus tells his disciples to turn the other cheek, Calvin rejects the Anabaptists' interpretation because "the object that Christ has in view is perfectly obvious."[40]

35. Matt. 5:15 and Mark 4:21 and Luke 11:33–34 (274).
36. Matt. 5:34 (294).
37. Matt. 7:6 (349); see also Matt. 7:12 (355).
38. Matt. 5:39 (299); see also Matt. 5:21 (282–83); Matt. 5:34 (295); Matt. 5:40 (299); Matt. 6:4 (310–11); Matt. 6:9 (316 [twice], 317); Matt. 6:12 (327); Matt. 7:1 (346); and Luke 13:26 (360).
39. Matt. 6:5 (312); Matt. 6:25 (339).
40. Matt. 5:39 (299); for other rejections of "caviling" or "quibbling" about words, see Matt. 5:34 (295); Matt. 5:40 (299); Luke 6:30 (301).

He urges readers to note the wider reference of some teachings, warning against restricting the reference of Christ's injunction to "perform to the Lord what we have sworn."[41] He acknowledges that Christ accommodated himself to the people's mistaken understanding of the law. Here Christ's "accommodation" seems to be his beginning with their misunderstanding, which he corrected by his teaching that God "spoke to the hearts" of Israel by the law.[42] He notes—and sometimes defines—tropes and figures of speech such as synecdoche, hyperbole, and an "exaggerated form of speech."[43] He explains that "opening his mouth, he taught them" is a "redundancy of expression" of the "Hebrew idiom."[44] He also cites "profane authors'" use of *hypokritai* ("hypocrites") and notes Jesus's use of the contemporary idiom in describing the publicans as stereotypical sinners.[45] He cautions that Jesus's promise of rewards from God for fasting, as also some of his earlier words about prayer, are "not strictly accurate" (trans. Pringle) or an "inexact expression" (trans. Morrison) (*impropria . . . loquutio*).[46]

Despite the breadth and depth of Calvin's knowledge of the literature of the Christian tradition, so evident in the successive editions of the *Institutes*, Calvin cites few authors and uses fewer sources in his commentaries.[47] His exposition of the Sermon of the Mount is no exception. He mentions Augustine only three times, and two of those are discussions of the same statement, within a few lines of each other.[48] Martin Bucer receives high praise at the end of the "Argument" when Calvin explains that he borrowed the harmony style from Bucer, but then he never mentions his late mentor in the course of these chapters.[49] Chrysostom is mentioned twice, once

41. Matt. 5:33 (294); see also Luke 6:35 (302).

42. Matt. 5:21 (284).

43. Synecdoche in Matt. 5:23 (287); see also Matt. 5:28 (290); Matt. 5:45 (307); Matt. 6:1 (309); hyperbole in Matt. 6:16 (331); and exaggeration in Matt. 5:29 (291).

44. Matt. 5:2 (259).

45. Matt. 6:2 (309); Matt. 5:47 (308).

46. Matt. 6:16 (331).

47. Thompson, "Calvin as a Biblical Interpreter," 64–67; idem, "Calvin's Exegetical Legacy," 32–39. Also see A. N. S. Lane, "The Sources of the Citations in Calvin's Genesis Commentaries," in his *John Calvin: Student of the Church Fathers* (Grand Rapids: Baker, 1999), 205–59.

48. Luke 6:24 (269); Matt. 5:39 (298, 299).

49. "Argument," *Harmony*, xl.

criticized for his "forced interpretation" and another time only to set aside his view.[50] Calvin likewise mentions Erasmus only to reject his view.[51] Several times he mentions that "some" or "others" interpret a passage in this way or that, but then discards their interpretation as wrong or declares it inconclusive. He mentions neither Melanchthon, whose commentaries he discussed in his "Dedicatory Epistle" to his Romans commentary, nor Luther.

Calvin's polemics against a series of opponents, who serve as foils for his exposition, constitute another aspect of Calvin's hermeneutics. His most frequent opponent, predictably, is Rome. The pope, popery, papists, papalists, monks, and other assorted terms occur throughout these chapters. Calvin also frequently targets Jews, as he expounds Jesus's condemnation of hypocrites, folly, and wickedness. However, whereas Jesus condemns actions or attitudes and the people who embody and practice them, Calvin's condemnation sometimes moves beyond that, apparently condemning the entire Jewish people for characteristic sinful traits. The Jews "had an inordinate love of themselves, and proudly despised God and his gifts."[52] The third most common target is also no surprise: the Anabaptists.[53] Calvin singles them out in the "Argument."[54] He twice mentions them by name when defending the use of swearing oaths in certain circumstances, rejecting their prohibition of all oaths.[55] He mentions them when he distinguishes between suffering persecution on Christ's account and those who receive just condemnation because they disturb the church with their "ravings."[56] They also seem to be the unstated foil throughout his discussion of law and gospel and the relation between the old and new covenants.

---

50. Matt. 7:1 (347); Matt. 6:13 (329).
51. Matt. 6:11 (322).
52. Luke 13:30 (361).
53. See Hiltrud Stadtland-Neumann, *Evangelische Radikalismen in der Sicht Calvins: Sein Verständnis der Bergpredigt und der Aussendungsrede (Matth. 10)*, Beträge zur Geschichte und Lehre der Reformierten Kirche (Neukirchen: Neukirchener Verlag, 1966), 15–41.
54. "Argument," *Harmony*, xxxviii.
55. Matt. 5:34 (294); Matt. 5:34 (291).
56. Matt. 5:12 (267).

The Moderate Calvin

Calvin's exposition quite consistently takes a moderate stance on the Sermon's commands.[57] (Anabaptists, then and now, might refer to his approach as "moderating" or "softening" the commands.) We see this, for example, on the permissibility of protecting oneself, taking legal action against another, lending for profit, judging, and swearing oaths and on the prohibition of anxiety. Though this may not fit popular stereotypes of Calvin's moral rigorism, this reading should not surprise us, given the Anabaptist association of more radical readings (especially in the sweeping, pejorative way that Calvin applied that label). He seeks to undermine their distinctive doctrines at every opportunity. For instance, Calvin assures us that the command to turn the other cheek does not require persons to remain under attack, offering themselves for further harm. This would constitute encouraging the assailant, furthering their propensities to injure others. Calvin rejects retaliation, however, including actions of self-defense against the attacker: "Christ does not permit his people to repel violence by violence."[58] He argues for the right to protect oneself by avoiding attack, particularly further attack, carefully interpreting a statement by Augustine: Christ's command does not prevent persons from turning aside "gently and inoffensively to avoid the threatened attack."[59]

Again, regarding the apparent prohibition of taking legal action, he argues: "None but a fool will stand upon the words, so as to maintain, that we must yield to our opponents what they demand before coming to a court of law, for such compliance would more strongly inflame the minds of wicked men to robbery and extortion; and we know that nothing was farther from the design of Christ."[60] Likewise, "We ought not to quibble about words, as if a good man were not permitted to recover what is his own, when God gives him the lawful means. We are only enjoined to exercise patience, that we may not be unduly distressed by the loss of our

---

57. As Holler observes, "perhaps the key word for Calvin's exposition is *moderatio*"; "Calvin's Exegesis of the Sermon on the Mount," 6.

58. Matt. 5:39 (298).

59. Matt. 5:39 (299).

60. Matt. 5:40 (299).

property, but calmly wait, till the Lord himself shall call the robbers to account."[61]

His moderation of the prohibition of anxiety is striking:[62] "Throughout the whole of this discourse, Christ reproves that excessive anxiety with which men torment themselves about food and clothing. . . . When he forbids them to be *anxious*, this is not to be taken literally, as if he intended to take away from his people all care. We know that men are born on the condition of having some care. . . . But immoderate care is condemned."[63] It is impossible and, more importantly, irresponsible not to be anxious over the appropriate cares of this life, he argues. The dangers and contingencies of this life, even more obvious in the sixteenth century, require our careful concern in order to provide for ourselves and those under our care.

Theological themes in Calvin's Exposition

The Theme of the Sermon on the Mount

The Sermon on the Mount compendium contains "the doctrine of Christ, which related to a devout and holy life."[64] Calvin's qualifying phrase, "which related to a devout and holy life," may indicate a specific subcategory of the large scope of Jesus's teaching. More often, however, he simply calls this "the doctrine of Christ." Calvin proposes nothing more specific for the theme of the Sermon. "A devout and holy life" may seem both too broad and too narrow. Is this sufficiently focused to be the theme? On the other hand, is this too narrow to embrace all that Jesus teaches in the gospels? Might some readers judge "a devout and holy life" to be an anthropocentric focus? On the other hand, what significance does the Sermon's anthology genre have for questions about thematic structure? Does it entail that we should not expect a more precise theme for the Sermon as a whole? How should this discussion

61. Luke 6:30 (301).
62. For the entire discussion, see his comments on Matt. 6:25–32 (339–44).
63. Introduction to Matt. 6:25–30 (339).
64. Matt. 5:1 (258).

141

affect our reading of Calvin's exposition? His exposition is not an integral unity; perhaps this is because he does not regard the Sermon as a unity.

Law and Gospel

Calvin perhaps gives more attention here to law and gospel (and the relationship between the old and the new covenants) than any other single doctrinal theme. He introduces this in his initial discussion of the three gospels, asserting that the Evangelists "had no intention or design to abolish by their writings *the law and the prophets*."[65] He rejects the "dreams" of some "fanatics" who claim that the Old Testament is superfluous now that Christ has come. "On the contrary," the gospel writers "admonish us to seek from him whatever is ascribed to him by *the law and the prophets*." Readers can gain the "full advantage from the gospel" only when they "connect it with the ancient promises."

In the course of his exposition, Calvin scarcely misses an opportunity to elaborate on this theme. He gives extended attention to this when commenting on Matthew 5:17: "Do not think that I have come to abolish the law and the prophets." In words that seem to shift back and forth from Christ's proclamation of the gospel in the first century to the Reformers' preaching in the sixteenth, he cautions against the inclination to extremes during times of change, especially of religious reforms. "As soon as any new method of teaching makes its appearance," people reject the entire established order "as if everything were to be overturned." The preaching of the gospel was no exception to this, for it "tended to raise the expectation that the Church would assume a totally different form. . . . They thought that the ancient and accustomed government was to be abolished." He notes, however, that "devout worshippers of God would never have embraced the Gospel if it had been a revolt from *the law*."[66] Calvin emphasizes that Christ "declares" that his doctrine is "so far from being at variance with *the law*, that it agrees perfectly

---

65. "Argument," *Harmony*, xxxviii.
66. Matt. 5:17 (276).

with *the law and the prophets*, and not only so, but brings the complete *fulfillment* of them."[67]

These reflections, including the reference to "ancient and accustomed government," bespeak both Calvin's theological caution and his sociopolitical caution. Mistaking reform for revolution or even anarchy jeopardizes social order and religious order alike. He soberly warns: "If we intend to reform affairs which are in a state of disorder, we must always exercise such prudence and moderation as will convince the people that we do not oppose the eternal Word of God or introduce any novelty that is contrary to Scripture."[68]

These words reflect the threat that he—and the other Magisterial Reformers—perceived in the Radical Reformers as well as their urgency to reject the Roman Catholic claims that the Reformers fostered religious and social disorder. Calvin strove to overcome Roman opposition, arguing strenuously that the lamentable state of the life and teaching of the sixteenth-century church called for profound reform to restore its fidelity. Yet he also deplored the destructive, disorderly radicalism that moved too far, too fast, often seeking to change what should not be changed. Here as elsewhere Calvin desired a *via media* that avoided errors on either side, employing what Ford Lewis Battles calls a *calculus fidei* to plot a trajectory through the dangers on either side.[69] Like many of the Magisterial Reformers, Calvin had a very high view of order and had a deep, almost visceral, fear of disorder. Calvin's legal and theological expertise gave him great respect for justice, but injustice was better endured than risk-producing disorder. We might say that, for Calvin, disorder was worse than any injustice, or the worst form of injustice, because it was so fundamental. At least in some cases, removing or drastically changing sociopolitical structures would do less to set things

67. Matt. 5:17 (275).
68. Matt. 5:17 (276–77).
69. "There is in Calvin a single principle, but it is expressed in many ways: every fundamental notion of his thought is defined in a field of tension—a true middle between false extremes"; Ford Lewis Battles, "*Calculus fidei*: Some Ruminations on the Structure of the Theology of John Calvin," in his *Interpreting John Calvin*, ed. Robert Benedetto (Grand Rapids: Baker, 1996), 140 (see 139–246 for the entire essay).

right than changing humans and their structural abuse. Yet he supported orderly change of structures by designated authorities, for example, laws outlawing begging and establishing church and civil support for the poor and the establishment of housing, education, and job retraining for religious refugees.[70]

Acknowledging a possible objection to his teaching on the continuity of the law, Calvin clarifies: "God had, indeed, promised a *new covenant* at the coming of Christ, but has at the same time showed that it would not be different from *the first*." "On the contrary, its design was to give a perpetual sanction to the covenant which he had made from the beginning with his people."[71] For Calvin, this is a *renewed* covenant, a clarified and restored covenant, not a substitute or replacement. As he states in the *Institutes*, the old covenant and the new covenant are two dispensations of the one covenant of grace, differing only in the mode of administration, not in their substance.[72]

Surely, however, *something* changes between the old and the new covenants, we might ask. Calvin clarifies the covenantal continuity and discontinuity of doctrine and ceremonies: "With respect to doctrine, we must not imagine that the coming of Christ has freed us from the authority of the law, for it is the eternal rule of a devout and holy life and must, therefore, be as unchangeable as the justice of God, which it embraced, is constant and uniform."[73] He grants that "there is some appearance of change having taken place" in the ceremonies, "but it was only the use of them that was abolished, for their meaning was more fully confirmed."

Does not the ceremonial change constitute some breaking of or deviation from the old covenant, so that Christ could be said to abolish at least the ceremonies? No, Calvin replies, for "that man does not break ceremonies, who omits what is shadowy, but

---

70. See, e.g., W. Fred Graham, *The Constructive Revolutionary: John Calvin and His Socio-economic Impact* (Richmond: John Knox, 1971); Robert M. Kingdon, "Social Welfare in Calvin's Geneva," *American Historical Review* 76 (1971): 50–69; William C. Innes, *Social Concern in Calvin's Geneva* (Allison Park, PA: Pickwick, 1983); and Jeanine Olsen, *Calvin and Social Welfare: Deacons and the Bourse Française* (Sellingsgrove, PA: Susquehanna University Press, 1989).

71. Matt. 5:17 (277).

72. *Institutes* 2.10.2.

73. Matt. 5:17 (277–78).

retains their effect."[74] This neatly maintains his point, but we may ask whether it does justice to the quantity and complexity of the covenantal stipulations, including the Levitical sacrificial and holiness stipulations. They are not immediately distinguished in old covenant legislation as merely shadow and of a quite different character than the doctrines. Perhaps the doctrines and ceremonies are more integrated than these categories suggest. Furthermore, Jesus's words in Mark 7 "declaring all foods clean" and Peter's vision in Acts 10 about unclean foods and unclean people seem more drastic than Calvin's language about shadows suggests.

Calvin urges: "Let us therefore learn to maintain inviolable this sacred tie between the law and the Gospel, which many improperly try to break."[75] The gospel summons and marks Christ's followers, but for Calvin, this does not imply any denigration of the eternal law of God, the law given to God's people Israel. Calvin clearly *distinguishes* law and gospel, but he does not make them *antithetical*. Rather he "maintains inviolable this sacred tie" between them. Christians do not turn from the law—either its doctrines or its ceremonies—in turning to the gospel, Calvin argues. The distinct functions of law and gospel do not warrant dispensing with the old in favor of the new.

Calvin then connects this to the kingdom of heaven, that is, "the renovation of the Church or the prosperous condition of the Church, such as was then beginning to appear by the preaching of the Gospel."[76] When Jesus begins his series of contrasts ("you have heard it said . . . but I say to you"), Calvin hastens to prevent misunderstandings of this "renovation of the church." He maintains that Christ neither corrected the law nor proposed a higher level of perfection for his disciples than that given to the nation Israel. He rejects suggestions that "the beginning of righteousness was laid down in the ancient law, but that the perfection of it is pointed out in the Gospel."[77] "But nothing could be farther from the design of Christ than to alter or innovate any thing in the commandments of the law. There God has

74. Matt. 5:19 (280).
75. Matt. 5:17 (278).
76. Matt. 5:18 (279).
77. Matt. 5:21 (282).

once fixed the rule of life which he will never retract."[78] Christ's intention, instead, is to "vindicate" the law from corruptions resulting from false expositions.

Calvin's comment indicates a crucial concern regarding the law, one central to his claim of the harmonious relationship between the law and the gospel. In the Decalogue God "fixed a rule of life" that he does not retract, even when the promised Messiah comes to establish the new covenant. For Calvin, the novelty of the new covenant is not that it discloses a new rule of life for God's people. Such a radical change in the *rule* of life would require a corresponding change in the *ruler* of life. God does not change, and therefore the rule of life for his people cannot change, for it embodies and reveals his eternal character in the form of the covenant's moral obligations. As the Sermon on the Mount is "a collection of the leading points of Christ's doctrine," exposition of it must stress the *continuity* of God's rule of life for his people. Christ's contrasts could not be between the law of God for Israel and the gospel for Jesus's disciples.

"Law" for Calvin is fundamentally the Decalogue. For most of his uses of "law" in this exposition, we could substitute "Decalogue" without altering the meaning. This helps to account for his easy distinction between doctrine and ceremonies. "Doctrine" is the Decalogue, the basic, enduring moral principles of human life because they state the eternal law based in God's character. Other nonceremonial stipulations are only applications or explications to human life, and the remainder of the covenant is ceremony. In Calvin's view, the Ten Commandments "briefly but comprehensively encompass the rule of a just and holy life," but, as David Wright notes, "Their supplementary appendages . . . add not the least to the substance of the law itself."[79]

This illustrates the seriousness of the Anabaptists' threat to the church. In Calvin's judgment, their teaching is not merely false to Scripture and the gospel, it is blasphemous, alleging that God

---

78. Matt. 5:21 (282).
79. "The Preface of John Calvin," *Commentary on the Four Last Books of Moses Arranged in the Form of a Harmony* (Edinburgh: Calvin Translation Society, 1852–55; repr. Grand Rapids: Baker, 1993), xvii–xviii; David F. Wright, "Calvin's Pentateuchal Criticism: Equity, Hardness of Heart, and Divine Accommodation in the Mosaic Harmony Commentary," *Calvin Theological Journal* 21 (1986): 49.

changes his rule of life from one covenant to the next and thus that God's moral character changes and develops from lower to higher. Such doctrine is unconscionable for Calvin, a violation of Christian truth in the most fundamental way. In short, he concludes, "We must not imagine Christ to be a new legislator who adds anything to the eternal righteousness of his Father. We must listen to him as a faithful expounder, that we might know what is the nature of the law, what is its object, and what is its extent."[80]

Inward Righteousness

A central claim of Calvin's exposition is that Jesus's teaching distinguishes between what he calls the outward, "carnal," political, or national keeping of the law, on one hand, and the inward keeping of the law, requiring "pure and holy affections of the heart."[81] The Jews "did wrong in viewing as a matter of civil law, the rule which had been given them for a devout and holy life."[82] "National laws are sometimes accommodated to the manners of men," he acknowledges, "but God, in prescribing a spiritual law, looked not at what men can do, but at what they ought to do. It contains a perfect and entire righteousness, though we want ability to fulfill it."[83] The Mosaic covenant, of course, was both the national *and* the spiritual covenant between Israel and its God and perhaps more integral than Calvin implies.

Calvin's doctrine of divine accommodation is well known. It pervades his theology, touching nearly every aspect of the transcendent God's relationship to his finite, temporal creation.[84] Accommodation characterizes not only *how* God has spoken on

80. Matt. 5:21 (283–84).
81. Matt. 5:27 (290).
82. Matt. 5:31 (292).
83. Matt. 5:31 (292).
84. See David F. Wright, "Calvin's 'Accommodation' Revisited," in *Calvin as Exegete: Papers and Responses Presented at the Ninth Colloquium on Calvin and Calvin Studies*, ed. Peter De Klerk (Grand Rapids: Calvin Studies Society, 1993), 171–90; and idem, "Calvin's Accommodating God," in *Calvinus sincerioris religionis vindex: Calvin as Protector of the Purer Religion*, ed. Wilhelm H. Neuser and Brian G. Armstrong, International Congress on Calvin Research 1994, Sixteenth Century Essays and Studies 36 (Kirksville, MO: Sixteenth Century Journal Publishers, 1997), 3–20.

a wide range of issues, but also *what* God has spoken (e.g., the doctrine of angels is mentioned in Scripture primarily to assure us of God's protection).[85] Moreover, it also is how God *acts*. The sacraments (especially the Lord's Supper), the use of angels, the use of human ministers to proclaim the word of God—these and other acts of God are his adaptation to our weakness and small capacity, as well as to our perversity. Significantly, Calvin acknowledges that at some points in Israel's history, because of "the people's irremediable hardness of heart," God accommodated his moral standards, making "concessions" or "tolerating" the moral defects of Israel.[86] These are the "national laws" that are "sometimes accommodated to the manners of men," but none of them involve God accommodating "the spiritual law."

This call to inward righteousness, "pure and holy affections," a "devout and holy life," pervades Jesus's doctrine, on Calvin's reading, and he reiterates it in his exposition at every opportunity. To follow Jesus is to submit to his teaching, to respond from the heart with faithful obedience born of love and gratitude in response to gracious redemption. In their several ways, Calvin seeks to show, the discourses collected in this Sermon consistently make this point. For instance, he identifies "the two leading points of the covenant": "the eternal salvation of the soul" and "the spiritual life," "in which all our salvation consists."[87] Christ included these two fundamental concerns in two petitions of the prayer he taught his disciples ("forgive us our debts" and "lead us not into temptation but deliver us from evil" [Calvin suggests rephrasing this as "that we may not be led into temptation, deliver us from evil"]).[88]

"Such is the corruption of our nature, that all our affections are so many soldiers of Satan."[89] Therefore, Calvin argues, for God to "deliver us from evil" requires that he transform us by writing the law on our hearts. This illustrates how integrally connected in Calvin's thought are the spiritual life, the law of God, and the Spirit's transforming work. We should not be surprised that, of

85. *Institutes* 1.14.6, 11.
86. See Wright, "Calvin's Pentateuchal Criticism," 39–45.
87. Matt. 6:12 (326).
88. Matt. 6:13 (327).
89. Matt. 6:10 (319).

the nearly eighty citations of these three Matthean chapters in the *Institutes*, about fifty of them occur in book 3, "The Way in Which We Receive the Grace of Christ," the book that primarily concerns the Spirit's work in Christians. Calvin's doctrine of word and Spirit also evidences this integral connection. The kingdom for which we pray comes "partly by the preaching of the word, and partly by the secret power of the Spirit. It is his will to govern men by his word, but as the bare voice, if the inward power of the Spirit be not added, does not pierce the hearts of men, both must be joined together in order that the *kingdom* of God may be established."[90] In those who turn to God by this renewing work of word and Spirit, he concludes, "The commencement of the *reign* of God in us is the destruction of the old man, and the denial of ourselves, that we may be renewed to another life."[91]

In this life, however, inward transformation does not completely remove sinfulness. Calvin makes this point regarding perfection in two ways. First he qualifies the "perfection" that Christ commands for his followers: "This *perfection* does not mean *equality*, but relates solely to resemblance. However distant we are from the perfection of God, we are said to be *perfect, as he is perfect*, when we aim at the same object, which he presents to us in Himself."[92] Second, he decisively rejects claims of sinlessness in this life because they effectively renounce Christ: "Those who dream of attaining such perfection in this world, as to be free from every spot and blemish, not only renounce their sins, but renounce Christ himself, from whose Church they banish themselves. For, when he commands all his disciples to betake themselves to him daily for forgiveness of sins, every one, who thinks that he has no need of such a remedy, is struck out of the number of the disciples."[93]

The Present Life in Relation to the Future Life

In distinguishing between inward and outward righteousness, Calvin admonishes his readers about the relation of this life to

90. Matt. 6:10 (320).
91. Matt. 6:10 (320).
92. Matt. 5:48 (308).
93. Matt. 6:12 (326).

the future life. Christ's followers should understand the transient nature of this life and live now in light of their future life in the fullness of the kingdom. As Calvin puts it in the *Institutes*, "meditation on the future life" is prerequisite to "the proper use of this life."[94] Christians' happiness or blessedness in this life depends on them submitting to Jesus's teaching about true happiness, the theme of the first of the gathered discourses of Jesus.[95]

"The leading object" of the Beatitudes, Calvin claims, is "to show that those are not unhappy who are oppressed by the reproaches of the wicked and subject to various calamities."[96] Christ demonstrates the error of measuring human happiness by the present state "because the distresses of the godly will soon be changed for the better." He "exhorts his own people to patience, by holding out the hope of a reward."[97] "As the condition of the godly, during the whole course of this life, is very miserable, Christ properly calls them to the hope of the heavenly life."[98] "Those things which relate to the present life are but favorable appendages, and ought to be reckoned greatly inferior to *the kingdom of God*."[99] In the face of wickedness and suffering, Calvin calls his readers to see this life in the light of the future, enduring with joy its suffering because of the great blessings to come.

Calvin not only calls the church to see this life in light of the future. He calls them to pray for their needs, the daily needs of this life, but also their supreme need, the coming of the kingdom. They display their gratitude to their heavenly Father for his past generosity and their utter dependence on him by refusing to seek help elsewhere. God's blessings of mercy and grace in this life of inequity turn our hearts to him for the fullness of the promised blessings.

Prayer too manifests Calvin's *via media*, the *calculus fidei*. He seeks to avoid both a fervency that ignores or violates Scripture's instructions and also a ritual formality devoid of the Spirit that

94. Institutes 3.9–10.
95. Matt. 5:1 (258–9).
96. Matt. 5:2 (260).
97. Matt. 5:2 (260).
98. Matt. 5:10 (266).
99. Matt. 6:33 (344).

comes from our lips but not our hearts. Calvin calls for heartfelt prayer, not mere words: "When prayer is offered with earnest feeling, the tongue does not go before the heart."[100] Yet, "All our affections being blind, the rule of prayer must be sought from the word of God."[101] Though prayer is "the most important exercise of piety, yet in forming our prayers, and regulating our wishes, all our senses fail us. No man will pray aright, unless his lips and heart shall be directed by the Heavenly Master."[102]

Calvin's discussion of prayer largely echoes the *Institutes*. However, his *Harmony* comments make more of the agency of prayer in God's provision. The *Institutes* emphasize prayer's benefits in turning our attention to God and increasing our dependence on him (our agency toward ourselves). The *Harmony* includes this emphasis as well, but there he more strongly acknowledges prayer as an agency in God's provision for us: "We must, therefore, maintain both of these truths," Calvin reminds us, "that He freely anticipates our wishes, and yet that we obtain by prayer what we ask."[103]

Conclusion

More could be said about each of these and about a number of other aspects of Calvin's exposition of this central scriptural passage, but this must suffice for this introduction. Calvin models for us what we may call an "ethic of interpretation," an attentive listening to Scripture as both human and divine, as the accounts by Matthew, Mark, and Luke and also as the word of God. He is more restrained than some others in staying close to the text of Scripture, seeking to provide the readers with a faithful exposition of what the authors wrote. Christ's message comes to us in Scripture, collected and arranged by humans. Calvin evidences no nervousness about the editorial work of the Gospel writers who "collected the leading points of Christ's doctrine," sometimes ignoring time and sometimes ignoring place, but faithfully presenting

100. Matt. 6:7 (313).
101. Matt. 7:11 (353).
102. Matt. 6:9 (316).
103. Matt. 6:8 (314).

Christ nonetheless, clear to those who have ears to hear, by the work of the Spirit.

Calvin's understanding of the edited character of the Sermon shapes his reading, for example, limiting his use of context as an interpretive guide. He evidences some of his humanist rhetorical training, but rather modestly and with little sign of his extensive reading of the Christian tradition. Calvin's concern is to understand what the authors wrote, but he expounds it with careful attention to the contemporary context. Indeed he understands Scripture in part by means of his agenda of avoiding prevalent errors in his contemporary context. He "calculates" the faithful path by marking the boundaries with misinterpretations and abuses. His contemporary opponents help to shape his hermeneutical lenses and establish the range of interpretation. Readings associated with them seem prejudged and discarded. He does not interpret Scripture solely in terms of itself.

Calvin's primary theological concern here is arguably law and gospel. The rule of life is as unchanging as the ruler of life. God gave his people Israel the eternal law, the eternal rule of a devout and godly life. The gospel of Christ cannot replace or alter that law without affronting the God who gave the law and sent Christ. Christ expounds the law, correcting misinterpretations and distortions. The Spirit writes the law on the hearts of God's people, thereby transforming them into Christ's image for faithful lives. For Calvin, only by keeping the law and the gospel together, maintaining the inseparable bond of word and Spirit, can the church walk faithfully in the present in light of the future, avoiding the pressing errors on either side.

John Wesley

Mark Noll

To John Wesley, the Sermon on the Mount was, as he put it in 1771, "the noblest compendium of religion which is to be found even in the oracles of God."[1] When he wrote these words in connection with a sermon preached at Oxford "in a room well filled with deeply attentive hearers," Wesley was nearing his seventieth birthday; he had been preaching on texts from the Sermon for more than forty-five years. The first of those sermons (on Matt. 6:33) was only the second one he ever wrote. As a time-pressed, recently ordained deacon in the Church of England he preached this early sermon in small village churches at least ten or twelve times in 1725, 1726, and 1727. Its message included much that would be characteristic of Wesley's preaching throughout his life, especially a concern for inner godliness and a stress on experiential holiness. Thus, in this early exposition of "seek ye first the kingdom of God, and his righteousness, and all these things

---

1. Unless otherwise indicated, all Wesley quotations are taken from *The Works of John Wesley: Bicentennial Edition*, ed. Frank Baker and Richard P. Heitzenrater (Nashville: Abingdon, 1975–) (hereafter WJW). The seven volumes of Wesley's journal (= WJW 18–24) were published in 1988–2003 and edited by W. Reginald Ward and Richard P. Heitzenrater (hereafter *Journal*). The four volumes of Wesley's sermons (= WJW 1–4) were published in 1984–87 and edited by Albert C. Outler (hereafter *Sermons*). This quotation is from *Journal V* for Oct. 17, 1771 (WJW 22.293).

shall be added unto you," Wesley urged his hearers not only to act properly but also "immediately [to] check any distrustful thoughts that may arise in your souls." And he repeatedly emphasized that the Christian's business was to honor God and serve the neighbor: "Consider in the beginning of every undertaking whether it be proper or likely in any degree to promote the glory of God, or peace and goodwill among men." Yet absent from this exhortation based on Matthew 6:33 was the intense concentration on works in relation to grace—life in relation to faith—that would make up so much of his mature discourses on the Sermon. At this early stage Wesley, though precociously fluent in pulpit exhortation and already a master of scriptural phrasing, was still primarily an Anglican moralist. Thus, he equated righteousness simply with "our duty to our neighbour" and defined fulfilling that duty as "the sum of the Christian religion." He described "the inestimable reward that remains eternal in the heavens" as belonging to "those who . . . behave themselves on earth" in accord with righteousness so defined. And in the Sermon's conclusion he quoted the stirring injunctions of Micah 6:8 ("what doth the Lord require of thee") as a sufficient description of the path leading to "eternal mansions of joy."[2] A lifetime of engagement with the Sermon on the Mount had begun, but there would be much development as that life went on.

After that early sermon in 1725 Wesley preached with great frequency throughout the rest of his life on texts from Matthew 5–7. During the memorable voyage that took him as a missionary to Georgia in the winter of 1736, he studied German with his Moravian shipmates in the morning, but then at other times exhorted the ship's company with texts from the Sermon.[3] In Georgia he used "a short paraphrase of our Lord's Sermon on the Mount" to instruct the children of Savannah.[4] After his return to England in 1738 Wesley's own records show that between 1739 and 1746 he preached over one hundred times from texts drawn from the Sermon.[5]

2. Wesley, "Seek First the Kingdom," in *Sermons IV* (WJW 4.216–23 at 218, 219, 220, 223).

3. Albert C. Outler, introduction to sermons 21–33, in *Sermons I* (WJW 1.467).

4. Wesley, Oct. 23, 1737, in *Journal I* (WJW 18.567).

5. Outler, introduction to sermons 21–33, in *Sermons I* (WJW 1.467).

The Sermon on the Mount also seems to have played an important part in Wesley's momentous decision to begin preaching out-of-doors, which in an England still uneasy about the long-past enthusiasm of the Cromwellian Revolution and jittery about the present possibility of a Jacobite invasion amounted to a provocation bordering on sedition. In early spring 1739 Wesley was in London when he received a message from George Whitefield writing from Bristol to say that his preaching was drawing more common-folk hearers than he could handle—could Wesley come and help? Whitefield had only just begun the practice of preaching out-of-doors, so Wesley knew that if he answered this summons, he too would likely end up preaching under the open sky. Against that choice for wild enthusiasm, several of his most trusted friends advised Wesley in no uncertain terms to beware. But go to Bristol Wesley did, and on Saturday, March 31, he met Whitefield, who explained why he had taken up this new seeker-sensitive strategy. In his journal Wesley wrote of that conversation: "I could scarce reconcile myself at first to this *strange way* of preaching in the fields, of which he set me an example on Sunday, having been all my life (till very lately) so tenacious of every point relating to decency and order that I should have thought the saving of souls *almost a sin* if it had not been done *in a church*." The next day, Sunday, April 1, Wesley preached (indoors) on "our Lord's Sermon on the Mount," which, however, he took pains to note was "one pretty remarkable precedent of *field preaching*, though I suppose *there were churches* at that time also." The very next day, Monday, April 2, Wesley used a phrase from 2 Samuel 6:22, which described David dancing before the Lord, to record the breakthrough that would lead on to systems of Methodist itinerancy that transformed the face of religion in Britain, the United States, and Canada: "At four in the afternoon I submitted to 'be more vile,' and proclaimed in the highways the glad tidings of salvation, speaking from a little eminence in a ground adjoining to the city, to about three thousand people."[6] Where Jesus with his Sermon on the Mount had pioneered, John Wesley—despite his establishmentarian DNA as

6. Wesley, March 31, April 1, April 2, 1739, in *Journal II* (WJW 19.46).

an orderly Anglican and his dignified status as a graduate of the University of Oxford—would follow.

Shortly thereafter, the Sermon figured again in one of the many memorable events from that remarkable revival summer of 1739. Wesley was preaching in Bath on Sunday, July 22, to an out-door crowd he estimated at three thousand auditors. His text was "blessed are the poor in spirit." While he was speaking a press gang came onto the scene and hauled away one of the young men listening to the sermon. The huge crowd remained peaceful, but Wesley was furious: "Ye learned in the law, what becomes of Magna Charta, of 'English liberty and property?' Are not these mere sounds, while, on any pretence, there is such a thing as a press-gang suffered in the land?"[7]

In subsequent years Wesley's preaching from the Sermon on the Mount also figured large in other signal circumstances. In Cardiff on October 19, 1739, he preached for three hours on the last six beatitudes. On June 13, 1742, he preached again on the Sermon for three hours "to a vast multitude gathered from all parts" as the last in a series of sermons in his father's own Epworth parish.[8]

As was his wont with many texts, Wesley knew how to turn preaching from the Sermon on the Mount toward polemical ends as well. In December 1740 we find him preaching twice on a Monday from the Sermon on the Mount in order to overcome the effects of predestinarian teaching. A few years later, he preached on Matthew 7:15 ("beware of false prophets") as a warning against unspiritual time-servers in the Church of England.[9]

Decades later he exploited sayings from the end of Matthew 7 to advance his doctrine of Christian perfection. In his journal Wesley recorded meeting several ordinary believers at Eccleshall who were "exceeding artless and exceeding earnest," but who had already been *saved from sin*," that is, come to experience entire sanctification. Immediately thereafter he preached on "the wise man that builds his house upon a rock" and applied the text to these ones who had been perfected. Now, however, in 1776, after

7. Wesley, July 21, 1739, in *Journal II* (WJW 19.81–82).
8. Wesley, Oct. 19, 1739, and June 13, 1742, in *Journal II* (WJW 19.108, 277).
9. Wesley, Dec. 15, 1740, and Jan. 30, 1743, in *Journal II* (WJW 19.174, 313).

long years of pondering the connection between faith and works, he stated his concluding application from the text with more nuance than he had shown in his early sermon from 1725: thus, to Wesley, the wise man was the one "who builds his hope of heaven on no other foundation than *doing these sayings* contained in the Sermon on the Mount—although in another sense, we build not upon his *sayings*, but his *sufferings*."[10]

As important as episodic preaching from the Sermon on the Mount was for Wesley's itinerant exhorting, the Sermon was even more significant for how it defined the central concerns of his theology. In a word, Wesley's understanding of the Sermon played a key role in his lifetime's effort to champion a religion marked by both free grace and practical holiness. In expounding the Sermon, as in much else, he pursued the preeminent but complex goal of his whole career, which Henry Rack well defines in these carefully chosen words: "Wesley [was] trying to find a solution to the old problem of how to reconcile the notion of salvation that depends on a divine act of grace to save fallen men with the desire for a positive and progressive attitude toward a recreation of the personality by a progressive realization of the mind of Christ in which men take an active part."[11]

Over the course of many decades Wesley himself restated time and again this twinned preoccupation with salvation bestowed by grace apprehended through faith and salvation experienced as holiness active in faith. In one of his most often repeated early sermons the note of grace was somewhat stronger over against the note of active love, but both were clearly present: "May we all thus experience what it is to be not almost only, but altogether Christians! Being justified freely by his grace, through the redemption that is in Jesus, knowing we have peace with God through Jesus Christ, rejoicing in hope of the glory of God, and having the love of God shed abroad in our hearts by the Holy Ghost given unto us!"[12]

Later came statements of careful balance. In 1746 he wrote a very long letter defending "The Principles of a Methodist," which

10. Wesley, April 26, 1776, in *Journal VI* (WJW 23.10).
11. Henry D. Rack, *Reasonable Enthusiast*, 3rd ed. (London: Epworth, 2002), 409.
12. Wesley, "The Almost Christian," in *Sermons I* (WJW 1.141).

he was able to sum up, with some exasperation, in a very short pair of sentences: "I have again and again, with all the plainness I could, declared what our constant doctrines are, whereby we are distinguished only from heathens or nominal Christians, not from any that worship God in spirit and in truth. Our main doctrines, which include all the rest, are three—that of Repentance, of Faith and of Holiness. The first of these we account, as it were, the porch of religion; the next the door; the third, religion itself."[13] That same year he spelled out the balance in the minutes of the Methodist conference: "In asserting salvation by faith we mean this: that pardon (salvation begun) is received by faith producing works; that holiness (salvation continued) is faith working by love; that heaven (salvation finished) is the reward of this faith."[14] Nearly three decades later he found an even more economical expression in exhorting one of his senior colleagues: "If we could bring all our preachers, itinerant and local, uniformly and steadily to insist on those two points, 'Christ dying for us' and 'Christ dying in us,' we should shake the trembling gates of hell."[15]

Albert Outler well catches this interpenetration of gracious yin and holy yang that defined the heart of Wesley's theology: "The Christian life in Wesley's view is empowered by the energy of grace: prevenient, saving, sanctifying, sacramental. [Yet] grace is always interpreted as something more than forensic pardon. Rather, it is experienced as actual influence."[16] For defining and promoting this theological center constituted by gracious holiness, the Sermon on the Mount was crucial.

The Sermon's central place for Wesley is indicated by its central place in his foundational teaching. In 1746 Wesley set about responding comprehensively to demands for a defining account of what his movement was about. The demands were coming from his itinerants, from many of the ordinary people who were joining

13. Wesley to Thomas Church, June 17, 1746, in *The Letters of the Rev. John Wesley*, ed. John Telford (London: Epworth, 1931), 2.267–68.

14. "The Third Annual Conference" (1746), in *John Wesley*, ed. Albert C. Outler (New York: Oxford University Press, 1964), 159.

15. Wesley to Charles Perronet, Dec. 28, 1774, in *Letters* (ed. Telford), 6.134.

16. Outler, introduction to *Sermons I* (WJW 1.33).

the Wesleyan societies, and from his opponents, who maintained a constant barrage of criticism. Wesley's answer was a three-volume set of formal discourses, entitled *Sermons on Several Occasions*, that was published at two-year intervals in 1746, 1748, and 1750. This set of originally thirty-seven sermons, which later grew to forty-three when a fourth volume appeared in 1760, eventually became known to Methodists as the *Standard Sermons*.[17] Shortly before Wesley in 1784 took the fateful step of personally ordaining superintendents for America—thereby, in effect, creating an American Methodist church separate from Anglicanism and putting the Methodist Connexion at home on a fast track toward separation from the Church of England—he bequeathed to the American movement a theological foundation in which his sermon collection came first: "Let all of you be determined to abide by the Methodist doctrine and discipline published in the four volumes of *Sermons* and the *Explanatory Notes upon the New Testament*, together with the *Large Minutes* of the Conference."[18] To Wesley and the Methodist movements on both sides of the Atlantic, these sermons were intended, in Outler's phrase, to "stand as a bloc and . . . define the evangelical substance of Wesley's message."[19] Wesley himself underscored the importance of these sermons at the very end of his life. In preparing instructions for his death, John Wesley left strict instructions to avoid all pomp and ostentation, but in a last will and testament providing for few other legacies he asked that copies of his sermons be distributed to all the Methodist preachers.[20]

Sermons on Several Occasions, or *Standard Sermons*, included many trademark discourses that were already renowned before they were collected into this edition. Just as all Methodist hymnals from the Wesleys' great 1780 edition of *A Collection of Hymns for the Use of the People Called Methodists* have led off with "Oh for

17. For the complicated publishing and editing history of the *Standard Sermons*, see Outler, introduction to *Sermons I* (WJW 1.38–45); and Thomas Oden, *Doctrinal Standards in the Wesleyan Tradition* (Grand Rapids: Francis Asbury/Zondervan, 1988), 89–97.

18. Wesley to the preachers in America, Oct. 3, 1783, in *Letters* (ed. Telford), 7.191.

19. Outler, introduction to *Sermons I* (WJW 1.98).

20. Rack, *Reasonable Enthusiast*, 532.

a thousand tongues to sing / My dear Redeemer's praise! / The glories of my God and King, / The triumphs of his grace!" so every edition of Wesley's *Standard Sermons* has begun with his memorable discourse entitled "Salvation by Faith." This was the sermon that Wesley declaimed as the Oxford University preacher on June 11, 1738, while he was still warmed by the white heat of his own grace-filled experience at Aldersgate in London less than three weeks earlier on May 24.[21] Other signature sermons in this collection included "The Almost Christian," "Scriptural Christianity," "Justification by Faith," and "The Witness of the Spirit." But at the center of this defining edition of sermons stood Wesley's exposition of the Sermon on the Mount—thirteen discourses in all, with five treating Matthew 5 and four each on Matthew 6 and Matthew 7. These thirteen discourses made up a quarter of the final edition of the *Standard Sermons*, and in the whole collection Wesley's sermons on the Beatitudes are among the longest.

The sermons are preeminent, not only for their sheer bulk in the middle of this defining collection, but because their exposition made up, in Outler's words, "the true centerpiece of the whole collection."[22] This judgment from a later scholar was also Wesley's judgment. In 1759 an Anglican rector, John Downes, fired off an intemperate tract that charged the Methodists with manifold depredations, including a scandalous neglect of good works. Wesley cannonaded right back with a vigorous point-by-point refutation. When he came to Downes's charge that the Wesleyans neglected good works, he waxed ironical in referring to the long-standing charge from his Calvinist opponents that Wesley and his followers taught good works without faith. To prove that his movement had always taught a faith active in love—faith and works together—Wesley adduced his published sermons and in so doing communicated his most basic understanding of the Sermon on the Mount: "We appeal to the whole tenor of our sermons, printed and unprinted; in particular to those upon 'Our Lord's Sermon on the Mount,' wherein every branch of gospel obedience is both asserted

21. Franz Hildebrandt and Oliver A. Beckerlegge, eds., *A Collection of Hymns for the Use of the People Called Methodists*, WJW 7 (Nashville: Abingdon, 1989), 79–81; and Wesley, "Salvation by Faith," in *Sermons I* (WJW 1.117–30).

22. Outler, introduction to *Sermons I* (WJW 1.45).

and proved to be indispensably necessary to eternal salvation."[23] "Gospel obedience" was the key phrase, since it communicated deep commitment to both salvation by grace through faith and holiness in obedience to God's will.

Wesley's discourses on the Sermon appeared at a moment in his career that was propitious for gauging his primary religious concerns, calmly considered. Wesley was never free from controversy, and his life was a scene of constant agitation, but in the late 1740s he exhibited as much theological equipoise as he would ever display. Although he had by this time broken decisively with the Moravians, the emphasis on justifying grace, which he had learned from Augustus Spangenberg, Peter Böhler, and their fellows, had become a fixture in his theology. Although Wesley had already made his differences with Calvinism crystal clear, his public debate with George Whitefield was past and the next round of ferocious Arminian-Calvinist disputation lay many years in the future. Although he had already published several statements defending his conception of Christian perfection, it was not until the 1760s that agitation over perfection rose to new heights. And although Wesley's ambiguity about the Anglican establishment was already clear for all to see, the traumas that led to the separation of Methodists from the Church of England were still far in the future. In other words, for a reflective account of Wesley's own Methodism there is no better place to look than the first edition of the *Sermons on Several Occasions*, and no more authoritative summary than Wesley's treatment of the Sermon on the Mount in that collection.[24] In what follows, I describe Wesley's understanding of the Sermon as a whole, then outline in more detail the three-part exposition he unfolded in

23. Wesley, "A Letter to the Reverend Mr. Downes," in *The Works of John Wesley*, ed. Thomas Jackson (London: Wesleyan Conference, 1872), 9.102.

24. For authoritative commentary on Wesley's theology as a whole, I have benefited especially from Rack, *Reasonable Enthusiast*, 381–470; Randy L. Maddux, *Responsible Grace: John Wesley's Practical Theology* (Nashville: Kingswood, 1994); Kenneth J. Collins, *The Scripture Way of Salvation: The Heart of John Wesley's Theology* (Nashville: Abingdon, 1997); and Herbert Boyd McGonigle, *Sufficient Saving Grace: John Wesley's Evangelical Arminianism* (Carlisle, U.K.: Paternoster, 2001). For useful commentary specifically on Wesley's discourses on the Sermon, see Ronald H. Stone, *John Wesley's Life and Ethics* (Nashville: Abingdon, 2001), 112–26.

his thirteen discourses, and finally close with an assessment. That assessment includes a historical judgment concerning the typicality of Wesley's concerns for the eighteenth century, an exegetical comment on the irrelevance of Wesley's concerns for contemporary New Testament scholarship, and a theological comment on the delicate balance that Wesley strove to maintain between grace and works in his sermons on the Sermon.

Several times in the course of his thirteen discourses, Wesley paused to outline his understanding of the Sermon as a whole. In Matthew 5 he found "the sum of all true religion . . . laid down in eight particulars, which are explained and guarded against the false glosses of man in the following parts of the fifth chapter." In Matthew 6 he discovered "rules for that right intention which we are to preserve in all our outward actions, unmixed with worldly desires." And in Matthew 7 he discerned "cautions against the main hindrances of religion" along with a closing "application of the whole,"[25] Later recapitulations of the whole Sermon added little to this summary.[26]

In one other place, however, Wesley did relate a slightly different sense of the Sermon's strategic importance. This was in his *Explanatory Notes* on the New Testament, which Wesley and later Methodists have placed with the *Standard Sermons* as definitive expressions of their theology.[27] In three short paragraphs for the *Explanatory Notes* on Matthew 5:2, Wesley underscored an experiential understanding of the Sermon by reading it as preoccupied with "happiness." Significantly, in his own modification of the King James Version that he printed with the *Explanatory Notes*, Wesley translated the *makarioi* of the Beatitudes, not as "blessed"

25. E.g., discourse X §1 (650–51); and discourse XIII preface, §1 (687). References to Wesley's thirteen discourses on the Sermon on the Mount are indicated by discourse number (a roman numeral) plus Wesley's paragraph numbers (sometimes section plus paragraph, sometimes only paragraph) plus the page number(s) in the Outler edition of the *Sermons*.

26. E.g., discourse X §1 (650–51); and discourse XIII preface, §1 (687).

27. On the formation and use of the *Explanatory Notes*, see Oden, *Doctrinal Standards*, 81–89.

but as "happy." Wesley's explanation for this translation took in his understanding of the whole Sermon: "To bless men; to make men happy, was the great business for which our Lord came to the world. . . . Our Lord therefore begins his Divine institution, which is the complete art of happiness, by laying down before all that have ears to hear, the true and only true method of acquiring it." Yet also in this brief summary of the Sermon, Wesley returned to a balanced understanding of the Christian life as marked by faith and works together: "Observe the benevolent condescension of our Lord. He seems, as it were, to lay aside his supreme authority as our legislator, that he may the better act the part of our friend and Saviour." By no means did Wesley want to lessen his stress on God's "will and our duty" as the key business of life, but he did take pains to stress the "gentle and engaging way" that the Redeemer used to move his followers from trust to action.[28]

In his discourses on the Sermon Wesley began with three long sermons on the Beatitudes, followed by two more on the verses immediately following in Matthew 5. Wesley's way of drawing out "the sum of all true religion" that he found in Matthew 5 was to expatiate on the Beatitudes, particularly by using the "you have heard . . . but I say to you" contrasts of the chapter's second half for his explanatory material. As he carries out this task, Wesley deliberately turns aside from critical or contextual issues in order to emphasize the implications of the Sermon for all who open themselves to its message. To Wesley, the diligent and constant student of Scripture, it was obvious that Jesus had never desired "at any other time or place, to lay down at once the whole plan of his religion, to give us a full prospect of Christianity, to describe at large the nature of that holiness without which no man shall see the Lord."[29] Wesley's citation here, early in the first discourse, of one of his favorite texts to support the doctrine of Christian perfection—Hebrews 12:14 ("that holiness without which no man shall see the Lord")—is intended to indicate without qualification how he thinks the Christian life should proceed. Christ came into

28. Wesley, *Explanatory Notes upon the New Testament* (1754; repr. Salem, OR: Schmul, n.d.), 19.
29. Discourse I preface, §7 (473).

the world to save sinners, but also to equip them for holy living. Still, as his discourses develop, Wesley's strong emphasis on holy living is matched by a strong emphasis on divine grace apprehended by faith.

Thus, in expounding the first beatitude ("blessed are the poor in spirit for theirs is the kingdom of heaven"), Wesley does not back down from his stress on holiness, but his emphasis on grace is much fuller than what he had preached in his first moralistic sermon on Matthew 6:33 from 1725. To be sure, Wesley interprets the first beatitude with his characteristic doctrinal emphases. There is, for instance, an early reference to prevenient grace: "Who then are the 'poor in spirit'? Without question, the humble . . . who are convinced of sin; those to whom God hath given that first repentance which is previous to faith in Christ."[30] It is also possible to catch a reference to infused righteousness when he speaks of "the image of God stamped upon the [believer's] heart."[31] And he intimates the Wesleyan caution about the possibility of losing salvation when he refers to Christ's righteousness as remitting "the sins that are past."[32]

Yet the clearest and most direct notes in his exposition of the first beatitude are Augustinian. Indeed, we might even call this exposition "Calvinistic in the main" if we did not know who had composed it. Thus, Wesley defines "poverty of spirit" as complete moral depravity—in his words, "a just sense of our inward and outward sins, and of our guilt and helplessness."[33] He then forthrightly describes entrance into the kingdom of God as made possible by an act of sheer grace—"'the redemption which is in Jesus,' the righteousness of Christ imputed to us for 'the remission of'" sins.[34] He then waxes lyrical in accounting for the believer's place in the kingdom as due solely to God's actions on the sinner's behalf—as "purchased for thee by the blood of the Lamb . . . 'who taketh away the sin of the world.'"[35] And he concludes by recapitulating

30. Discourse I §1.4 (477).
31. Discourse I §1.11 (481).
32. Discourse I §1.11 (481).
33. Discourse I §1.7 (479).
34. Discourse I §1.11 (481).
35. Discourse I §1.12 (482).

what "poverty of spirit" means: it "begins where a sense of our guilt and of the wrath of God ends; and is a continual sense of our total dependence on him for every good thought or word or work; of our utter inability to all good unless he 'water us every moment.'"[36] True religion, as described by Wesley in these terms, is a gift of God *simpliciter*. Whatever else Wesley wants to make of the Sermon, he reads it first as a message concerning human depravity and gratuitous divine mercy.

Wesley's second discourse treats the next three beatitudes ("blessed are the meek . . . they which do hunger and thirst after righteousness . . . the merciful"). In them he finds the Christian ideal defined by the righteousness for which the redeemed hunger and thirst. In Wesley's wording, this righteousness can be equated with love from God and love to God and neighbor. It is "the image of God, the mind which was in Christ Jesus. It is every holy and heavenly temper in one; springing from as well as terminating in the love of God as our Father and Redeemer, and the love of all men for his sake."[37] When he discusses this righteousness, Wesley spells out clearly his expectation that consistent pursuit of sanctification will bring the believer to perfection, "the entire renewal of thy soul in that image of God wherein it was originally created."[38] The themes of meekness, hungering for righteousness, and mercy allow Wesley to ratchet up his demands on all believers. In discourses that consistently envision a very high level of Christian exertion, this discourse takes first place for earnestness. Yet amid a flood of exhortation, Wesley also pauses with a note of reassurance for the believer who is searching wholeheartedly for God: to be purified means to practice "the religion, the righteousness he [the believer] thirsts after." But it is a religion that, as Wesley quotes Augustine's famous line from *The Confessions*, offers great consolation: "Nor can he [the believer] rest till he thus rests in God."[39]

This second discourse closes with a noteworthy application of the Sermon on the Mount to present affairs. In reading "blessed

36. Discourse I §1.13 (482).
37. Discourse II §2.2 (495).
38. Discourse II §2.6 (498).
39. Discourse II §2.4 (497).

are the meek," Wesley makes an extensive detour to critique the bellicose nation-states of eighteenth-century Europe. His interests are ultimately spiritual, so the detour that begins by condemning warfare ends by denouncing ecclesiastical infighting, but this memorable passage does indicate how Wesley can use the Sermon on the Mount for sharp social criticism:

> You may pour out your soul, and bemoan the loss of true genuine love in the earth. Lost indeed! . . . These Christian kingdoms that are tearing out each other's bowels, desolating one another with fire and sword! These Christian armies that are sending each other by thousands, by ten thousands, quick into hell! These Christian nations that are all on fire with intestine broils, party against party, faction against faction! These Christian families, torn asunder with envy, jealousy, anger, domestic jars—without number, without end! Yea, what is most dreadful, most to be lamented of all, these Christian churches!—churches ("Tell it not in Gath"; but alas, how can we hide it, either from Jews, Turks, and pagans?) that bear the name of Christ, "the Prince of Peace," and wage continual war with each other![40]

More of such social criticism would come later in the discourses, especially when Wesley addresses questions of wealth and status.

Wesley's third discourse includes lengthy consideration of "blessed are the pure in heart," which he illustrates from the rest of the chapter through Jesus's comments on anger, lust, divorce, swearing, revenge, and hatred. Wesley's consideration of purity again offers him the chance to show how the free grace of redemption naturally entails wholehearted Christian holiness: "'The pure in heart' are they whose hearts God hath 'purified even as he is pure'; who are purified through faith in the blood of Jesus from every unholy affection; who, being 'cleansed from all filthiness of flesh and spirit, perfect holiness in the' loving 'fear of God.' They are, through the power of his grace, purified from pride by the deepest poverty of spirit" and from other sinful dispositions. The end result is that "now they love the Lord their God with all their heart, and with all their

---

40. Discourse II §2.18 (507–8).

soul, and mind, and strength."[41] When Wesley has finished his account of what the "pure in heart" are, and then also what they do (make for peace, bear up under persecution, rejoice in God), he can summarize by proclaiming: "Behold Christianity in its native form, as delivered by its great Author! This is the genuine religion of Jesus Christ."[42]

Wesley's last two discourses on Matthew 5 expand on what he calls "the beauty of holiness . . . that inward man of the heart which is renewed after the image of God."[43] In these discourses he pauses to criticize those, like the Moravians, who urge inactivity as a way of being still before God.[44] He reiterates the indissoluble bond he sees between "the root of religion . . . in the heart, . . . the inmost soul . . . the union of the soul with God" and "the branches" of that inward root reflected in "outward obedience."[45] And he again urges Christians to spare no pains—"renounce all superfluities. Cut off all unnecessary expense, in food, in furniture, in apparel. . . . Cut off all unnecessary expense of time"—so that they can "enlarge [their] ability of doing good."[46] Along the way he attacks as murderers those ministers who lead their charges astray.[47] In equally strong terms he condemns those who claim that grace abolishes the necessity of the law.[48] Instead, in a culminating statement of everything he has argued from Matthew 5, Wesley holds that the highest respect for free grace and the highest respect for God's law must stand together. In fact, as Wesley sees it, "it is impossible indeed to have too high an esteem" for the reality of faith inspired by free grace as spelled out in Titus 1:1; Ephesians 2:8–9; and Acts 16:31. "But at the same time," he insists, "we must take care to let all men know we esteem no faith but that which 'worketh by love'; and that we are not 'saved by faith' unless so far as we are delivered from the power as well as the guilt of sin."[49]

41. Discourse III §1.2 (510–11).
42. Discourse III §4 (530).
43. Discourse IV preface, §1 (531).
44. Discourse IV preface, §3 (532).
45. Discourse IV §3.1 (541–42).
46. Discourse IV §4.4 (548–49).
47. Discourse V §3.5 (557).
48. Discourse V §3.7 (558–59).
49. Discourse V §3.9 (559–60).

It is noteworthy that in the discourses of the *Standard Sermons*, Wesley does not go out of his way to stress the perfectionistic implications of Matthew 5:48 ("be ye therefore perfect, even as your Father which is in heaven is perfect"). He does not consider this text directly in his thirteen discourses on the Sermon. In the *Explanatory Notes* on the New Testament, however, Wesley does devote two short, but intense, paragraphs to this important verse—and that after altering the King James translation from an injunction into a promise ("ye *shall be* perfect, as your Father who is in heaven is perfect" [emphasis added]). To Wesley, this text refers to everything that had been recommended at the beginning of Matthew 5 as "happiness" and now at the end as "holiness." As he views it, God in his grace and wisdom provides this promise at this place in the Sermon as a whole. To Wesley it is "even the proper promise of the Gospel! That he will *put* those *laws in our minds and write them in our hearts*! He well knew how ready our unbelief would be to cry out, this is impossible! And therefore stakes upon it all the power, truth, and faithfulness of him to whom all things are possible."[50] In the discourses Wesley does underscore many times his understanding of entire sanctification. In the *Explanatory Notes* he takes advantage of Matthew 5:48 to make an especially strong statement of the doctrine.

If Wesley's interpretation of Matthew 5 defines true religion as free grace manifested in holy life, his treatment of Matthew 6, which unfolds in the sixth through ninth of his thirteen discourses, spotlights the sanctification of human intention or motivation. The material in this chapter on almsgiving, prayer, fasting, not serving two masters, and anxiety is, in Wesley's view, designed by Jesus "to show . . . how all our actions . . . , even those that are indifferent in their own nature, may be made holy and good and acceptable to God, by a pure and holy intention."[51] To Wesley, "the necessity of this purity of intention"[52] is a theme of greatest importance: for him, purity of intention defined both the gracious goal to which a

---

50. Wesley, *Explanatory Notes*, 24.
51. Discourse VI preface, §1 (573).
52. Discourse VI preface, §1 (573).

merciful God called his children and the extraordinary exertions that those children should demand of themselves.

Wesley divides his consideration of Matthew 6 in two: (1) purity of intention with respect to the religious activities of almsgiving, prayer, and fasting; and (2) purity of intention with respect to dispositions and attitudes toward money and life in general. Yet for both considerations, he views the fruit of good works as always arising organically from God's work of grace in Christ. Thus, the heart of Wesley's exposition of the Lord's Prayer is his reflection on "forgive us our trespasses, as we forgive them that trespass against us." It is when "our debts are forgiven . . . through the free grace of God in Christ" that "the chains fall off our hands," and we are numbered "among those which are sanctified, by faith which is in him."[53] Similarly, fasting is not a way to merit favor with God, but "is only a way which God hath ordained wherein we wait for his *unmerited* mercy; and wherein, without any desert of ours, he hath promised *freely* to give us his blessing."[54] It is the same with the injunctions of Matthew 6:33, about seeking first the kingdom of God. In words very different from his early sermon on this text, Wesley stresses that righteousness is first "the righteousness of Christ, imputed to every believer," which then serves as the ground for "that inward righteousness of that holiness of heart, which is with the utmost propriety termed 'God's righteousness,' as being both his own free gift through Christ, and his own work, by his almighty Spirit."[55] In every case—prayer, fasting, seeking the kingdom—heavy emphasis on the Christian's purity of intention begins with concentration on the divine intention, as Wesley puts it at the end of his ninth discourse, to sanctify "me and all the elect people of God."[56]

Yet if divine grace extended to unworthy sinners is the *cantus firmus* of Wesley's exposition of Matthew 6, almost all of the driving counterpoint is the Christian's effort. So we hear an extended

---

53. Discourse VI §2.13 (586), quoting Acts 26:18.

54. Discourse VII §4.2 (609).

55. Discourse IX §21 (643). After controversy with Calvinists reemerged later in Wesley's career, he resolved not to use the term *imputation* any longer. See Outler, in *Sermons I* (WJW 1.643n72).

56. Discourse IX §29 (649).

discussion on how *not* to pray with vain repetitions;[57] we learn how fasting should improve the life of prayer;[58] we are enjoined through thousands of words about the danger of trusting in wealth;[59] and we find out why giddiness and sloth should have no part in the lives of those who seek first the kingdom of God.[60] Throughout, Wesley does not hold back, as in the strongest terms he urges readers to higher planes of disciplined holiness.

In sermons filled with interesting reflections on Matthew 6, three particular matters may justify special mention. First is Wesley's reading of the petition "give us this day our daily bread" from the Lord's Prayer as "all things needful, whether for our souls or bodies." In this petition Wesley discerns not only physical provision, but what he calls "sacramental bread also."[61] Wesley, the father of evangelical movements that would come to deemphasize the sacraments, was himself a lifelong advocate of frequent, even daily, communion, which he held to be the estimable practice of the primitive church.

Another striking element of these discourses is the frequent contrast that Wesley draws between life lived in vain and life lived purposefully for the glory of God. Nowhere is that contrast etched more sharply than in his discourse on fasting, where he contrasts the follies that many converts have gladly abandoned with the purposefulness that conversion makes possible. On the one hand is "that sprightly folly, that airiness of mind, that levity of temper, that gay inattention to things of the deepest concern, that giddiness and carelessness of spirit, which were no other than drunkenness of soul."[62] In sharpest contrast, on the other hand, is the abiding desire "to glorify our Father which is in heaven; to express our sorrow and shame for our manifold transgressions of his holy law; to wait for an increase of purifying grace, drawing our affections to things above; to add seriousness and earnestness to our prayers; to avert the wrath of God, and to obtain all the great and precious

57. Discourse VI §2.4 (576–77).
58. Discourse VII §2.6 (600), §4.6 (610).
59. All of discourse VIII.
60. Discourse IX §16 (639).
61. Discourse VI §2.11 (584).
62. Discourse VII §2.3 (599).

promises which he hath made to us in Christ Jesus."[63] In Wesley's mind, the Sermon on the Mount provides Jesus's definitive statement concerning what kind of life to avoid as well as what kind of life to seek.

A final noteworthy feature of Wesley's interpretation of Matthew 6 is his extensive commentary on the hazards of seeking wealth. Although he was not yet as obsessive on this matter as he became in his old age, when Methodists were increasingly confronted by the perils of their own prosperity, Wesley's remarks from the late 1740s are challenging enough. In fact, when he comes to apply passages like "lay not up for yourselves treasures upon earth" (6:19) or "where your treasure is, there will your heart be also" (6:21), Wesley may speak even more powerfully to our wealth-fixated age than to his own. He begins with a most unflattering comparison between "the heathen . . . of Africa or America . . . who desires and seeks nothing more than plain food to eat and plain raiment to put on" with so-called Christian Europe where it is difficult to find any professed believers who are not eager to lay up as much treasure for themselves as possible.[64] But this stern beginning is only a warm-up. Wesley, of course, thought there was nothing wrong for men providing life's necessities for wives and children, but "not delicacies, not superfluities . . . for it is no man's duty to furnish them . . . with the means either of luxury or idleness."[65] Even closer to home, Wesley holds that the person who has enough to meet daily needs and yet worries about gaining more wealth "lives in open habitual denial of the Lord that bought him. He hath practically 'denied the faith, and is worse than' an African or American 'infidel.'"[66] Again, "to trust in riches for happiness is the greatest folly of all that are under the sun!"[67] And yet again, "if you will add house to house, or field to field, why do you call yourself a Christian? You do not obey Jesus Christ. You do not design it. Why do you name yourself by his name? 'Why call ye me, Lord, Lord,' saith he himself, 'and do

63. Discourse VII §4.1 (608).
64. Discourse VIII §9 (617–18).
65. Discourse VIII §11 (619).
66. Discourse VIII §12 (620).
67. Discourse VIII §20 (625).

not the things which I say?"[68] These hard words were perhaps slightly easier to take in the mid-eighteenth century than they have become in the early twenty-first. But for readers then and now, Wesley provides a cup of cooling refreshment alongside a hammer of indignation. At the very end of these strenuous denunciations, he concludes by pointing once again away from supports that must fail to the one support who does not fail: "The great foundation indeed of all the blessings of God, whether temporal or eternal, is the Lord Jesus Christ, his righteousness and blood, what he hath done, and what he hath suffered for us. . . . Therefore, 'labour' thou, 'not for the meat that perisheth, but for that which endureth unto everlasting life.'"[69] At the dawn of the modern age Wesley's attacks on the delusions of self-sufficient economic security manifest a rare prescience.

In general, his interpretation of Matthew 6 constructs a very high standard for truly Christian intention. But even when Wesley fulminates against the piling of riches, he does so by also referring to the grace that God has bestowed in Christ to purify even the most threatened of holy intentions.

Wesley's last four discourses on the Sermon treat Matthew 7, which he expounds as describing "the main hindrances of this religion" that Jesus had proclaimed in Matthew 5–6.[70] They are the shortest of Wesley's sermons on the Sermon and can be summarized succinctly.

The hindrances to true religion, as Wesley describes them, follow the pattern of his comments on purity of intention. Although individuals may be led astray by the deeds they perform, the most debilitating hindrances are attitudinal. Prayer, as explained in his comments on Matthew 7:7–11, is a prime means to keep from judging others, which usually takes place when one forgets one's own faults, a sin that Wesley epitomizes in his comment on 7:3 as "the grand beam, . . . supine carelessness and indifference."[71] His summary of the golden rule (7:12), which also brings his tenth discourse to a close, offers first an exquisitely balanced restatement:

68. Discourse VIII §22 (627), quoting Luke 6:46.
69. Discourse VIII §28 (631), quoting John 6:27.
70. Discourse X §1 (650).
71. Discourse X §7 (654).

"And we may reasonably desire that [others] should do us all the good they can do without injuring themselves; yea, that in outward things . . . their superfluities should give way to our conveniences, their conveniences to our necessities, and their necessities to our extremities. Now then, let us walk by the same rule."[72] Then, however, Wesley provides an even stronger evangelical statement about how it is possible to live up to the golden rule: "Be it observed, none can walk by this rule . . . , none can love his neighbour as himself, unless he first love God. And none can love God unless he believe in Christ, unless he have redemption through his blood, and the Spirit of God bearing witness with his spirit that he is a child of God. Faith therefore is still the root of all, of present as well as future salvation. . . . Thou wilt love the Lord thy God because he hath loved thee; thou wilt love thy neighbour as thyself."[73]

Wesley's last three discourses on the Sermon feature strong recapitulation of what has gone before. To enter the "narrow way, which leadeth unto life" (7:13) means to live by the Beatitudes: "The way of poverty of spirit, the way of holy mourning, the way of meekness, and that of hungering and thirsting after righteousness."[74] To guide oneself by the way of the world is to curry destruction: "In whatever profession you are engaged, you must be singular or be damned. The way to hell has nothing singular in it; but the way to heaven is singularity all over."[75] To know when to abandon "false prophets" (7:15) requires a careful evaluation of "experience" to determine when attending to ungodly ministers "hurts your soul."[76] And to know the truth it is necessary to exercise constant vigilance: "In particular reject with the utmost abhorrence whatsoever is described as the way of salvation that is either different from, or short of, the way our Lord has marked out in the foregoing discourse."[77]

Wesley treats the parable of the wise man and the foolish man at the end of Matthew 7 as a final opportunity to show how Christian-

72. Discourse X §26 (662).
73. Discourse X §27 (662–63).
74. Discourse XI §2.3 (668).
75. Discourse XI §3.4 (672–73).
76. Discourse XII §3.9 (683).
77. Discourse XII §3.9 (684).

ity demands full trust in Christ, but also fully intentional holiness. He describes building on sand as resting hope for life in "my orthodoxy or right opinions," "my belonging" to the right church, my own "innocence," my "not living" in known sin, my "attending all the ordinances of God," my "good works," and even my preaching, prophesying, driving out devils, and converting sinners to God.[78] All of these estimable actions, in Wesley's view, constitute nothing but building on sand if God's mercy to myself as a sinner is set aside. But then, in typical fashion, Wesley hastens on to say that when faith in that divine grace is being exercised, it will lead on to "inward and outward holiness" and "the whole of the religion described in the foregoing chapters."[79] Such words are a fitting conclusion for what Wesley describes as the hindrances to "gospel obedience," which in both its parts (gospel plus obedience) and the two parts together define for him the central meaning of the Sermon on the Mount.

In assessing Wesley's treatment of the Sermon on the Mount, it is useful to begin by responding to modern critical concerns about the Sermon, as recently summarized by Graham Stanton:[80]

1. Is the Sermon on the Mount given for all Christians everywhere, or does it represent a set of special provisions for either the age before the giving of the Spirit (dispensationalism) or the short period immediately before the return of Christ (modern apocalyptic)? For Wesley the Sermon is definitely for all Christians everywhere.
2. Are the injunctions of the Sermon meant to be taken literally, or are some hyperbolic in their intent? For the most part, Wesley reads the Sermon not as providing counsels of perfection for a holy few, but as revealing the standard guidelines for ordinary Christian life.

78. Discourse XIII §3.1–4 (694–95).
79. Discourse XIII §3.5 (695–96).
80. G. N. Stanton, "Sermon on the Mount/Plain," in *Dictionary of Jesus and the Gospels*, ed. Joel B. Green, Scot McKnight, and I. Howard Marshall (Downers Grove, IL: InterVarsity, 1992), 740.

3. Is the Sermon directed to all people or only to Christians? Wesley holds that most of the Sermon is for Christians, but that significant parts apply to all people as well.[81]

4. Does Jesus present the Sermon as the fulfillment and natural extension of the Mosaic teaching or as the abrogation of that teaching and the inauguration of a radical new law as from "the new Moses"? For Wesley, the Sermon represents the natural development of Mosaic teaching. In this regard it is noteworthy that Wesley's exposition of the Sermon consists primarily of citations from other parts of the Scripture, with references to the Old Testament intermingled freely with the New. In his preface to the *Standard Sermons*, Wesley famously expressed his devotion to the Scriptures in what sound like hyperbolic terms:

> I want to know one thing, the way to heaven—how to land safe on that happy shore. God himself has condescended to teach the way: for this very end he came from heaven. He hath written it down in a book. O give me that book! At any price give me the Book of God! I have it. Here is knowledge enough for me. Let me be *homo unius libri*. Here I am, far from the busy ways of men. I sit down alone: only God is here. In his presence I open, I read his Book; for this end, to find the way to heaven.[82]

When Wesley expounded the Sermon on the Mount, he came close to fulfilling his own hyperbole. In these expositions he has perfected his lifelong habit of citing, alluding to, paraphrasing, referencing, and quoting other parts of Scripture as his primary way of expositing the texts in view for any particular discourse. Thus, in the first of Wesley's thirteen sermons of about eight thousand words on Matthew 5:1–4, his modern editor identifies 153 allusions or quotations to other Scriptures. In the thirteenth discourse of about five thousand words on Matthew 7:21–27, there are over 100 such allusions or quotations (or about one for every fifty words). As with Charles in the hymns, so with John in these discourses—the Wesleys could not think without deploying a nearly global mastery of the Bible.

81. E.g., discourse X §6 (652).
82. Wesley, "The Preface," in *Sermons I* (WJW 1.105–6).

With regard to Wesley's treatment of the scriptural text itself, it is also pertinent to note that his approach is completely precritical. He simply assumes that Matthew presents the quoted words of Jesus that he delivered as a unified and direct address.[83] I do not believe there is even any reference to what modern scholars see as the parallel Sermon on the Plain of Luke 6:17–49.

Wesley's treatment of the Sermon on the Mount is important historically for what it reveals about the character of eighteenth-century evangelical religion in the English-speaking world. Of many significant matters, perhaps the most interesting is how close Wesley comes in his thirteen discourses to the main emphases of Jonathan Edwards, his American contemporary and Wesley's only serious rival as the guiding theological light of emerging evangelical religion. The well-schooled student of the eighteenth century would certainly turn to Edwards's *Nature of True Virtue*, his "Personal Narrative," or one of his famous "Miscellanies" on the sublime beauty of God when hearing, for example the following exalted expressions describing "the genuine religion of Jesus Christ": "What beauty appears in the whole! How just a symmetry! What exact proportion in every part! How desirable is the holiness here described! How venerable, how lovely the holiness!"[84]

The same student would instinctively turn to Edwards's *Treatise on Religious Affections* when hearing the following statements about the character of true religion or about the signs in a person's life that may or may not provide secure evidence concerning the presence of true religion:

Our great Teacher has fully described inward religion [as] those dispositions of soul which constitute real Christianity; the tempers contained in that holiness "without which no man shall see the Lord"; the affections which, when flowing from their proper

---

83. On Wesley's precritical assumptions, see Outler, in *Sermons I* (WJW 1.468) ("obviously there is no interest, in any of these sermons, in critical textual problems or in the historical context"); and Warren S. Kissinger, *The Sermon on the Mount: A History of Interpretation and Bibliography* (Metuchen, NJ: Scarecrow/ATLA, 1975), 38 ("being free from the findings of later critical, biblical scholarship, Wesley believed that Jesus delivered the Sermon as a unified and systematic public address").

84. Discourse III §4 (530). For much the same, see discourse VIII §4 (612).

fountain, from a living faith in God through Christ Jesus, are intrinsically and essentially good, and acceptable to God.[85]

A true prophet, a teacher sent from God, does not bring forth good fruit sometimes only, but always; not accidentally, but by a kind of inner necessity.[86]

Even more certain this reader would be that the following passage was taken from Edwards's *End for Which God Created the World*: "Believing in God . . . implies . . . to trust in God as our end; to have an eye to him in all things; to use all things only as means of enjoying him; wheresoever we are, or whatsoever we do, to see him that is invisible looking on us well-pleased, and to refer all things to him in Christ Jesus."[87] Yet all these sentences, and more that could be piled up, come from Wesley's discourses on the Sermon on the Mount, and they have not been wrenched out of context.

This display of Wesley's "Edwardsean" theology should alert observers of the eighteenth century to an important reality. Differences there certainly were in the nascent evangelical world, and far from insignificant: Calvinist versus Arminian, Anglican versus Congregationalist versus Baptist versus Presbyterian, learned versus enthusiast, and more. Yet an overriding reality was that the search for true religion over against the specter of hollow religious formalism revealed remarkable similarities across a wide spectrum. Edwards and Wesley had their real differences, but what joined them together—especially in defining true religion as God-oriented affections longing for the beauty of an infinitely holy God—constituted a much deeper commonality.

Wesley's treatment of the Sermon on the Mount reveals the characteristic weaknesses of his mature ministry as the key early Methodist. Wesley is more attuned to the spiritual needs of ordi-

85. Discourse X §2 (651). For almost the same phrasing, see discourse VI preface, §1 (573).

86. Discourse XII §3.4 (681). For similar reasoning about the marks of a true Christian, see discourse XIII §2.1 (691) and discourse XIII §3.4 (695).

87. Discourse IX §4 (635). For very similar comments, see discourse IX §29 (649), discourse X §7 (653), and discourse XIII §2.2 (692) (where Wesley quotes with approval the first question and answer of the Westminster Shorter Catechism).

nary people than was any leader of his day, but he is also as close to humorless as it is possible to be. He is the great advocate of perfect love, but his unrelenting exhortations lack the patience, kindness, slowness to find fault, and willingness to bear a slight that the apostle Paul spells out so clearly as the marks of charity in 1 Corinthians 13. He is the keenest evangelist of his age in sensing the profoundly new demands, both intellectual and experiential, of the Enlightenment, yet he is also driven by a demon of the Enlightenment to parse every human activity and every human emotion into a clearly phrased set of unambiguous rules. Most importantly, Wesley is one of the great preachers of God's grace in the entire history of Christianity, but in his treatment of the Sermon he is never able to communicate the peace of soul that receiving the grace of Christ can bestow.

But if there are weaknesses in Wesley's exposition of the Sermon on the Mount, they are overmatched by great strengths. Wesley shows convincingly that Jesus's ethical teachings are thoroughly compatible with the great themes of both Testaments and the great themes of both law and gospel. Wesley displays a special wisdom in his unusually incisive critique of the love of riches, for this was a critique perfectly suited to an industrializing age when the dream of economic self-sufficiency had become a veritable Dagon. And in a theological universe so thickly populated with vapid verbosity, Wesley's simple and direct prose stands out as a delightful exception. He claimed to speak "plain truth for Plain people"[88]—to "speak rough, plain truths, such as none can deny who has either understanding or modesty left"[89]—and he did.

But the most significant contribution of Wesley's exposition of the Sermon concerns the last of Stanton's questions about its interpretation: How does the Sermon on the Mount relate the practice of righteousness with the New Testament's teaching on justification by faith? The great marvel of Wesley's thirteen discourses is how consistently they maintain both an exalted view of divine grace and a full dedication to active holiness—and without compromising one by the other. I am not sure if Wesley, even with

88. Wesley, "The Preface," in *Sermons I* (WJW 1.104).
89. Discourse XII §1.1 (676).

an Enlightenment demon driving him to ever more exact exertions for clarity, has come as close as he hoped to detailing exactly the schema, or formula, or clear-cut means by which living faith and loving service can nurture, instead of undercut, each other. But he has certainly done as well as any other major Christian thinker in expounding with relentless energy the bonded scriptural message of purity of heart bestowed by grace and sanctification of life pursued through works.

For myself, as a Calvinist with Lutheran proclivities, I can only conclude that, whatever quarrels I may want to pick with John Wesley, they do not concern his concluding words on the Sermon on the Mount. It is not a devotee of works-righteousness far gone into self-pampering moralism that I hear when Wesley, seeming to paraphrase Martin Luther's discrimination between a theology of glory and a theology of the cross, proclaims: "Now the way to heaven . . . is the way of lowliness, mourning, meekness, and holy desire, love of God and of our neighbour, doing good, and suffering evil for Christ's sake. They are . . . false prophets who teach as the way to heaven any other way than *this*."[90]

Even more centrally, it is not a sectarian enthusiast giddy with fantasies of perfection who closes his expositions on the Sermon with an extensive description of "a wise man, which built his home upon a rock" (Matt. 7:24). It is rather a biblical Christian who speaks with all other biblical Christians through the ages—whether called Calvinist, Arminian, Pentecostal, Holiness, Roman Catholic, Eastern Orthodox, Apostolic, or whatever—in grounding his understanding of faith and works, and his hope for now and the future, in the only enduring foundation:

> What is the foundation of *my* hope? Wherein do I build my expectation of entering into the kingdom of heaven? . . . Then go and learn what thou hast so often taught, "By grace ye are saved, through faith." "Not by works of righteousness which we have done, but of his own mercy he saveth us." Learn to hang naked upon the cross of Christ, counting all thou hast done but dung and dross. . . . Now, seeing thou canst do all things through Christ strengthening thee, be merciful as thy Father in heaven is merciful. Love thy neighbour

90. Discourse XII §1.4 (677).

179

as thyself. . . . Enjoy whatsoever brings glory to God, and promotes peace and goodwill among men. . . . Let thy soul be filled with mildness, gentleness, patience, long-suffering towards all men, at the same time that all which is in thee is athirst for God, the living God; longing to awake up after his likeness, and to be satisfied with it. Be thou a lover of God and of all mankind. In this spirit do and suffer all things. Thus show thy faith by thy works: thus "do the will of thy Father which is in heaven." And as sure as thou now walkest with God on earth, thou shalt reign with him in glory.[91]

91. Discourse XIII §3.1, 4, 10, 12 (694–68).

Charles Haddon Spurgeon

Timothy Larsen

"The Prince of Preachers"

Charles Haddon Spurgeon (1834–92) began his series on the Beatitudes with the observation that the Sermon on the Mount commends itself to us by coming from "the Prince of preachers."[1] Ironically, Spurgeon himself has been called the "prince of preachers" far more often than has his divine master. At least nine different books about Spurgeon have been published with the phrase *prince of preachers* in their very title, and virtually all of the numerous other books about Spurgeon employ the phrase somewhere. Spurgeon had an unrivaled reputation as a preacher in his own day, and this position has held up remarkably well ever since. An English Baptist, Spurgeon became a widely celebrated minister in London—then the greatest city in the Western world—by the age of twenty-one. Already by 1858, when he was only twenty-four, the *North American Review* was reporting that when Americans returned from a trip to England they were almost

---

1. *Metropolitan Tabernacle Pulpit* 55.361 (1909). The sermons were originally published in London by Passmore & Alabaster and have since been reprinted by other publishers. In addition to my coeditors, I am grateful to the following colleagues and friends for reading a draft of this paper and commenting on it: Ian Randall, Jon Vickery, Daniel Treier, Daniel Master, and Michael Graves.

invariably asked two questions: "Did you see the Queen?" "Did you hear Spurgeon?"[2]

Week by week, decade after decade, a sermon of Spurgeon's was published, with sales averaging 25,000–30,000 copies. No building in London was large enough to hold the crowds who wished to hear him. In 1861, the purpose-built Metropolitan Tabernacle was opened. The largest Protestant place of worship in the world at that time, it seated close to six thousand people, and Spurgeon kept it full week in and week out for the rest of his life. Its formal membership also made him the pastor of the largest Protestant congregation in the world. During the early 1870s, the period in which he delivered his series on the Beatitudes, the Metropolitan Tabernacle was growing at the rate of five hundred new members a year. David Bebbington observes, "By common consent he was the greatest English-speaking preacher of the century."[3] Spurgeon has continued to inspire many Christians ever since. Someone as unlikely as German Lutheran theologian Helmut Thielicke enthused in 1964: "Sell all that you have (not least of all some of your stock of current sermonic literature) and buy Spurgeon (even if you have to grub through the second-hand bookstores)."[4] Moreover, one need not worry about getting grubby, as the standard sixty-three volumes of Spurgeon's published sermons is just the beginning of the list of publications of his that are still in print. If someone chose to read a Spurgeon sermon every day, it would take them a decade to get through all the ones in print. One could then begin on other Spurgeon classics, such as his commentary on the Psalms (*The Treasury of David*) or his *Lectures to My Students*, both of which are also multivolume works. It is therefore particularly apt in an exploration of how figures in the history of Christianity encountered the Sermon on the Mount that we should look at what this preeminent preacher saw in this greatest of all sermons.

2. Patricia Stallings Kruppa, *Charles Haddon Spurgeon: A Preacher's Progress* (New York: Garland, 1982), 250.

3. David W. Bebbington, *The Dominance of Evangelicalism: The Age of Spurgeon and Moody* (Downers Grove, IL: InterVarsity, 2005), 40.

4. Helmut Thielicke, *Encounter with Spurgeon* (Cambridge: James Clarke, 1964), 45.

Spurgeon as Reformed Baptist Evangelical

The standard collection includes twenty-five Spurgeon sermons on texts from Matthew 5–7. The earliest one is from September 1858, and the last one was preached thirty-one years on, in September 1889.[5] Often the entire chapter was read before he spoke, and Spurgeon would refer to other parts of the Sermon on the Mount beside his primary text. Most of these sermons were free standing, but he did deliver a series on the Beatitudes in 1873. Moreover, Spurgeon died just after he had completed the manuscript for his commentary *The Gospel of the Kingdom: A Popular Exposition of the Gospel according to Matthew*. This source therefore not only provides us with literally his last word on the subject—his final reading of the Sermon on the Mount—but also with a text in which he addresses the meaning of the whole discourse verse by verse. Spurgeon's widow, Susannah, saw *The Gospel of the Kingdom* through the press the year following her husband's death and commended it as almost otherworldly in a way that might strike many today as a reflection of Victorian sentimentality—perhaps even sugary to the point of revulsion:

> During two previous winters in the South of France, a great part of dear Mr. Spurgeon's leisure had been devoted to the production of this Commentary . . . and till within a few days of the termination of his lovely and gracious life, he was incessantly occupied in expounding this portion of God's Word. . . . Much of the later portion of the work, therefore, was written on the very Border-land of Heaven, amid the nearing glories of the unseen world, and almost "within sight of the Golden Gates."[6]

Spurgeon was a straight-shooting, conservative evangelical, Calvinist Baptist, and his reading of the Sermon on the Mount

5. Spurgeon's sermons were recorded by an authorized shorthand writer. As he preached several times a week but prepared only one of these texts for publication, numerous unpublished sermons were left over when Spurgeon died in 1892, and the series continued on into 1917. The citations given here refer to the date when the sermon was published and should not be confused with the date when the sermon was originally delivered.

6. C. H. Spurgeon, *The Gospel of the Kingdom: A Popular Exposition of the Gospel according to Matthew, with Introductory Note by Mrs. C. H. Spurgeon* (London: Passmore & Alabaster, 1893), iii–iv.

amply reflects these identities. He repeatedly refers to his Calvinism or reveals it by what he says. In a sermon on Matthew 5:47 he even offered three biblical quotations in order to defend the doctrine of limited atonement, despite it being often the first petal of the tulip to fall off when figures search for a more moderate form of Calvinism.[7] A sermon on Matthew 7:7 prompted Spurgeon to explain how he could give a general evangelistic invitation while holding to Calvinist doctrine:

> You may knock, and you may expect to see the door open. I know the blessed doctrine of election, and I rejoice in it; but that is a secret with God, while the rule of our preaching is,—"Preach the gospel to every creature." . . . The Lord knows who will knock, for "the Lord knoweth them that are his." But knock, my friend, knock now, and it will soon be seen that you are one of God's chosen ones. . . . So the secret counsel of the Lord is revealed to our faith when it gets Christ in possession, and not before. Knock at once. If you are predestined to enter, I know you will knock, and knock till you are admitted.[8]

Spurgeon's Calvinism was also demonstrated through occasional swipes at Wesleyan theology. He was careful to insist, for example, that Christ's warning that although "ye are the salt of the earth," salt that loses its flavor is "good for nothing, but to be cast out" (Matt. 5:13) should not be read as affirming the possibility of a true believer losing his or her salvation:

> What unscriptural nonsense to talk of a man's being born again, and yet losing the divine life, and then getting it again. Regeneration cannot fail: if it did, the man must be for ever hopeless. He could not be born again, and again, and again: his case would be beyond the reach of mercy. But who is hopeless? . . . The great lesson is, that if grace itself fails to save a man, nothing else can be done for him.[9]

A sermon on Matthew 5:18 entitled "The Perpetuity of the Law of God" provoked this anti-Wesleyan grumble: "No wonder that

7. *Metropolitan Tabernacle Pulpit* 18.16 (1872).
8. *Metropolitan Tabernacle Pulpit* 29.310 (1883).
9. Spurgeon, *Gospel of the Kingdom*, 24.

men talk of perfect sanctification if the law has been lowered."[10] Spurgeon's Baptist identity is less on display, although in a sermon on Matthew 5:14 entitled "The Light of the World" he did declare:

> We as Baptists bear that testimony by our very peculiarity. We do not believe a person to be baptised except it be by his own wish and request. We consider all religion by proxy to be an unmitigated farce, if not worse. The man must do it himself: it must be his personal repentance, his personal faith, his personal baptism, his personal everything, or else it is good for nothing.[11]

In a sermon on the text "lead us not into temptation" (Matt. 6:13), he mentioned as an example of a standard temptation having to deal "with cruel tongues in a church-meeting," but I will leave it to others to decide whether that reference reveals a Baptist distinctive.[12] Being a Baptist meant that he was also a resolute Dissenter or Nonconformist, and this is reflected in various jibes at the Church of England. Here, for example, is a tirade against the standard form of address for peers spiritual (those who sat in the House of Lords on the basis of their episcopal office) leading on to a protest against church establishments in principle:

> "Lord Bishop" is an expression suitable for Babylon, or Rome, but not for the new Jerusalem. I challenge the whole world to find any apostolic title of the kind, or anything approaching to it in the days of the apostles. It is as contrary to Christianity as hell is contrary to heaven. . . . And the church takes care, when she is in a right state, that there shall never be any legislator for her except Christ. He is her law-maker, and not Parliaments or kings. Jesus walks in the midst of the churches, among his golden candlesticks, to observe and prescribe her order; he tolerates no other lawgiver or ruler in spiritual things. . . . It was a brave thing for the Covenanters of Scotland to be ready to die for the headship of Christ in his church . . . to preserve the crown-right of our exalted Lord.[13]

10. *Metropolitan Tabernacle Pulpit* 28.286 (1882).
11. *Metropolitan Tabernacle Pulpit* 19.244 (1873).
12. *Metropolitan Tabernacle Pulpit* 9.272 (1863).
13. *Metropolitan Tabernacle Pulpit* 20.99–100 (1874).

Most of all, however, Spurgeon is revealed in these sermons to be a conservative evangelical. Negatively, this identity is manifest in disparaging remarks about two alternatives, Roman Catholicism and theological liberalism. Indeed, anti-Catholic remarks are sprinkled throughout this material. In his commentary, Spurgeon, in effect, adapted Matthew 6:7 to read, "When ye pray, use not vain repetitions, as the papists do," going on explicitly to apply this text to the use of the rosary.[14] At his worst, Spurgeon could use a ridiculous and revolting piece of Protestant propaganda to illustrate the kind of person who might cry out "Lord, Lord" (Matt. 7:21) on the grounds of their own religiosity, but who nevertheless will not enter the kingdom of heaven. We are apparently meant to believe a tale about a "Catholic in Spain" who had murdered hundreds of people in the course of committing robbery without it troubling his conscience. He went to confession with a "very serious sin" weighing him down; however, when in the course of murdering a man the blood spurting from his victim's wound accidentally sprayed him on the lips thereby causing him inadvertently to violate the prohibition against eating meat on a Friday.[15]

Theological liberalism sometimes was also a target that came into view. Matthew 5:17 ("think not that I am come to destroy the law or the prophets") prompted Spurgeon to reflect that unlike "modern critics," "the Lord Jesus knew nothing of 'destructive criticism.'"[16] The Sermon on the Mount offered a particular gift for these purposes in an English context, as the standard name for the theologically liberal wing of Anglicanism at that time was "Broad Church," leading Spurgeon to reflect upon Christ's words about the broad versus the narrow way (Matt. 7:13–14):

> There may come other days, when the many will crowd the narrow way; but, at this time, to be popular one must be *broad*—broad in doctrine, in morals, and in spirituals. . . . Lord, deliver me from the

14. Spurgeon, *Gospel of the Kingdom*, 34.
15. *Metropolitan Tabernacle Pulpit* 20.102 (1874). Alas, Spurgeon's mind was so taken with this story that he even rehearsed it again in another of these sermons: *Metropolitan Tabernacle Pulpit* 28.285 (1882).
16. Spurgeon, *Gospel of the Kingdom*, 25.

temptation to be *"broad,"* and keep me in the narrow way though few find it![17]

In another place, Spurgeon asserts that theological liberals sit around engaging in unsound speculations while the evangelicals are "up to their necks in work among the poor and sinful": "There is nothing like work to keep a man soundly evangelical. When a fellow has nothing to do, the devil puts it into his head to write an essay against the orthodox faith."[18] The Baptist prince of preachers did not hesitate to use other Christian traditions as examples of things that Jesus warned against in the Sermon on the Mount.

Spurgeon's credentials as a straight-shooting conservative evangelical are also on display in his unabashed and frequent references to the work of Satan and the reality of hell. In the peroration of his sermon on the wise and foolish builders (Matt. 7:24–27), Spurgeon cried out, "The lake of fire! and souls cast into it! The imagery is dreadful. 'Ah,' says one, 'that is a metaphor.' Yes, I know it is, and a metaphor is but a shadow of the reality."[19] Even the beatitude regarding those who hunger and thirst after righteousness could lead Spurgeon to contemplate "the dreadful truth of the eternal perdition of the wicked."[20] Spurgeon's conservative evangelical identity led him frequently to introduce the themes of justification by faith and substitutionary atonement. He often did this even in contexts where these subjects do not seem readily to arise from the text or discussion at hand. At his most breezy, for example, in a sermon on Matthew 5:8, he informed his hearers that they should not be "rebelling against the doctrine of vicarious sacrifice . . . The pure in heart see no difficulty in the atonement." Moreover, if you evaded that censure, see how you do with this follow-up: "Impure minds . . . see reasons for doubting whether Paul wrote the Epistle to the Hebrews."[21] More substantively, as the Sermon on the Mount is so concerned with moral formation, Spurgeon was careful not to allow this mes-

17. Ibid., 43.
18. *Metropolitan Tabernacle Pulpit* 19.248 (1873).
19. *Metropolitan Tabernacle Pulpit* 16.132 (1870).
20. *Metropolitan Tabernacle Pulpit* 35.489 (1889).
21. *Metropolitan Tabernacle Pulpit* 55.413, 416 (1909).

sage to be misconstrued as one of salvation by works. In a telling move, he began a sermon entitled "A Call to Holy Living," which had as its text Matthew 5:47, with a disclaimer:

> It is a very great fault in any ministry if the doctrine of justification by faith alone be not most clearly taught. I will go further, and add, that it is not only a great fault, but a fatal one; for souls will never find their way to heaven by a ministry that is indistinct upon the most fundamental of gospel truths. We are justified by faith, and not by the works of the law. The merit by which a soul enters heaven is not its own; it is the merit of our Lord and Saviour Jesus Christ. I am quite sure that you will all hold me guiltless of ever having spoken about this great doctrine in any other than unmistakable language; if I have erred, it is not in that direction. . . . At the same time . . . Sanctification must not be forgotten.[22]

What makes Spurgeon's evangelicalism all-pervasive, however, is his unwavering commitment to evangelism, to preaching for conversions. Spurgeon counseled the students in his Pastors' College (now Spurgeon's College), "Do not close a single sermon without addressing the ungodly. . . . On such occasions aim distinctly at immediate conversions."[23] While he did not follow his own advice legalistically, it is nevertheless true that the vast majority of these sermons end with a direct appeal to the unconverted, irrespective of the intended audience for the main body of the address. A sermon on Matthew 6:31–33, for example, was delivered as a communion address, and that context was made explicit throughout much of it. Nevertheless, the end moved from speaking to believers who were preparing to receive the elements to providing an answer to those who might be asking, "What must I do to be saved?"[24] Spurgeon's commitment to plain speaking on these matters is evident in a sermon on Matthew 7:21–23 entitled "The Disowned." Early on, he warns his hearers that his goal is "solemnly to talk to you about your immortal soul, and to stir you up to see to its future destiny, lest Christ should come, and you should be as un-

22. *Metropolitan Tabernacle Pulpit* 18.13 (1872).
23. C. H. Spurgeon, *Lectures to My Students: Second Series* (London: Passmore & Alabaster, 1877), 188.
24. *Metropolitan Tabernacle Pulpit* 52.72 (1906).

prepared for his coming as the men in the days of Noah were for the flood which swept them all away." Having fulfilled this plan, his final appeal includes these words: "It may be that my words upon this solemn theme distress you, but how much more will his words distress you when his own dear lips shall say, 'I never knew you!'"[25] In a manner that one might find either endearing or exasperating, Spurgeon concedes at the outset of his sermon on Matthew 7:8 ("to him that knocketh it shall be opened") that the text was "intended for God's believing people" before launching into a sermon that nevertheless uses it as an invitation to unbelievers.[26] Spurgeon's appeals were often a straightforward demand for an immediate response:

> Soul! wilt thou have Christ or not? Young men, young women, ye may never hear this word preached in your ears again. Will ye die at enmity against God? Ye that are sitting here, still unconverted, your last hour may come, ere another sabbath's sun shall dawn. . . . Come, give some answer this morning—ay, this morning. Thank God thou canst give an answer. Thank God that thou art not in hell.[27]

A sermon on Matthew 5:15–16 (not hiding one's light under a bushel) led Spurgeon unapologetically to affirm his commitment to a notion of conversion that has sometimes led evangelicalism to be criticized as being marred by individualism:

> Sin is personal, and so must grace be. We are individually in the darkness, and must be individually kindled into light. One by one each man must accept the light. . . . There must be an individual appropriation of the light. . . . There is no way by which individuality can be destroyed and men saved *en masse*.[28]

A related feature of Spurgeon's preaching was his commitment to speak straight to his hearers' hearts. He was never far from application, running it throughout a sermon in a determined refusal ever to give an uninterrupted block of time to presenting

25. *Metropolitan Tabernacle Pulpit* 48.578, 586 (1902).
26. *Metropolitan Tabernacle Pulpit* 29.301 (1883).
27. *Metropolitan Tabernacle Pulpit* 7.600 (1861).
28. *Metropolitan Tabernacle Pulpit* 27.220 (1881).

background or even purely didactic material. In the sermons, his references to the thoughts of scholars, writers, and prominent figures in the Christian tradition or to the original Greek are minimal. Robert H. Ellison, the leading authority on Victorian preaching, observes that Victorian homiletic theory in general insisted that "the sermon be practical and persuasive, rather than merely abstract or informative."[29] This tendency to foreground calls to respond can be seen even in Spurgeon's written commentary, *The Gospel of the Kingdom*. The seemingly unpropitious first verse of Matthew's Gospel, "the book of the generation of Jesus Christ, the son of David, the son of Abraham," fails to tempt the celebrated preacher to get bogged down in presenting information on matters Davidic and Abrahamic. Instead, after literally only a few short sentences of set-up, Spurgeon bursts into a prayer of application: "Lord Jesus, make us each one to call thee, 'My God and King!' As we read this wonderful Gospel of the Kingdom, may we be full of loyal obedience, and pay thee humble homage!"[30] Sometimes he could seem almost brutal in his plain-speaking application: "I have heard a father saying that his child should never darken his door again. Does that father know that he can never enter heaven while he cherishes such a spirit as that?"[31] This trait would seem to be the secret of the sermons' success and the key to their abiding worth. Spurgeon was not a seminal theological mind or biblical scholar: his genius was an ability not to let his hearers and readers ever forget that the word of God is coming to them in that moment and is demanding a response.

Moral formation is an important aspect of the Sermon on the Mount, and any reading of it must take some approach in regards to the apparently absolutist standards that it presents. Spurgeon takes these sayings on a case-by-case basis, explaining some in a way that softens their impact while insisting that others must be adhered to literally despite their not being standard interpretation in his context. First, let us look at examples of his softening pas-

29. Robert H. Ellison, *The Victorian Pulpit: Spoken and Written Sermons in Nineteenth-Century Britain* (Selinsgrove: Susquehanna University Press, 1998), 18; see also 24, 64–65.

30. Spurgeon, *Gospel of the Kingdom*, 1.

31. *Metropolitan Tabernacle Pulpit* 53.546 (1907).

sages. Spurgeon quite sensibly asserts flatly that Matthew 5:29–30 ("if thy right eye offend thee pluck it out," etc.) is never to be taken literally.[32] Victorian respectability with its culture of hard work, prudence, and thriftiness meant that the take-no-thought-for-tomorrow tone of the last part of Matthew 6 seemed to strike the wrong note. The London preacher therefore approached this text with a barrage of disclaimers and found its meaning in comparative rather than literal statements:

> Certainly, *we are not to understand it in the sense of the idler.* . . . *Neither did our Lord Jesus Christ intend to inculcate prodigality*, when he said, "Take no thought, saying, What shall we eat?" and so on. This is what the young spendthrift does when he comes into possession of his estate. . . . With what singular economy did the Saviour always behave! . . . He fed five thousand men, beside women and children; but, equally economical, he said to his disciples, "Gather up the fragments that remain, that nothing be lost." . . . *Neither did our Lord forbid a certain amount of forethought.* . . . I think that he meant, first, "*Do not let provision for your temporal wants be the chief end of your life*" . . . you are not to make this search the sole end and aim of your life . . . he meant, *as compared with the service of God.*[33]

A text from the Sermon on the Mount that Spurgeon consistently softened was the counsel to avoid taking your adversary to court (Matt. 5:25–26). He insisted that this advice reflected the context of the times in which it was first uttered and therefore need not apply today. Indeed, at times he would even go so far as to invert it: "The courts of our Lord's day were vicious; and his disciples were advised to suffer wrong sooner than appeal to them. Our own courts often furnish the surest method of solving a difficulty by authority."[34]

Much of the time, however, Spurgeon insisted that the absolutist claims of the text not be weakened. He preached on Matthew 5:18, for example, in order to emphasize that not one jot of the law had been abolished:

32. Spurgeon, *Gospel of the Kingdom*, 28.
33. *Metropolitan Tabernacle Pulpit* 52.62–64 (1906) (emphasis original).
34. Spurgeon, *Gospel of the Kingdom*, 30.

I should like to say to any brother who thinks that God has put us under an altered rule: "Which particular part of the law is it that God has relaxed?" Which precept do you feel free to break? Are you delivered from the command which forbids stealing? My dear sir, you may be a capital theologian, but I should lock up my spoons when you call at my house.[35]

Spurgeon was human enough to concede that turning the other cheek is counterintuitive: "No doubt, there is some pleasure in knocking a fellow down who insults you." Nevertheless, he insisted that nonretaliation is the gospel rule: "'Love your enemies, and pray for them that despitefully use you.' He does not insert a clause to the effect that we are only to do this where we are sure that it will not be abused. No, it is absolute."[36] In one particularly delightful passage Spurgeon encourages his hearers to imagine that, however much it seems to go against our own expectations of outcomes, nonretaliation could lead to triumph in the end: "There has been a long enmity, as you know, between the wolves and the sheep; and the sheep have never taken to fighting, yet they have won the victory, and there are more sheep than wolves in the world to-day. In our own country, the wolves are all dead, but the sheep have multiplied by tens of thousands."[37] Over the decades, Spurgeon frequently raised his voice against the possibility of Britain going to war. On December 8, 1861, he preached a sermon on Matthew 5:9 entitled "The Peacemaker" in order to dissuade Britain from allowing indignation over the Trent Affair (in which American troops from the Union side forcibly stopped and boarded a British ship in order to intercept Confederate envoys) to lead it into a war.[38] In a sermon to London bankers, "seek first the kingdom" (Matt. 6:33) was a text that the minister of the Metropolitan Tabernacle would not allow to be relaxed in the light of business realities:

"Well," cries one, "but, you know, we must live." I am not sure about that. There are occasions when it would be better not to live. An

35. *Metropolitan Tabernacle Pulpit* 28.283–84 (1882).
36. *Metropolitan Tabernacle Pulpit* 24.282–84 (1878).
37. *Metropolitan Tabernacle Pulpit* 53.547 (1907).
38. *New Park Street Pulpit* 7.593–600 (1861). For Spurgeon's antiwar activities at some other moments of current affairs, see Kruppa, *Charles Haddon Spurgeon*, 333–41.

old heraldic motto says, "Better death than false of faith." I am, however, quite clear about another necessity—*we must die*; and we had better take that "must" into consideration, and not quite so often repeat the cant phrase, "We must live."[39]

Perhaps the most intriguing absolutist stance that Spurgeon takes is on the question of oaths:

> Notwithstanding much that may be advanced to the contrary, there is no evading the plain sense of this passage, that every sort of oath, however solemn or true, is forbidden to a follower of Jesus. Whether in court of law or out of it, the rule is, *"Swear not at all."* Yet, in this Christian country we have swearing everywhere, and especially among law-makers. Our legislators begin their official existence by swearing. . . . Christians should not yield to an evil custom, however great the pressure put upon them; but they should abide by the plain and unmistakable command of their Lord and King.[40]

Such a pronouncement has Spurgeon siding with a Quaker rather than a Baptist perspective on this issue in England, though Spurgeon would have claimed a spiritual affinity with the Anabaptists rather than the Society of Friends. Moreover, he is certainly right to note that Baptists were routinely swearing in the course of civil duties and responsibilities in Victorian society. Bebbington identifies nineteen Baptists who served as members of Parliament in the nineteenth century, some of whom were among the most prominent and well-respected laypeople in the denomination.[41] They would have been swearing an oath at the start of each new Parliament. Far more common for ordinary Baptists would have been the practice of swearing an oath before giving evidence in a court of law. Indeed, there is a kind of ironic tension in Spurgeon's relaxing of the advice against going to court being coupled with his exacting interpretation of the prohibition regarding oaths.

To round off this section, Spurgeon seems most awkward when endeavoring to expound the meaning of the bald demand: "Be ye

39. *Metropolitan Tabernacle Pulpit* 31.560 (1885) (emphasis original).
40. Spurgeon, *Gospel of the Kingdom*, 29 (emphasis original).
41. D. W. Bebbington, "Baptist M.P.s in the Nineteenth Century," *Baptist Quarterly* 29.1 (Jan. 1981): 3–24.

therefore perfect, even as your Father which is in heaven is perfect" (Matt. 5:48). He seems unwilling either to gloss over the statement or to concede the Wesleyan notion that sinless perfection is possible, and he ends up trying to square this circle in ways that, to this reader, at the very least, lack force, if not coherence.[42]

Spurgeon and Catholic Mystical Traditions

Having earlier identified Spurgeon as a straight-shooting, conservative evangelical, anti-Catholic, Calvinist Baptist, it is now time to problematize that portrait. Spurgeon's work on the Sermon on the Mount reveals that he was drawing upon pre-Reformation Christian traditions to a surprising extent, not least medieval Catholicism. Indeed, the language and approaches that Spurgeon uses in this material repeatedly strike me as having affinities with the stream of medieval mysticism stemming from the Neoplatonic theme of ascent that was appropriated in the Christian tradition in a seminal way in the writings of Pseudo-Dionysius the Areopagite. Although the secondary literature on Spurgeon is vast, a connection with medieval Catholic thought is almost never made. J. C. Carlile, however, in his important biography, did include an entire chapter entitled "Spurgeon the Mystic." Carlile saw a resemblance between Spurgeon's language and thought and that of fourteenth-century Dominican mystic Johannes Tauler, asserting (alas, without giving examples): "Many of [Spurgeon's] passages contain not only the same faith but almost the same phrasing" as remarks by Tauler.[43] In Spurgeon's material on the Sermon on the Mount, the most striking convergence with the language and patterns of thought of medieval mysticism comes in the Baptist preacher's handling of the Beatitudes. Spurgeon taught that the Beatitudes were sequential and cumulative: that is, the peacemaker was inevitably someone who had already attained, each in turn, the blessedness of the preceding states such as poverty of spirit and meekness. Spurgeon persistently referred to the Beatitudes as a "celestial

42. Spurgeon, *Gospel of the Kingdom*, 31–33.
43. J. C. Carlile, *C. H. Spurgeon: An Interpretative Biography* (London: Religious Tract Society, 1933), 271.

ascent" and a "ladder of light." Although John R. W. Stott would not hesitate to observe that there were nine beatitudes—and even Augustine conceded that there were eight—Spurgeon was determined to find only seven in order to capitalize on the symbolic import of the number of perfection. In this manner, one arrives in Spurgeon's thought, as in Dante's *Purgatorio*, at a view of the Beatitudes as markers of a seven-storied ascent to perfection. In short, Spurgeon is presenting this portion of the Sermon on the Mount as a complete path to moral formation. In his sermon on Matthew 5:3, the pastor of the Metropolitan Tabernacle claims that the first beatitude is "thus placed at a suitably low point, where it may be reached by those who are in the earliest stages of grace."[44] His descriptions of this process can sometimes sound remarkably like Benedictine spirituality: "In proportion as men rise in the reception of the divine blessing, they sink in their own esteem, and count it their honour to do the humblest works."[45] Spurgeon even refers in this sermon to the classic mystical ascent passage—Jacob's ladder to heaven—and names explicitly the final goal to be reached: "Their's [*sic*] the beatific vision, their's [*sic*] the eternal ecstasy."[46]

While the language of ascent runs throughout Spurgeon's handling of the Beatitudes, he does not confine sequential thinking to that portion of the Sermon on the Mount. Instead, it bursts forth seemingly wherever it possibly can. In a 1863 sermon on Matthew 6:13, Spurgeon presented the Lord's Prayer as "a Prayer of Degrees." Here, for example, is his description of the progression from the first phrase of the prayer to "hallowed be thy name": "This child-like spirit soon perceives the grandeur of the Father 'in heaven,' and ascends to devout adoration."[47] Later in the same sermon, Spurgeon explains another aspect of the alleged cumulative nature of the prayer in the realm of spiritual formation:

> This is a petition for men already pardoned, for those who know their adoption, for those who love the Lord and desire to see his

44. *Metropolitan Tabernacle Pulpit* 55.374 (1909).
45. *Metropolitan Tabernacle Pulpit* 55.366 (1909).
46. *Metropolitan Tabernacle Pulpit* 55.382 (1909).
47. *Metropolitan Tabernacle Pulpit* 9.265 (1863).

kingdom come. Taught of the Spirit to know their pardon, adoption, and union to Jesus, they can cry, and they alone—"Lead us not into temptation, but deliver us from evil."[48]

Perhaps it is not too far-fetched to hear in "pardon, adoption, and union" a kind of evangelical Protestant alternative to and echo of the classic Dionysian triad: purgation, illumination, and union. In a sermon on the same text given fifteen years later, Spurgeon was still finding a spiritual journey in the prayer, even referring to it as "a ladder," but by then he had decided that it was a descent rather than an ascent. Nevertheless, like the apophatic theology of Dionysian mysticism, he concluded that descent might be a more profound approach to personal formation: "At any rate the down-going process of the prayer might equally well illustrate the advance of the divine life in the soul."[49] Spurgeon even found a triad of ascent—or at least a positive progression—in the asking, seeking, knocking of Matthew 7:8.[50]

A wider issue to bring into view on this point is Spurgeon's fondness for allegorical interpretations of Scripture. He published an entire lecture to his students at the Pastors' College in which he defended this practice in defiance of the prohibition against it that had been pronounced by various Protestant thinkers. Spurgeon preferred to refer to this hermeneutical method as "spiritualizing," but he made it explicit that this is a synonym for allegorizing. With typical Victorian prudery, he coyly told his students that they should positively avoid the literal meaning of the Song of Songs.[51] This did not mean, however, as it often does today, that this book of Scripture receded into the background. To the contrary, Spurgeon's emphasis on it ought to have been sufficient to win the approbation of Bernard of Clairvaux himself. In his published corpus, no less than sixty-three sermons have a passage from the Song of Songs as their primary text. That is more than all of the following ten books of the Old Testament

48. *Metropolitan Tabernacle Pulpit* 9.265 (1863).
49. *Metropolitan Tabernacle Pulpit* 24.134 (1878).
50. *Metropolitan Tabernacle Pulpit* 29.301 (1883).
51. C. H. Spurgeon, *Lectures to My Students: First Series* (London: Passmore & Alabaster, 1875), 107.

combined: Ezra, Nehemiah, Esther, Ecclesiastes, Joel, Jonah, Nahum, Habakkuk, Zephaniah, and Haggai. This disproportionate attention even holds true for the New Testament. Texts from all of the Pastoral Epistles combined, for example, resulted in only fifty-one sermons—a dozen fewer than the Song of Songs. The Sermon on the Mount does not provide nearly the same kind of potential for allegorizing as Hebrew love poetry, but a spiritualizing tendency does leaven much of Spurgeon's reading of even Matthew 5–7. Spurgeon was delighted with the spiritual significance of the mount itself:

> Exalted doctrine might well be symbolized by an ascent to the mount; at any rate, let every minister feel that he should ascend in spirit when he is about to descant upon the lofty themes of the gospel. . . . Besides, mountains have always been associated with distinct eras in the history of the people of God; mount Sinai is sacred to the law, and mount Zion symbolical of the Church. . . . The open space was in keeping with his large heart, the breezes were akin to his free spirit.[52]

The eye mentioned in Matthew 6:22–23 admittedly must be a metaphor for something, but a certain *sensus plenior* instinct is arguably betrayed by Spurgeon's unapologetic willingness to expound five different meanings in a single sermon.[53] In a sermon on Matthew 7:8 entitled "Knock!" Spurgeon can even give us two different allegorical meanings of the physical door knocker attached to the door (the promises of God and the name of the Lord Jesus Christ), never mind that there is not even a door knocker in the text.[54] The features of the storm that tests the houses built on the rock and the sand are spiritualized as follows:

> The rain typifies *afflictions from heaven*. . . . But there will also arise *trials from earth*—"the floods came." . . . Then there will come *mysterious trials* typified by "the winds." The prince of the power of the air will assail you, with blasphemous suggestions, horrible

---

52. *Metropolitan Tabernacle Pulpit* 55.363 (1909).
53. *New Park Street Pulpit* 6.389–95 (1860). The five meanings are the conscience, the understanding, the heart, our faith, and our obedience.
54. *Metropolitan Tabernacle Pulpit* 29.307 (1883).

temptations, or artful insinuations. He knows how to cast clouds of despondency over the human spirit.[55]

These examples will suffice, but they do not exhaust the spiritualizing that Spurgeon did when reading even such an unpropitious portion of Scripture for these purposes as the Sermon on the Mount.

Spurgeon's Sources

So where did these influences come from? I would like to offer an answer rooted in specific sources here, but I shall return to a more general theory toward the end of this essay. One concrete answer must be that Spurgeon was influenced by his reading. Spurgeon was a typical Victorian autodidact who read voraciously and more widely than a person formally trained would typically do. He built up a personal library of some twelve thousand volumes. However, as has already been said, Spurgeon quoted theologians, scholars, past Christian leaders, and other sources in his sermons only sparingly. He even read the conclusion of the Sermon on the Mount ("for he taught them as one having authority, and not as the scribes"; Matt. 7:29) as revealing that Jesus set the practice that he aspired to follow: "Not quoting Rabbi So-and-so, to show how well he was acquainted with his writings, but speaking as one who knew what he had to say, and who spoke, out of the fullness of his heart, truth that was evidently inspired; and his hearers felt the force of the solemn message which he thus delivered."[56] Nevertheless, the occasional citations that Spurgeon did give reveal how wide ranging his reading was. In two of these sermons, for example, he found occasion to cite John Chrysostom. During the opening sermon in the series on the Beatitudes in which he made general remarks on the Sermon on the Mount as a whole, this evangelical Baptist pastor even said explicitly that he was quoting the *Catena aurea*, a collection of sayings by church fathers and authorities compiled by Thomas Aquinas. The quotation he gave is a Pseudo-Chrysostom saying.[57] In one of these sermons,

55. *Metropolitan Tabernacle Pulpit* 16.129 (1870) (emphasis original).
56. *Metropolitan Tabernacle Pulpit* 48.588 (1902).
57. *Metropolitan Tabernacle Pulpit* 55.362 (1909).

Spurgeon even quotes approvingly the allegorizing of Matthew 5:15–16 done by an early medieval monk:

> The venerable Bede, when he was interpreting this text, said that Christ Jesus brought the light of Deity into the poor lantern of our humanity, and then set it upon the candlestick of his church that the whole house of the world might be lit up thereby. So indeed it is.[58]

A list of the books in Spurgeon's library reveals other patristic and medieval authors as well. For example, as the seven-storied ascent was mentioned earlier, it should be noted that he possessed two different translations of Dante.[59] Spurgeon owed a far greater intellectual debt, however, to Puritan authors, and it is likely that many of these seemingly medieval influences were mediated to him through seventeenth-century English Protestants. Spurgeon found warrant for allegorizing, for example, in the elaborate spiritualizing of the furnishings of Solomon's Temple that had been done by John Bunyan.[60] One of the books in Spurgeon's library was a collection of sermons on the Beatitudes by Puritan Robert Harris. While this theme is much more muted in Harris than it is in Spurgeon, the seventeenth-century divine also spoke of the Beatitudes as steps that lead on from one to the next.[61] However anti-Catholic he might have been, Spurgeon continued to draw upon the great tradition generously.

Spurgeon and Charismatic Ministry

If Spurgeon's identity as a conservative evangelical Calvinist Baptist is problematized by the way that his thought reaches back into

58. *Metropolitan Tabernacle Pulpit* 27.227–28 (1881).

59. I am grateful to Angela Stiffler (William Jewel Library, William Jewel College, Liberty, Missouri) for providing me with a photocopy of a typescript of the books in Spurgeon's personal library in the possession of William Jewel College. It should be noted, however, that many of Spurgeon's books were dispersed before this core was purchased and kept together.

60. Spurgeon, *Lectures to My Students: First Series*, 112–14.

61. Robert Harris, *The Way to True Happiness: Delivered in Twenty-four Sermons upon the Beatitudes*, ed. Don Kistler (Morgan, PA: Soli Deo Gloria Publications, 1998 [originally 1653]), 176.

medieval resources, it is also given a surprising flavor by the ways in which his life, ministry, and thought seemed to foreshadow features of Pentecostal and charismatic spirituality. Although it has rarely been commented upon, Spurgeon was also known in his own day for a ministry of divine healing. There are a whole series of specific stories about this including, for example, one about the complete healing of a man who had paralysis resulting from a stroke. There is also an account of Spurgeon successfully performing an exorcism.[62]

Spurgeon spoke openly and unapologetically about a word over his life that had been given to him when he was only ten years old by an eminent missionary. Richard Knill prophesied that the boy would someday preach the gospel to great multitudes and that he would preach in "the chapel of Rowland Hill," that is, Surrey Chapel, one of the largest Nonconformist places of worship in London. Knill was so far from being double-minded about his prophecy, that he charged the boy to have the hymn "God moves in a mysterious way, his wonders to perform" sung on the occasion of its fulfillment. Spurgeon cherished this word in his heart, and when, having become a preacher, he was asked to speak at Surrey Chapel he made the singing of that hymn a condition of his coming. He reflected on this moment in his autobiography: "My emotions on that occasion I cannot describe, for the word of the Lord's servant was fulfilled. . . . To me it was a very wonderful thing, and I no more understood at that time how it came to pass than I understand to-day why the Lord should be so gracious to me."[63]

Spurgeon's own ministry was marked by what in the Pentecostal-charismatic tradition is sometimes referred to as "word of knowledge," that is, he would suddenly seem to know something that he had not learned in a natural way. There are a whole series of

62. Jon Vickery, "The Unexpected Healer: C. H. Spurgeon and the Ministry of Healing," unpublished paper. I am grateful to Jon for sharing his research with me. The main published source on Spurgeon's ministry of healing is Russel H. Conwell, *Life of Charles Haddon Spurgeon: The World's Greatest Preacher* (Philadelphia: Hubbard, 1892), 173–211.

63. C. H. Spurgeon, *Autobiography*, vol. 1: *The Early Years, 1834–1859* (London: Banner of Truth, 1962), 27–28.

such stories, and some of them contain a level of detailed information to rival any televangelist downloading street addresses. For example, Spurgeon once interrupted his sermon to point at someone and declaim: "There is a man sitting there who is a shoemaker; he keeps his shop open on Sundays; it was open last Sabbath morning. He took ninepence and there was fourpence profit on it: his soul is sold to Satan for fourpence."[64] In his autobiography, Spurgeon himself told the story of the time when a member of his congregation came to him in distress because her unconverted husband had deserted her and fled the country. He prayed with her and felt emboldened to give her this prophetic word of encouragement: "Do not fret about the matter. I feel sure your husband will come home; and that he will yet become connected with our church."[65] At that same moment, the story goes, the man, while on a ship, happened upon a published sermon by Spurgeon himself. It triggered his conversion to Christ, he reunited with his wife and duly became a sound and grateful member of the Metropolitan Tabernacle.

The literature on Spurgeon is at a loss to account for these stories. His wife explained (or failed to explain) one famous "word of knowledge" outburst in which Spurgeon had pointed to a specific hearer in his audience and told of his secrets by saying, "The preacher had drawn the bow at a venture, but the arrow struck the target for which God intended it."[66] Baptist minister J. C. Carlile offered as an explanation: "Spurgeon was a psychic man."[67] Given such a level of analysis in the existing literature, perhaps it will at least be conceded that I have done no worse, if I postulate the possibility that these extraordinary occurrences might have been the work of the Holy Spirit. What is indisputable is that Spurgeon himself had a pronounced pneumatological emphasis in his thinking and preaching. Lecture one of the

64. W. Y. Fullerton, *C. H. Spurgeon: A Biography* (London: Williams & Norgate, 1929), 249.
65. C. H. Spurgeon, *Autobiography*, vol. 2: *The Full Harvest, 1860–1892* (London: Banner of Truth, 1973), 356.
66. C. H. Spurgeon, *C. H. Spurgeon's Autobiography* (London: Passmore & Alabaster, 1899), 3.89.
67. Carlile, *C. H. Spurgeon*, 12.

second series of his *Lectures to My Students* was entitled "The Holy Spirit in Connection with Our Ministry." In it, Spurgeon spoke of a recent prayer meeting in which the Holy Spirit was so present that "bodily frames were quivering."[68] He went on to argue: "The lack of distinctly recognizing the power of the Holy Ghost lies at the root of many useless ministries."[69] This was not limited to public ministry: "A very important part of our lives consists in praying in the Holy Ghost." If the Spirit was at work, then there was no need for a scripted service: "Certain weaklings have said, 'Let us have a liturgy!' Rather than seek divine aid they will go down to Egypt for help. Rather than be dependent upon the Spirit of God, they will pray by a book!"[70] This emphasis is reflected in Spurgeon's reading of the Sermon on the Mount. He refers in this material far more often to the Spirit than to the Father, despite the fact that the Spirit is not explicitly mentioned in Matthew 5–7, while the Father is named seventeen times. Even in a sermon entitled "The Fatherhood of God," which took the first phrase of the Lord's Prayer as its text (Matt. 6:9), Spurgeon enthused: "I must pour out my heart in the language which his Spirit gives me; and more than that, I must trust in the Spirit to speak the unutterable groanings of my spirit, when my lips cannot actually express all the emotions of my heart."[71]

Spurgeon's sermons were taken down by a shorthand writer, but he then edited them for publication. Beside any changes that he wanted to make to clarify his message or rein himself in, he routinely had to either cut or expand the text in order to fit the twelve-page format used for publication. I do not know whether Spurgeon was more apt to delete these spontaneous asides or leave them in. On one occasion he was clearly addressing a specific hearer impromptu in the Matthew 5–7 material. In his sermon entitled "The Sixth Beatitude," he cried out, "Oh, that that troubled young man over there could come and trust in Jesus!"[72] That is perhaps small beer compared to the stories offered above, but the preacher clearly did

68. Spurgeon, *Lectures to My Students: Second Series*, 8.
69. Ibid., 12.
70. Ibid., 13–14.
71. *New Park Street Pulpit* 4.386 (1858).
72. *Metropolitan Tabernacle Pulpit* 55.420 (1909).

not know the man and therefore could not be sure of the nature of his situation. There are many occasions in these sermons when Spurgeon names specific cases in the clear hope that, as his wife put it, God would cause the arrow to strike its mark. In another one of the classic mysterious stories in which Spurgeon's words reflected the situation of one of his hearers with uncanny precision, the preacher testified that while he was speaking "an idea haunts my mind that I have been drawing somebody's portrait."[73] One wonders how often applications to precisely delineated circumstances in these sermons on Matthew 5–7 were also accompanied by such an impression. One time, Spurgeon suddenly used two personal names in the appeal, "Mary, he calleth thee! John, he calleth thee!"[74] These are common enough names, but this was the only occasion in these sermons when he used them. Moreover, he was far from his main theme at that moment, as the primary goal of this sermon (on the text "blessed are the peacemakers") was to dissuade Britain from declaring war on the United States of America. These sermons are filled with examples of the preacher speaking to very specific cases. For example, in a sermon on Matthew 5:45 Spurgeon spoke in the appeal to the case of someone who was fifty years old and had heard sermons his or her whole life but had never yet accepted Christ.[75]

Moreover, Spurgeon occasionally "prophesied" in these sermons, that is, he spoke extrabiblical words from God to his congregation. In a sermon on Matthew 5:47 he has Christ say to them: "Inasmuch as I have loved you thus, and have redeemed you with such a price, and have begotten you unto myself by the power of my Spirit, what manner of people ought ye to be in all holy conversation?"[76] In his sermon on Matthew 5:45, Spurgeon tells his Victorian audience that he believes God is saying this to them: "This is the day of free grace; this is the time of mercy." In the same sermon, he told with approval the story of a contemporary who had a vision in which Christ said to him: "I did all this for thee, what hast thou done for me?"[77] In his sermon entitled "The Peacemaker," Spur-

73. Spurgeon, *Autobiography*, 2.59.
74. *Metropolitan Tabernacle Pulpit* 7.600 (1861).
75. *Metropolitan Tabernacle Pulpit* 24.286 (1878).
76. *Metropolitan Tabernacle Pulpit* 18.17 (1872).
77. *Metropolitan Tabernacle Pulpit* 24.280, 285 (1878).

geon informed his audience that he could hear "Christ speaking to you now": Christ was saying, "Soul, I love you; I love you from my heart; I would not have you at enmity with my Father."[78] If it be said that such utterances may be excused because they stick so closely to biblical thoughts and words, then bear in mind that such a proviso would also give warrant to the standard prophetic words delivered in many Pentecostal and charismatic settings. No doubt Spurgeon would have had substantive differences with Pentecostal-charismatic theology and practice as it emerged in the twentieth century and beyond, but these phenomenological affinities serve to remind us that it might sometimes be more illuminating to think of these more dramatic and controversial forms of ministry as existing on a continuum.

Finally, I wish briefly to mention one more fascinating way in which Spurgeon seems to leap out of his situatedness in these sermons: this Victorian Baptist had a remarkable commitment to speaking in gender-inclusive ways. Here, for example, is a list of phrases he used in his sermon on Matthew 6:31–33:

dear brothers and sisters
O beloved brethren and sisters
you young lads and lasses
O brothers and sisters
brothers and sisters
our brethren and sisters
my brethren and sisters
my sister
my dear sister
says a brother
brethren and sisters[79]

Throughout all these sermons on Matthew 5–7 his standard practice is to refer to sisters as well as brothers and to be careful not continually to assume that an example figure is male. In this pas-

78. *Metropolitan Tabernacle Pulpit* 7.599 (1861).
79. *Metropolitan Tabernacle Pulpit* 52.61–72 (1906).

sage, for example, Spurgeon uses pronouns in a way that we are still sometimes told is too jarring to recommend:

> The poorest Christian possesses more than the richest unbeliever. You shall set before me now the pauper who is a believer, and the emperor who has no faith in Christ, and I am persuaded that the poor, aged pauper would not exchange her lot though the imperial purple should be offered her. She would refuse to leave her Saviour though the world were offered her. . . . The poor believer feels that his God is his portion he dispises [sic] rather than covets the glories of the world.[80]

So what is going on here? This leads me to the general theory that I promised earlier. What medieval allegorizing, evangelical evangelistic preaching, charismatic ministry, and gender-inclusive language all have in common is a prioritizing of making an immediate, relevant connection with the hearer—they are traditions and practices that demand a payoff applicable at that moment, manna for the day. This was Spurgeon's overriding concern. Spurgeon used language that referred to women as well as men because he wanted to see women as well as men come to Jesus. He allegorized because it made the text speak more directly to the human condition. He "prophesied" and named specific cases because he wanted the gospel to hunt down individuals and arrest them in their tracks. Spurgeon's deepest desire was that his preaching on the Sermon on the Mount would occasion spiritual conversion and moral formation. Moreover, he was convinced that the original speaker of this greatest of all sermons was aiming at the same effect.

---

80. *Metropolitan Tabernacle Pulpit* 18.17–18 (1872).

Dietrich Bonhoeffer and John Howard Yoder

Stanley Hauerwas

Bonhoeffer and Yoder on the Visibility of the Church

In *Performing the Faith: Bonhoeffer and the Practice of Nonviolence* I argued that the heart of Dietrich Bonhoeffer's work from *Sanctorum Communio* to *Letters and Papers from Prison* was animated by his conviction that the significance of the visibility of the church must be recovered. I suggested, moreover, that his stress on the visibility of the church made Bonhoeffer and John Howard Yoder allies.[1] Lutherans and Anabaptists are, of course, strange bedfellows, but Bonhoeffer's observation concerning the consequences of Luther's doctrine of grace and the implications that doctrine had for shaping an understanding of how Christians should live in the world sounds very much like something Yoder might say:

> Thus in his own way Luther confirms Constantine's covenant with the church. As a result, a minimal ethic prevailed. Luther of course wanted a complete ethic for everyone, not only for monastic orders. Thus the existence of the Christian became the existence of the citizen.

---

1. Stanley Hauerwas, *Performing the Faith: Bonhoeffer and the Practice of Nonviolence* (Grand Rapids: Brazos, 2004), 33–54.

The nature of the church vanished into the invisible realm. But in this way the New Testament message was fundamentally misunderstood, inner-worldliness became a principle.[2]

Bonhoeffer's observation concerning the effects of Luther's understanding of grace correspond to Yoder's understanding of one of the results of the Constantinian shift. Yoder notes that after Constantine the meaning of the description *Christian* changes. Prior to Constantine, it took exceptional conviction to be a Christian. After Constantine, it took exceptional courage to be a pagan. According to Yoder this development resulted in "the doctrine of the invisible church." Before Constantine, Christians knew as a fact of everyday experience that the church was under God's care, but they had to have faith that God was governing history. After Constantine, Christians assumed that God was governing history through the emperor, but one had to take it on faith that within the nominally Christian mass there was a community of true believers. No longer could being a Christian be identified by church membership, because many in the church clearly did not belong to Christ. To be a Christian was transmuted to "inwardness."[3]

Bonhoeffer and Yoder in quite similar ways were intent on a recovery of the visibility of the church. Yet their understanding of the importance of the church's visibility was a correlative of similar christological convictions. That the church must take up space in the world is necessary because God in Jesus Christ occupied space in the world.[4] Thus Bonhoeffer argues "and so, too, the church of

2. Dietrich Bonhoeffer, *No Rusty Swords*, ed. Edwin Robertson (New York: Harper & Row, 1965), 87.

3. John Howard Yoder, *The Priestly Kingdom: Social Ethics as Gospel* (Notre Dame: University of Notre Dame Press, 2001), 135–49.

4. Yoder and Bonhoeffer were deeply influenced by Karl Barth, but their understanding of the necessity of the visibility suggests that they developed some of Barth's themes in a manner that defied Barth's dialectic. For example, Bonhoeffer observes: "Only if the concept of God is understood to be comprehensible when exclusively connected to the concept of the church is it permitted, for technical reasons of presentation, to 'derive' the latter from the former. In order to establish clarity about the inner logic of theological construction, it would be good for once if a presentation of doctrinal theology were to start not with the doctrine of God but with the doctrine of the church"; *Sanctorum Communio*, trans. Reinhard Krauss and Nancy Lukens (Minneapolis: Fortress, 1998), 134. Bonhoeffer and Yoder seem to have been more willing than Barth to risk "being Catholic" in terms of their ecclesiology.

Jesus Christ is the place, in other words the space in the world, at which the reign of Jesus Christ over the whole world is evidenced and proclaimed."[5] Yoder is as insistent as Bonhoeffer that "the politics of Jesus" requires a people exist that constitute a politics capable of being an alternative to the politics of the world.[6]

Yoder and Bonhoeffer shared the fundamental christological conviction that the person and work of Christ cannot be separated. Accordingly they are critical of theologies that stress the saving work of Christ, often understood in terms of satisfaction theories of the atonement, in which Jesus's teachings become an afterthought. Satisfaction theories of the atonement reflect an accommodated church that has lost the eschatological character of Jesus's proclamation of the kingdom. As a result the radical character of discipleship depicted by Jesus in the Sermon on the Mount is lost in the interest of sustaining an account of salvation concerned primarily with whether we have a "personal relationship" with Jesus.

Such accounts of salvation Bonhoeffer called "cheap grace." By cheap grace he meant an understanding of grace "as a doctrine, as principal, as system. It means forgiveness of sins as a general truth; it means God's love as merely a Christian idea of God. Those who affirm it have already had their sins forgiven."[7] Grace so understood, according to Bonhoeffer, leads to the assumption that since the whole world is justified by grace Christians should

5. Dietrich Bonhoeffer, *Ethics*, ed. Clifford Green, trans. Reinhard Krauss, Charles West, and Douglas Stott (Minneapolis: Fortress, 2005), 61–64. Bonhoeffer's understanding of the worldliness of the church, one of the most misunderstood aspects of Bonhoeffer's work, is a correlative of his Christology. Thus he says, "The worldliness of the church follows from the incarnation of Christ. The church, like Christ, has become world. It is a denial of the real humanity of Jesus and also heretical to take the concrete church as only a phantom church or an illusion. . . . Real worldliness consists in the church's being able to renounce all privileges and all its property but never Christ's Word and the forgiveness of sins. With Christ and the forgiveness of sins to fall back on, the church is free to give up everything else"; *A Testament to Freedom: The Essential Writings of Dietrich Bonhoeffer*, ed. Geffrey Kelly and Burton Nelson (San Francisco: Harper, 1990), 89–90.

6. *The Politics of Jesus* (Grand Rapids: Eerdmans, 1995) is Yoder's best known work that develops the interconnection of Christology and ecclesiology, but equally important is his *Christian Witness to the State* (Scottdale, PA: Herald, 2002).

7. Dietrich Bonhoeffer, *Discipleship*, trans. Barbara Green and Reinhard Krauss (Minneapolis: Fortress, 2001), 43.

live like the rest of the world. Such a view of grace, a view often legitimated by the alleged Pauline tension between law and gospel, is shared by conservative and liberal Christians who otherwise think they are in deep disagreement. But they differ only in the way they think Christians should conform to the world; that is, they have confused being Christian with the liberal and conservative options dictated by the world.

In contrast Yoder and Bonhoeffer focus on the Sermon on the Mount to remind us that the salvation wrought in Christ has a distinct shape constituted by discipleship. Accordingly the Sermon is not some ideal given only to make us guilty, but rather the Sermon is the very form of life necessary to witness to the reality of the new age begun in Christ. The one who preached the Sermon and the Sermon are one.[8] In Bonhoeffer's words,

> the Sermon on the Mount is the word of the one who did not relate to reality as a foreigner, a reformer, a fanatic, the founder of a religion, but as the one who bore and experienced the nature of reality in his own body, who spoke out of the depth of reality as no other human being on earth ever before. The Sermon on the Mount is the word of the very one who is the lord and law of reality. The Sermon on the Mount is to be understood and interpreted as the word of God who became human. That is the issue at stake when the question of historical action is raised, and here it must prove true that action in accord with Christ is action in accord with reality. Action in accord with Christ does not originate in some ethical principle, but in the very person of Christ. This is because everything real is summed up in Christ, who, by definition is the origin of any and all action that is in accord with the reality of the Sermon.[9]

The visibility of the church for Bonhoeffer and Yoder is, however, not an end in itself. The church exists to give testimony to Jesus Christ. To so testify requires that the church be holy. Sanctification

8. Bonhoeffer, *Ethics*, 231. It is not surprising therefore that a few pages later (235) Bonhoeffer notes that "the sayings of Jesus in the Sermon on the Mount are the interpretation of his existence, and thus the interpretation of that reality in which history finds its fulfillment in God's becoming human, in the reconciliation of the world with God."

9. Ibid., 231.

names the way the church becomes visible because sanctification is not just something that happens to individuals, but rather is the "seal of the Holy Spirit" placed on "the church in the midst of struggle."[10] Yoder and Bonhoeffer, therefore, reject Reinhold Niebuhr's contention that individuals can be moral in a manner that a social grouping cannot. The reverse is true. The church must be and is a community of holiness without which individual sanctification is impossible.[11]

Bonhoeffer's and Yoder's ecclesial understanding of sanctification as the necessary condition for the recovery of the visibility of the church is exhibited in how they read the Sermon on the Mount. Bonhoeffer's reflections on the Sermon are more extensive than Yoder's, but I hope to show that Bonhoeffer's reading of the Sermon often parallels themes in Yoder's work. Bonhoeffer and Yoder would have not been particularly interested in whether their reading of the Sermon was in agreement. They would not have wanted attention directed to their positions, but rather to the Sermon itself. Accordingly in what follows I have tried to focus attention on the Sermon itself rather than a comparison of Bonhoeffer's and Yoder's hermeneutics of the Sermon.

The Sermon as a Manual for Discipleship

Bonhoeffer's reflections on the Sermon on the Mount inform everything he wrote, but his most extended reflections on the Sermon are to be found in his book *Discipleship*. Bonhoeffer thought

10. Bonhoeffer, *No Rusty Swords*, 261–62.

11. Yoder puts it this way: "In view of Niebuhr's interest in history it is surprising that the concept of the church is quite absent from his thought; when he mentions the word 'church' it is only to criticize the medieval synthesis of Catholicism. This omission is highly significant for understanding what is wrong with Niebuhr's social ethics. For the body of Christ differs from other social bodies in that it is not less moral than its individual members. If being a perfectly loyal American, a freemason, or a bourgeois, identifies a man with that group egoism in such a way as to make him less loving than he would be as an individual, the contrary is true of being a member of Christ. Thus the thesis of *Moral Man and Immoral Society* falls down in the crucial case, the only one which is really decisive for Christian ethics"; *Reinhold Niebuhr and Christian Pacifism* (Scottdale, PA: Herald, 1968), 21. Bonhoeffer makes a very similar criticism of Niebuhr in his *Ethics*.

discipleship was the key to the Sermon because, though the crowd heard the Sermon, Jesus primarily addresses his disciples who will have to learn to live in tension with the crowd. Bonhoeffer observes that the disciples

> have visibly left the people to join him. He has called each individual one. They have given up everything in response to his call. Now they are living in renunciation and want; they are the poorest of the poor, the most tempted of the tempted, the hungriest of the hungry. They have only him. Yes, and with him they have nothing in the world, nothing at all, but everything with God. So far, he has found only a small community, but it is a great community he is looking for, when he looks at the people. Disciples and people belong together. The disciples will be his messengers; they will find listeners and believers here and there. Nevertheless, there will be enmity between the disciples and the people until the end. Everyone's rage at God and God's word will fall on the disciples, and they will be rejected with him. The cross comes into view. Christ, the disciples, the people—one can already see the whole history of the suffering of Jesus and his community.[12]

Therefore for Bonhoeffer the Sermon is not a list of requirements, but rather a description of the life of a people gathered by and around Jesus. To be saved is to be so gathered. Therefore the Beatitudes are the interpretative key to the whole Sermon. Yoder and Bonhoeffer emphasize that the Beatitudes are not recommendations.[13] Yoder, for example, argues that the Beatitudes are misinterpreted as a scheme of performances and rewards when they are separated from the annunciation of the new regime begun in Christ: "One cannot simply, by making up his mind, set out to 'mourn' or to 'be persecuted for righteousness' sake.' Jesus is saying, 'There are some who hunger and thirst after righteousness: *good for them*! For the kingdom is at hand and they shall be filled. There are those who make peace; *good for them*! For the kingdom is at hand and it will be known that they are sons of God.'"[14]

12. Bonhoeffer, *Discipleship*, 100–101.
13. Yoder's most extended reflections on the Sermon on the Mount are in his "The Political Axioms of the Sermon on Mount," in *The Original Revolution: Essays on Christian Pacifism* (Scottdale, PA: Herald, 2003), 34–51.
14. Ibid., 40.

As a way to call attention to the character of the Beatitudes, Bonhoeffer reads them through Jesus's claim that the disciples are to be a light to the world and a city on a hill that cannot be hidden. Bonhoeffer observes that any Israelite could not help but be reminded of Jerusalem, but the city that Jesus calls into the world is that constituted by a community of disciples. Accordingly,

> the followers of Jesus are no longer faced with a decision. The only decision possible for them has already been made. Now they have to be what they are, or they are not following Jesus. The followers are the visible community of faith; their discipleship is a visible act which separates them from the world—or it is not discipleship. And discipleship is as visible as light in the night, as a mountain in the flatland. To flee into invisibility is to deny the call. Any community of Jesus which wants to be invisible is no longer a community that follows him.[15]

Bonhoeffer and Yoder, therefore, do not speculate about who may be poor in spirit or who may be those who mourn, the meek, those who hunger and thirst, the merciful, the pure in heart, the peacemakers, those persecuted. It is from Jesus we know what it means to have any of the characteristics named in the Beatitudes. Jesus is "poor in spirit" because Jesus, though he was in the form of God, emptied himself, taking the form of a slave (Phil. 2:5–8). Jesus's blessing of the poor is, therefore, according to Bonhoeffer totally different from its caricature that takes the form of a political-social program. The antichrist also declares that the poor are blessed, but he does so not for the sake of the cross. It is only in the poverty of the cross that the visible majesty of the kingdom of heaven is revealed.[16] Each beatitude when seen in the light of Christ's life cannot help but deepen the breach between the disciples and the crowd, thus making the visibility of the disciples unavoidable.

In like manner Jesus, speaking about himself for the first time, makes clear that he has not come to abolish the law or the prophets. He has not come to abolish the law, but rather he is the fulfillment

---

15. Bonhoeffer, *Discipleship*, 112–13.
16. Ibid., 103.

of the law. He is so because he is the only one who could teach the law and to show what it means for the law to be fulfilled, for the fulfillment of the law can come about only by his being nailed to a cross as a sinner. The "better righteousness" of Jesus's disciples, therefore, is that which comes from the righteousness of Jesus's crucifixion.[17]

Throughout the Gospel of Matthew the scribes and Pharisees will be criticized for neglecting the weightier matters of the law, for greed and self-indulgence, and for hypocrisy. Yet what cannot be overlooked is the politics at the heart of the antitheses that follow Jesus's claim that the righteousness of his followers must exceed that of the scribes and Pharisees. The antitheses are the description of the order of the new community that Jesus calls into the world. Yoder observes that Jesus does what God had done in calling Abraham, Moses, Gideon, or Samuel, that is, he gathers people around his law so that a society comes into being like no society the world has ever seen:

1. This was a voluntary society: you could not be born into it. You could come into it only by repenting and freely pledging allegiance to its king. It was a society with no second-generation members.
2. It was society that, counter to all precedent, was mixed in its composition. It was mixed racially, with both Jews and Gentiles; mixed religiously, with fanatical keepers of the law and advocates of liberty from all forms and with both radical monotheists and others just in the process of disentangling their minds from idolatry; mixed economically, with members both rich and poor.
3. When he called his society together Jesus gave its members a new way of life to live. He gave them a new way to deal with offenders—by forgiving them. He gave them a new way to deal with violence—by suffering. He gave them a new way to deal with money—by sharing it. He gave them a new way to deal with a corrupt society—by building a new order, not smashing the old. He gave them a new pattern of relation-

17. Ibid., 115–20.

ship between man and woman, between parent and child, between master and slave, in which was made concrete a radical new vision of what it means to be a human person. He gave them a new attitude toward the state and toward the "enemy nation."[18]

Bonhoeffer and Yoder, therefore, do not speculate whether the antitheses are impossible to follow. They are impossible only if the antitheses are abstracted from the new people made possible by Jesus's life, death, and resurrection. The antitheses serve, just as did the Beatitudes, to spell out, to describe, the kind of community the law requires. Jesus is clear that the law is to be observed, so murder, adultery, divorce, oaths, retaliation, and hatred of enemy are forbidden. Yet the community that Jesus calls into existence cannot be determined by what it avoids, but rather what is avoided is avoided because of the character of the community that is to exemplify Christ's life.

Perhaps nothing is more indicative of the unexpected world that Jesus reveals and community that he calls into existence than his suggestion that some of his followers will not marry. The community called into existence by Jesus does not grow by biological ascription, but by witness and conversion. Jesus's teaching on adultery and divorce, therefore, reflect the new body made ours through his crucified body. Bonhoeffer observes:

> Jesus does not make either marriage or celibacy into a required program. Instead, he frees his disciples from infidelity within and outside marriage, which is a sin not only against one's own body, but a sin against the very body of Christ (I Corinthians 6:13–15). Even the body of the disciple belongs to Christ and discipleship; our bodies are members of his body. Because Jesus, the Son of God, assumed a human body, and because we are in communion with his body, that is why infidelity is a sin against Jesus' own body. Jesus' body was crucified. The apostle says of those who belong to Christ that they have crucified the flesh with its passions and desires (Galatians 5:24). Thus, the fulfillment of even this Old Testament commandment becomes true only in the crucified, martyred body

18. Yoder, *Original Revolution*, 28–29.

215

of Jesus Christ. The sight of that body, which was given for us, and our communion with it provide the disciples with the strength for the chastity Jesus commands.[19]

Any community capable of sustaining singleness as a way of life must also be a community of trust made possible by speaking the truth to one another. Bonhoeffer observes that oaths are a sign that we live in a world of lies. If we could trust ourselves to tell the truth not only to others but especially to ourselves, then oaths would not be needed. Christians, as the Mennonites have long tried to practice, are therefore committed to plain speech. No more should be said than needs to be said. To so speak requires training and, in particular, training that makes possible truthful confession of sin. Such truthfulness, according to Bonhoeffer, comes only through the cross, because those whose lives are constituted by the "cross can do without the oath as a command-ment establishing truthfulness, for they exist in the perfect truth of God. There is no following Jesus without living in the truth unveiled before God and other people."[20]

Yoder and Bonhoeffer, moreover, assume that such a people will have enemies. Jesus, however, commands that his followers not only not retaliate against their enemies, but he even says we must love our enemies. In doing so he does not promise if we turn the other cheek that we will not be hit again.[21] Nonretaliation is not a strategy to get what we want by other means. Rather Jesus calls us to practice nonretaliation because that is the form that God's care of us took in his cross.

The eschatological character of the Sermon is nowhere more apparent than in Jesus's charge that we are not to retaliate against those who seek to do us harm as well as his demand that we are to

---

19. Bonhoeffer, *Discipleship*, 127. In *Letters and Papers from Prison* (New York: Touchstone, 1971), 376, Bonhoeffer observes that "the essence of chastity is not the suppression of lust, but the total orientation of one's life toward a goal. Without such a goal, chastity is bound to become ridiculous. Chastity is the *sine qua non* of lucidity and concentration."

20. Ibid., 131.

21. Yoder reflects on the command to love the enemy in numerous places in his work, but one of my favorites is his chapter "The Way of Peace in a World at War," in *He Came Preaching Peace* (Scottdale, PA: Herald, 1985), 17–29.

love our enemies. To so live requires the patience made possible through the cross. It is the patience that animates those blessed in the Beatitudes, that is, blessed are they who have time in an unmerciful world to be merciful. To be a disciple of Jesus, to be ready to be reconciled with those with whom we are angry, to be faithful in marriage, to take the time necessary to tell the truth are habits that create the time and space to be capable of loving our enemies.

Yoder therefore argues that the patience required by the Beatitudes and the antitheses makes no sense if, as we are told in the Revelation of John, it is not true that "the lamb that was slain is worthy to receive power!" The heart of the Sermon on the Mount is the conviction

> that the cross and not the sword, suffering and not brute power determine the meaning of history. The key to the obedience of God's people is not their effectiveness but their patience. The triumph of the right is assured not by the might that comes to the aid of the right, which is of course the justification of the use of violence and other kinds of power in every human conflict. The triumph of the right, although it is assured, is sure because of the power of the resurrection and not because of any calculation of causes and effects, nor because of the inherently greater strength of the good guys. The relationship between the obedience of God's people and the triumph of God's cause is not a relationship between cause and effect but one of cross and resurrection.[22]

Yoder and Bonhoeffer, therefore, unapologetically maintain that we are called to be perfect. Perfection, however, does not mean that we are sinless or that we are free of anger or lust. Rather, to be perfect is to learn to be part of a people who have the time to take the time to live without resort to violence to sustain their existence. To so live requires habits like learning to tell one another the truth, to be faithful in our promises to one another, to seek reconciliation. To so live can be called pacifism and/or nonviolence, but such descriptions do not do justice to the form of life described in the Beatitudes and antitheses. The form

22. Yoder, *Politics of Jesus*, 232.

of life to which the Beatitudes and antitheses point is possible if it is true that "in Christ the Crucified and his community, the 'extraordinary' occurs."[23]

Bonhoeffer is well aware that this way of reading the Sermon on the Mount has been challenged by those who have sought to be responsible for the social order. For example, Frederick Dale Bruner commenting on the command not to take oaths observes that obedience "to this Command will eventually raise serious questions about how far disciples can participate in government service where oaths are frequently required and administered. What of military service and its oaths?"[24] That question has often been answered by drawing a distinction between responding to injury done to one personally and harm done that affects one as a bearer of an office. Personally, I am to act as Jesus would have me act, but to the extent I bear the responsibility for maintaining order I am obligated to use violence in the name of that order.

Bonhoeffer observes, however, that the distinction between the private person and the bearer of an office is unknown to Jesus. Indeed such a distinction leads to the invisibility that the Sermon on the Mount challenges. We are never a private person but, Bonhoeffer argues, we exist as people constituted by responsibilities. Yet Jesus asks his disciples to leave behind even their responsibilities as sons to follow him. Such a leaving is necessary if evil is to be resisted with the weapons of the Spirit. Those weapons, moreover, are those shaped by the suffering of the cross:

> Only those who there, in the cross of Jesus, find faith in the victory over evil can obey his command, and that is the only kind of obedience which has the promise. Which promise? The promise of community with the cross of Jesus and of community with his victory. . . . In the cross alone is it true and real that suffering love is the retribution for and the overcoming of evil. Participation in the cross is given to the disciples by the call into discipleship. They are blessed in this visible community.[25]

23. Bonhoeffer, *Discipleship*, 145.
24. Frederick Dale Brunner, *The Christbook: Matthew 1–12*, rev. ed. (Grand Rapids: Eerdmans, 2004), 235.
25. Bonhoeffer, *Discipleship*, 136–37.

Practicing Prayer

I have argued that Bonhoeffer and Yoder share a common commitment to recover the visibility of the church. I have tried to exhibit how that commitment works by displaying how they read Matthew 5. However, there are two more chapters to the Sermon on the Mount. Moreover Matthew 6 begins by warning against practicing our piety before others in order to be seen. How are we to understand Jesus telling us in 5:16 that our light should shine before others and that we are to give alms in secret? Bonhoeffer argues that this is not a contradiction if we attend to whom the visibility of discipleship is to be kept hidden. According to Bonhoeffer the hiddenness that should characterize the disciple's action applies to the disciple. The disciple should "keep on following Jesus, and should keep looking forward to him who is going before them, but not at themselves and what they are doing. The righteousness of the disciples is hidden from themselves."[26]

As far as I know Yoder does not comment on Jesus's admonition against the display of piety, but the general thrust of his position is quite similar to Bonhoeffer's suggestion that the hiddenness required is that peculiar to the disciple's way of life. Yoder, like Bonhoeffer, has little use for pietistic accounts of the Christian life. Their common christological focus means that attention is directed to Jesus, not to ourselves. Therefore, for Yoder, following Jesus requires that we lose our overpowering sense of self. Such a loss often accompanies participation in a grand movement, but the kind of forgetfulness required to follow Jesus is different from that which is for a time exhilarating but lost through time. Rather the forgetfulness Jesus makes possible is that constituted by the reality of the kingdom, which makes possible our participation in God's time.[27]

Bonhoeffer, therefore, suggests that "the genuine deed of love is always a deed hidden to myself."[28] Jesus calls us not to attend to our own goodness or our loves, but rather to follow him. Not to let our left hand know what our right hand does when alms

26. Ibid., 149.
27. Yoder, *Original Revolution*, 31–33.
28. Bonhoeffer, *Discipleship*, 151.

are given is possible only by the overwhelming that comes from Jesus's call to discipleship. We can give only what we have been given. Our overwhelming comes as a gift through our being called to follow the one who alone knows and therefore can make known the Father.

Jesus directs our attention to prayer as the discipline necessary for becoming a disciple, for when we pray we no longer know ourselves, but, Bonhoeffer observes, we know only God to whom we call. Prayer is part of the hiddenness because prayer is directed solely to God.[29] That is why Jesus tells us to pray to God "in secret" and why the Father will reward us "in secret." To so pray requires that we pray to the one whom Jesus makes known. Discipleship and prayer are inseparable because Jesus is the Father's prayer for us. Thus Jesus taught his disciples not only how they should pray, but what they should pray.

Bonhoeffer argues that we should not be surprised that after teaching us to pray Jesus advises that we fast. To be a disciple "requires strict external discipline."[30] Fasting is a necessary discipline for prayer, because satiated flesh is unwilling to pray. Fasting, moreover, is the necessary discipline for us to learn to live without security, without storing up treasures. To so live means, as Yoder argues, that we must learn to live depending on others. Indeed the whole purpose of the Sermon is to teach us that we cannot live alone, but rather we must trust one another if we are to live as disciples of Christ.

It is, therefore, not surprising that the Sermon on the Mount concludes with a description of how those who would follow Jesus must live together. Bonhoeffer puts it this way: "The fifth chapter spoke of the extraordinariness of discipleship, while the sixth chapter spoke of the disciples as hidden, in simple righteousness. In both aspects the disciples were separated from the community to which they had previously belonged and bound solely to Jesus. The boundary became clearly visible."[31] But this boundary might tempt the disciples to believe that their being set apart gives them

29. Ibid., 153.
30. Ibid., 159.
31. Ibid., 176.

special rights or authority. Jesus's admonition against judging challenges anyone who might draw such a conclusion. The disciples, no more than the lilies of the field, are to judge as God judges.

The disciples are not to judge, because any judgment that needs to be made has been made, for those who follow Jesus cannot presume to determine what is good and what is evil on their own. The appropriate stance for the acknowledgment of evil is the confession of sin. We quite literally cannot see clearly unless we have been trained to see "the log that is in our eye." But it is not possible for us to see what is in our eye because the eye cannot see itself. That is why we are able to see ourselves only through the vision made possible by Jesus.

If we are to follow Jesus we are required to recognize that the one I am tempted to judge is, like me, a person who has received the forgiveness manifest in the cross. The recognition that the other person is, like me, in need of forgiveness prevents those who would follow Jesus from trying to force others to follow Jesus. It means quite simply that disciples are not called to be effective, to make the world conform to the gospel, but rather the disciples are schooled in patience—which means, as Bonhoeffer puts it, that the gospel is not a "conquering idea" that neither knows nor respects resistance. Rather "the Word of God is so weak that it suffers to be despised and rejected by people. For the Word, there are such things as hardened hearts and locked doors. The Word accepts the resistance it encounters and bears it."[32]

Bonhoeffer and Yoder were pacifists, but as I suggest above, this description is inadequate. "Pacifism" suggests a position that can be abstracted from what it means to be a disciple of Jesus. Bonhoeffer and Yoder understand nonresistance to be the refusal to respond to evil in kind, but to resist evil by using the weapons provided by the Sermon on the Mount.[33] To so live requires our willingness to join Jesus on a journey that takes place on a road called discipleship. Jesus does not try to entice us to undertake the journey by telling us it will be easy or that many will join us on the way. Rather he tells us that the gate is narrow and that the

32. Ibid., 136.
33. For Yoder's account of nonresistance, see *Original Revolution*, 48–49.

road is hard. Even worse, the journey will be made more difficult by false prophets who are quite good at disguising themselves as fellow travelers. Bonhoeffer bluntly tells us:

> To give witness to and to confess the truth of Jesus, but to love the enemy of this truth, who is his enemy and our enemy, with the unconditional love of Jesus Christ—that is the narrow road. To believe in Jesus' promise that those who follow shall posses the earth, but to encounter the enemy unarmed, to prefer suffering injustice to doing ill—that is the narrow road. To perceive other people as being weak and wrong, but to never judge them; to proclaim the good news to them, but never to throw pearls before swine—that is a narrow road. It is an unbearable road.[34]

When Jesus had finished "saying these things" the crowds were "astonished." Bonhoeffer and Yoder, however, make clear that Jesus does not want our admiration. What Jesus has taught, who Jesus is, requires nothing less than our lives. We cannot serve two masters. Like those Athenians who heard Paul preach, we would like to respond to Jesus's Sermon saying, "We will hear you again about this." But Jesus teaches as one having authority. That authority, moreover, extends to asking us to be willing to lose our lives for his sake (Matt. 16:25). Bonhoeffer and Yoder defeat all attempts to separate the Sermon on the Mount from the one who alone had the authority to preach the Sermon. I am convinced that they have taught us why and how the Sermon must be read if the church is to be seen to be a visible alternative to the world.

---

34. Bonhoeffer, *Discipleship*, 176.

Pope John Paul II and Leonardo Boff

William T. Cavanaugh

11

The two figures discussed in this essay represent opposite ends of theological opinion within the Catholic Church. Pope John Paul II is regarded by many as a saint, both for his personal sanctity and for his forceful leadership of the church, a beacon of clarity amid confusion. Leonardo Boff is regarded by others as a martyr, a tireless advocate for the downtrodden who was silenced by John Paul II and eventually hounded out of the priesthood.[1] Partisans on both sides of this issue tend to reduce it to a simple morality play, either of the wise and courageous pastor protecting the flock from a grandstanding communist or of the power-hungry defender of the status quo throwing the prophet down a well. Neither of these caricatures does justice to the case, of course, in part because John Paul II and Boff share so much in their views

---

1. Boff was summoned before Joseph Ratzinger (who has since become Pope Benedict XVI, but was then in charge of the Congregation for the Doctrine of the Faith) in 1984 to answer charges stemming from his 1981 book *Igreja: carisma e poder*, published in English as *Church: Charism and Power*, trans. John W. Diercksmeier (New York: Continuum, 1985). The book argues for a liberation of the church from the grip of ecclesiastical abuses of power. In 1985, the congregation imposed a one-year period of silence on Boff. He left the Franciscan order and the priesthood in 1992.

of modern society and its ills. Both speak out forcefully against contemporary abuses of the dignity and rights of human persons. Both look out at the world and decry what John Paul II called "the culture of death." Where they differ profoundly is in their theological diagnoses of the problem.

The Sermon on the Mount is a good place to compare and contrast these two figures. Both consider it to be the heart of Jesus's moral teaching and therefore the key to the resolution of social ills. Their treatments of law and eros in the Sermon on the Mount provide good examples of their views. Their theological differences over the Sermon on the Mount may be seen in terms of their contrasting diagnoses of the evils of modern society.

Law

When Boff reads the Sermon on the Mount, he is inclined to ignore the way Matthew presents Jesus as the new Moses and concentrate instead on Matthew's depiction of Jesus as the scourge of the Pharisees. For Boff, the Sermon on the Mount is in fundamental discontinuity with the Judaism of Jesus's day:

> In the Jewish religion at the time of Jesus, everything was prescribed and determined, first relations with God and then relations among human beings. Conscience felt itself oppressed by insupportable legal prescriptions. Jesus raises an impressive protest against all such human enslavement in the name of law. . . . [For Jesus] the law possesses merely a human function: one of order, one of creating the possibilities for harmony and understanding among human beings. Because of this, the norms of the Sermon on the Mount presuppose love, a new person free for greater things.[2]

The problem is not limited to Jesus's day; for Boff, Pharisaism is a perennial problem inherent in the nature of law itself. The church has, throughout the history of the West, erroneously equated "a morality of laws and commandments with the Sermon on the

2. Leonardo Boff, *Jesus Christ Liberator: A Critical Christology for Our Time*, trans. Patrick Hughes (London: SPCK, 1980), 63.

Mount."[3] For Boff, there is something deeply problematic about the Old Testament itself in its emphasis on the law. In his book on the Lord's Prayer, he goes so far as to make the Marcionite-sounding claim: "The God of Jesus is no longer the God of the Torah, the Law. He is the God of mercy, of unlimited goodness, and of patience for the weak who recognize that they are weak and start on the road back to God."[4]

At least once Boff calls the law a "crutch" and implies that it can be discarded once the person is healthy.[5] Usually, however, Boff does not dismiss the law entirely. Law has the human function of creating order and therefore the possibility of cooperation among people.[6] Nevertheless, law is essentially negative, a necessary evil. In his book on St. Francis of Assisi, Boff applauds Francis's rule for employing a "minimum of law and a maximum of spirituality."[7] Francis recognized the "constant tension between the Gospel and the rule, between the Sermon on the Mount and the order."[8] According to Boff, Francis acknowledged the necessity of the two poles, but always held primarily to the former in each pair.

What is most crucial about the Sermon on the Mount for Boff is the way that it displays Jesus's complete freedom before the law. The lesson of the six antitheses from Matthew 5:21–48 is the "liberty and nonconformity" of Jesus with regard to the law.[9] Boff would not like the language of "hypertheses" that some scholars use for these six sayings of Jesus, because he does not see Jesus as simply ratcheting up the demands of the law. This is why Boff finds wanting some of the typical responses to the Sermon on the Mount: the norms are there to break our pride, or Jesus is

3. Ibid., 41.

4. Leonardo Boff, *The Lord's Prayer: The Prayer of Integral Liberation*, trans. Theodore Morrow (Maryknoll, NY: Orbis, 1983), 92.

5. Boff, *Jesus Christ Liberator*, 76–77: "The golden rule is: treat others as you would like them to treat you (Matt. 7:12). The distinction between pure and impure no longer exists outside of the human person, but depends on you, on the intentions of your heart, wherein lies the root of your actions. In this regard, the support given by the crutch of law no longer exists."

6. Ibid., 70–71.

7. Leonardo Boff, *St. Francis: A Model for Human Liberation*, trans. John W. Diercksmeier (New York: Crossroad, 1989), 101.

8. Ibid., 156.

9. Boff, *Jesus Christ Liberator*, 68.

focused on intention only, or the norms are meant as an interim ethic. According to Boff, all these solutions see the Sermon on the Mount as a more severe law, and they despair of trying to fulfill its demands.[10] For Boff, the message of the Sermon on the Mount is this: "The love that saves is superior to all laws and reduces all norms to absurdity."[11] This liberty before the law does not release people to libertinism, however, but rather equips them for love, which creates even stronger bonds among people than does the law. For example, one is free to work on the Sabbath if it is to help someone; those who profane the Sabbath for frivolous reasons are condemned.[12] When the primacy of love over law is recognized, the individual subject is free to bend the law to the higher purpose of love: "The clear and juridical vision of the law no longer exists. Jesus offers a clear objective, expressed in the Sermon on the Mount: an objective of total giving that will demand exertion, generosity, responsibility, creativity, and initiative on our part. Jesus permits us to observe traditions insofar as they do not harm but favor the principal objective (Matt. 5:19–20; 23:23)."[13] Along with Boff's antinomianism comes a dose of what he calls "ecclesiological skepticism," that is, readiness to accept the fallibility of church structures.[14]

The fifth chapter of Boff's influential book *Jesus Christ Liberator* bears the title "Jesus, a Person of Extraordinary Good Sense, Creative Imagination, and Originality." Boff cites with approval Ernst Käsemann's declaration that Jesus was a "liberal," because he interpreted the law, Scriptures, and dogmatics from the point of view of love.[15] Jesus does not deal in "prefabricated notions."[16] According to Boff, Jesus does not "theologize" or appeal to "superior moral principles" or engage in casuistry. His words rather

10. Ibid., 70.
11. Ibid., 71.
12. Ibid., 67–68.
13. Ibid., 77.
14. Ibid., 44. For a more extended critique of church structure, see Boff, *Church: Charism and Power*.
15. Boff, *Jesus Christ Liberator*, 94. The reference is to Ernst Käsemann's chapter "Was Jesus Liberal?" in his *Der Ruf der Freiheit* (Tübingen: Mohr, 1968); see *Jesus Means Freedom* (Philadelphia: Fortress, 1970) for English translation.
16. Boff, *Jesus Christ Liberator*, 93.

"bite into the concrete world," forcing us to make a decision.[17] The attributes of creativity and imagination are meant to apply not only to Jesus, but to his followers as well: "Imagination postulates creativity, spontaneity, and liberty. It is precisely this that Christ demands when he proposes an ideal like the Sermon on the Mount."[18] Boff puts a lot of emphasis on personal decision as the context within which creativity and freedom are exercised in the moral life. According to Boff, Jesus himself never used the word *obedience*, though it appears eighty-seven times in the New Testament:[19] "Obedience for him is not a question of fulfilling orders, but a firm decision in favor of what God demands within a concrete situation. The will of God is not always manifested in the law. Normally it reveals itself in the concrete situation where conscience is caught unawares by a proposal that demands a response."[20]

Jesus's teaching demands a decision of each individual, but according to Boff, Jesus does not make demands based on higher authority. Jesus's teachings "possess an internal evidence."[21] Rabbis appeal to Scripture; Jesus appeals to experience: "He draws his doctrine from the common experiences that all live and can verify. His listeners understand immediately. The only presuppositions demanded of them are good sense and sound reason."[22] Boff continues by citing examples from the Sermon on the Mount: everyone knows that a city on a hill cannot be hidden (Matt. 5:14), that each day has its

17. Ibid., 81–82.

18. Ibid., 95.

19. For how Boff deals with various texts that apparently contradict this claim, see ibid., 305n11.

20. Ibid., 92. Let me cite a couple more examples of Boff's emphasis on decision: "Obedience is a question of having our eyes open to the situation; it consists in deciding for and risking ourselves in the adventure of responding to God who speaks here and now. The Sermon on the Mount, which is not a law, is addressed to everyone, inviting us to have extremely clear consciences and an unlimited capacity for understanding people, sympathizing with them, being tuned into them, and loving them with all their limitations and realizations" (93). "Security does not come from a minute observance of the laws and unreserved adherence to social and religious structures, but from the vigor of one's interior decision and from the responsible autonomy of those who know what they want and why they live" (78).

21. Ibid., 83.

22. Ibid., 82.

troubles (6:34), that we cannot turn a single hair white or black (5:36), that we cannot add an hour to our lives (6:27), that people are worth more than birds (6:26), and so on.[23] Jesus says "rational things that people can understand and live."[24] Christ did not come to bring a new morality, but merely to bring to light what people already knew, but had lost because of their alienation.[25] Here we see Boff's democratic impulses in play. Boff does not wish the revolution that Jesus brings—the kingdom of God—to be something esoteric, something in which the common people are not invested. What Christ brings to the people is much like what Paulo Freire's pedagogue brings: the ability to discover latent possibilities in oneself.[26] The liberation of the oppressed is not a matter of heteronomy, obedience to something or someone wholly other than oneself, but rather the discovering in oneself of one's own proper autonomy, one's own law. Christ, therefore, is not wholly other than common humanity, but the fulfillment of humanity's potential. In his teaching, Christ "joins the long line of great sages" who occupied themselves with the nature of humanity.[27] The divinity of Christ is discovered in his "extraordinary good sense, in his singularly creative imagination, and in his unequalled originality."[28] Christ's divinity seems to be a quantitative, not a qualitative, leap from the human.

The radicality of Jesus is therefore based in the mundane; the Sermon on the Mount tells us what we already knew, but had been unable to see. There is a strong sort of natural law in Boff, although he does not use that term, perhaps because of his aversion to law in general. The terms he does use are "good sense" and "sound reason." The command to love our enemies is an example of these, for all can see that the rain falls on the good and bad alike.[29] Boff assumes that, with the exercise of

23. Ibid., 82–83.
24. Ibid., 83.
25. Ibid.
26. See Paulo Freire, *Pedagogy of the Oppressed*, trans. Myra Bergman Ramos (New York: Continuum, 1970), esp. chaps. 1–2. The relationship, of course, is not coincidental. Freire's work had a tremendous impact on the development of liberation theology in Brazil and throughout Latin America.
27. Boff, *Jesus Christ Liberator*, 84.
28. Ibid., 97.
29. Ibid., 84–85.

sound reason, people will see that the love of enemies naturally follows the common observation that rain falls on all alike. Boff often writes of the immediacy of Jesus's message, such that his followers grasp his meaning without the need for training or learning or discipline. For Boff, there is no need for community practices of training in the virtues. Jesus "emancipates the message of God from its connection to one religious community and directs it to all people of good will."[30] Boff's version of natural law, he believes, allows the true spontaneity of Jesus to blossom in each person.

The contrast with Pope John Paul II is stark. When John Paul II discusses the Sermon on the Mount, it is almost always in the context of law. The verse from the Sermon that he seems to quote most frequently is Matthew 5:17: "Do not think that I have come to abolish the law or the prophets; I have come not to abolish but to fulfill."[31] The starting point for John Paul II's discussion of the Sermon on the Mount is typically its relationship to the Decalogue. When John Paul II gave a homily in March 2000 on the Mount of the Beatitudes in Israel, traditional site of the Sermon on the Mount, he immediately began talking of how Jesus's listeners would have had the memory of another mountain in their hearts: "These two mountains—Sinai and the Mount of the Beatitudes— offer us the roadmap of our Christian life and a summary of our responsibilities to God and neighbour."[32] The Ten Commandments may seem negative, the pope says, but in fact they point positively forward to the law of love. After citing Matthew 5:17, the pope said that the Sermon on the Mount "leads what went before to its fullest potential."[33]

---

30. Ibid., 98.

31. For examples, see John Paul II, "General Audience, 1 March 2000" §5, http:// www.vatican.va/holy_father/john_paul_ii/audiences/2000/documents/hf_jp-ii_aud_ 20000301_en.html; idem, "Address at Devotion to the Sacred Heart of Jesus, Sunday, 6 June 1999" §3, http://www.vatican.va/holy_father/john_paul_ii/travels/documents/ hf_jp-ii_hom_06061999_elblag_en.html; idem, "General Audience, 7 April 1999" §3, http://www.vatican.va/holy_father/john_paul_ii/audiences/1999/documents/hf_jp-ii_ aud_07041999_en.html.

32. "Homily of John Paul II, Israel—Korazim, Mount of the Beatitudes" §2, http:// www.vatican.va/holy_father/john_paul_ii/travels/documents/hf_jp-ii_hom_20000324_ korazim-israel_en.html.

33. Ibid.

This fulfillment of the law is by no means a superseding of law. John Paul II observed that in the Sermon on the Mount "the Ten Commandments make themselves heard through [Jesus's] voice."[34] Furthermore, "we cannot think of being faithful to God if we do not observe his Law."[35] In his *Catechesis on the Sermon on the Mount*, John Paul II made clear that the fulfillment of the law must fully correspond to the meaning of the exterior norms of the individual precepts of the Decalogue: "Only this fulfillment constructs that justice which God the Legislator willed."[36] At the same time, the Sermon on the Mount penetrates into the "depth" of each of the norms to "descend within the man-subject of morality."[37] Jesus overcame the legalism of the old law, but the problem was not with the old law itself. The problem was with a kind of casuistry that built up around the old law and concentrated on finding or closing loopholes in the exterior observance of the law. In the Sermon on the Mount, Christ shifts the emphasis to the "interior man," without, however, simply doing away with the exterior precepts.[38]

John Paul II develops this view of the law most extensively in his 1993 encyclical on the foundations of moral theology entitled *Veritatis Splendor*. The pope begins his account of the moral life with the story of the rich young man, taken from Matthew's Gospel. Jesus first tells the young man that he must keep the commandments. This is necessary but not sufficient, for the commandments themselves point forward to the new covenant, fulfilled in Christ himself. In the Sermon on the Mount, which *Veritatis Splendor* calls "the *magna charta* of Gospel morality," "Jesus brings God's commandments to fulfillment . . . by interiorizing their demands and by bringing out their fullest meaning. Love of neighbor springs from a loving heart which, precisely because it loves, is ready to live out the loftiest challenges."[39] John Paul II continues on to say

34. John Paul II, "General Audience, 1 March 2000" §5.
35. Ibid., §2.
36. John Paul II, *Blessed Are the Pure of Heart: Catechesis on the Sermon on the Mount and Writings of St. Paul* (Boston: St. Paul Books, 1983), 21.
37. Ibid., 23.
38. Ibid., 24, 91–92.
39. John Paul II, *Veritatis Splendor* [The splendor of truth] (Boston: St. Paul Books, 1993), §15.

that the commandments are not to be understood negatively as a minimum limit to human action, but rather as pointing forward toward the perfection of love.[40] The "Sermon on the Mount demonstrates the openness of the commandments and their orientation toward the horizon of the perfection proper to the Beatitudes."[41]

The overcoming of legalism by love leaves the commandments behind, but not in the sense of inaugurating a kind of individual creativity or looseness with regard to the law. Love leaves the commandments behind only in the sense that the commandments abide as a kind of foundation out of which the perfection of love develops in a more advanced direction. *Veritatis Splendor* develops these reflections in the context of a response to objections of "physicalism" against traditional Catholic moral theology. Some moral theologians argue that the moral species of an act cannot be determined by the physical act itself; its meaning is determined by the freedom of the moral subject, taking into account the intention and circumstances of the act.[42] For John Paul II, however, the fulfillment of the law does not mean flexibility with regard to the law. The negative precepts of the law are universally valid and allow of no exceptions, regardless of the circumstances. This does not mean that positive precepts are less important than the negative ones. It is simply that "the commandment of love of God and neighbor does not have in its dynamic any higher limit, but it does have a lower limit, beneath which the commandment is broken."[43] The interiorization of the law in the Sermon on the Mount is not to be understood as putting the human subject in the place of legislator or judge of the law. It is rather a more complete conformity of the whole person to the law, a conformity of the heart to the law, so that the law may be practiced more perfectly. As John Paul II emphasizes, the gift of grace in Jesus Christ "does not lessen but reinforces the moral demands of love."[44]

40. Ibid.
41. Ibid., §16.
42. Ibid., §§47–48.
43. Ibid., §52.
44. Ibid., §24. See also John Paul II, "General Audience, 7 April 1999," whose theme is the demanding nature of God's love and how the Sermon on the Mount reinforces those demands.

For John Paul II, there is no abrupt discontinuity between different epochs of the law. There is rather a progressive penetration of the law, and therefore of love, into the human person, beginning at creation with the natural law, proceeding through the covenant at Sinai, and reaching its summit in the Sermon on the Mount.[45] The natural law is not superseded any more than the old law is. It remains "the light of understanding infused in us by God, whereby we know what must be done and what must be avoided."[46] The pope is careful to emphasize, however, that the natural law does not make a person his or her own legislator. The natural law is simply the eternal law implanted in rational beings; practical reason is essentially *responsive* to the promptings of God's law in the human conscience. Reason must therefore be enlightened by revelation, beginning with the commandments on Sinai.[47] The "rightful autonomy" that the natural law creates in the human person therefore "cannot mean that reason itself creates values and moral norms."[48] The pope's concern here is to counteract what he calls a "'creative' understanding of moral conscience" in the work of some moral theologians. Such theologians argue that the complexity of different situations and the rigidity of moral norms requires a certain flexibility in making use of those norms. Norms provide a general perspective, but cannot replace the importance of personal free *decision*. Moral discernment is not just a matter of response and judgment, but decision; there is a creative moment in conscience, allowing for the possibility of exceptions to the norms, not simply the application of general norms to particular cases.[49] John Paul II rejects the "creative" conscience as in fact a recapitulation of the attitude of the Pharisee in Luke 18:9–14. The Pharisee is self-justified, finding a subjective justification for each of his actions.[50] Thus, in an interesting twist, John Paul II throws the charge of Pharisaism back on those who believe that

45. John Paul II, *Veritatis Splendor* §12.
46. Ibid. Here John Paul II is quoting from Thomas Aquinas's *In duo praecepta caritatis et in cecem legis praecepta*.
47. Ibid., §44.
48. Ibid., §40.
49. Ibid., §§54–56.
50. Ibid., §§104–5.

the Sermon on the Mount introduces a new flexibility with regard to the law.

In his discussion of freedom in *Veritatis Splendor*, John Paul II emphasizes that the rich young man's commitment to abide by all the moral demands of the Decalogue is the "absolutely essential ground" in which love and the desire for perfection can take root.[51] Authentic freedom, therefore, depends on the maturity that can be gained only by obedience to the law. There can be no opposition of freedom and law. Freedom is not the merely negative absence of limits. It is rather a positive disposition toward the truth, embodied in God's law: "Man's genuine moral autonomy in no way means the rejection but rather the acceptance of the moral law."[52] God's law is not imposed on humans heteronomously, but rather human beings come to the fullest realization of their freedom by what *Veritatis Splendor* calls "participated theonomy," that is, the real participation of the human person in God's law.[53] In John Paul II's view, the more one is caught up in the will of God, manifested in God's eternal law, the freer one is.

Eros

Pope John Paul II's "Catechesis on the Sermon on the Mount and Writings of St. Paul" was published in English under the title *Blessed Are the Pure of Heart*. The catechesis was presented by the pope as a series of weekly general audiences early in his pontificate, from April 16, 1980, to May 6, 1981. To call it a "Catechesis on the Sermon on the Mount" is a little misleading, because it is actually focused on just two verses, Matthew 5:27–28, which deal with lust as adultery in the heart. The pope, however, does not regard these verses as dealing with just one isolated issue, but sees in them a key to understanding the whole of the Sermon on the Mount and Jesus's ethical teaching in general. What Jesus does is to drive the law deep into our hearts, so that every true desire is ultimately a desire for God.

51. Ibid., §17.
52. Ibid., §41.
53. Ibid.

A controversy erupted over the pope's remarks in his general audience of October 8, 1980. John Paul II stated that a man could commit adultery in the heart with regard to his own wife if he looked upon her lustfully.[54] The secular media worldwide reported the story with barely concealed eye-rolling, more evidence of the Catholic Church's phobia of sexuality and hatred of the body. For John Paul II, however, the point was precisely the opposite. Because the "body manifests the spirit,"[55] it cannot be reduced to something merely physical. Adultery in the heart can take place even within marriage if the man treats his wife "only as an object to satisfy instinct."[56] Lust is the objectification of the other[57] and is therefore the opposite of true desire. True desire seeks to unite, rather than divide into relations of objectification and domination. As John Paul II puts it, concupiscence is "an interior separation from the nuptial meaning of the body."[58]

This account of desire has implications beyond sexual ethics, for the body is a manifestation of the spirit for John Paul II. The central point toward which John Paul II drives is the status of the heart. The purity of heart to which Jesus refers in the Beatitudes (Matt. 5:8) is the key to the redemption of the body and indeed redemption in general: the "good is 'purity of heart,' of which Christ speaks in the same context of the Sermon on the Mount. From the biblical point of view, 'purity of heart' means freedom from every kind of sin and guilt, and not just from sins that concern the 'lust of the flesh.'"[59] Purity of heart for John Paul II is not just an attempt to fight against natural desires. Indeed what is most

---

54. John Paul II, *Blessed Are the Pure of Heart*, 142–49. *L'osservatore romano's* response to the controversy is reprinted on pages 150–52.

55. Ibid., 162.

56. Ibid., 145. John Paul II stays with the example of a man lusting after a woman and does not write directly about the opposite case, presumably because Jesus's own example is of the man's lust for the woman. In his response in *L'osservatore romano*, Claudio Sorgi represents the pope's remarks as a defense of the dignity of women over against those men who would objectify and use them. Sorgi adds, "Obviously what is said of the man with regard to the woman also holds true vice versa" (152). This is a plausible interpretation of the pope's intent, since he stresses the mutual donation of the marriage relationship.

57. Ibid., 130.

58. Ibid., 123.

59. Ibid., 256; also see 198–204.

natural, what is embedded in the depths of the heart from creation, is the desire for purity and union:

> The words of Christ, who in the Sermon on the Mount appeals to the "heart," induce the listener, in a way, to this interior call. If he lets them act in him, he will be able to hear within him at the same time almost the echo of that "beginning," that good "beginning" to which Christ refers on another occasion, to remind his listeners who man is, who woman is, and who we are for each other in the work of creation.[60]

The heart is not just the locus of adultery, then, but also the locus of a deeper attraction to the good, a deep desire to return to the beginning, to return to an original union with others. The heart is the locus of a truly erotic desire.[61] John Paul II acknowledges the common tendency to reduce eros to its bodily, sensual meaning. Eros is commonly reduced to lust. The pope, on the other hand, refers to the Platonic definition of eros as the force that compels the human spirit toward what is true and good and beautiful. In this sense the ethos of Jesus is not opposed to eros; indeed, it is lust that is opposed to eros: "If we admit that 'eros' means the interior force that 'attracts' man towards what is true and good and beautiful, then, within the sphere of this concept, the way towards what Christ wished to express in the Sermon on the Mount, can also be seen to open."[62] Eros and ethos are not opposed to each other, but meet in the human heart. The pope emphasizes that the Sermon on the Mount is not primarily negative, not primarily about prohibitions, but is about eros for "the really deep and essential values"[63] and, ultimately, eros for God.

It is instructive to compare this account with Boff's discussion of eros in his book on St. Francis, who, Boff says, "places us immediately before the Gospel and the Sermon on the Mount."[64] For Boff, Francis is a model for the integration of logos and eros. For too long the world has been ruled by logos, that is, instrumental-

60. Ibid., 173.
61. Ibid., 176–83.
62. Ibid., 180–81.
63. Ibid., 181–82.
64. Boff, *St. Francis*, 155.

technocratic rationality, to the detriment of pathos, or sympathy, and eros, defined as "fraternal communication and tenderness."[65] Boff wants to get beyond the battle between affectivity and reason, love and power, and integrate the two. Indeed, integration and union is the driving force of eros, which is why eros is more elemental and prior to reason: "In the beginning is Eros and not Logos."[66] Eros is not just passion, but *com*passion, an entering into communion: "What is proper to Eros is to unite subject with object; but to unite with compassion, with enthusiasm, with desire. There is fire and heat in Eros. Everything that is tied to Eros must see with fantasy, with creativity, bursting forth toward the new, the surprising, the wonderful."[67] Rather than set up an opposition between lust and eros, as does John Paul II, Boff distinguishes between sex and eros, which he says are related, but not the same thing. Sex pursues gratification and the relief of tension, while eros expresses itself supremely in oblative love, a concern for and service of the other for the other's own sake. Boff alters the Platonic formulation somewhat, with eros as that which compels us toward "the higher, the more beautiful, the more true, the more just, and the more human."[68] Despite the addition of the human to the transcendentals, Boff acknowledges the Platonic-Augustinian tradition of eros as that which pushes us toward God and toward ecstasy.[69]

The rule of eros over logos does not mean the vanquishing of logos. The potentially destructive enthusiasm of eros needs to be disciplined by logos, but when logos is brought into the service of eros—and not vice versa—the result is a combination of gentleness and strength. The creative spontaneity of eros issues in fidelity.[70] For Boff, St. Francis is the epitome of this happy accord between logos and eros. Francis's asceticism, for example, is the channeling of his insatiable desire by the discipline of logos. It is crucial for

65. Ibid., 6.
66. Ibid., 13. Though this seems to overturn the priority of the logos in John 1, Boff does not appear to have the christological connotations of logos in mind here. Boff appears to be using the term *logos* as a general principle of instrumental reason.
67. Ibid., 11.
68. Ibid., 12.
69. Ibid.
70. Ibid., 12–14, 18–19.

Boff, however, that channeling is not denial. Boff understands the harsh penances that Francis imposed on himself as the necessary means of directing his powerful eros outward toward God. Boff rejects the ideal of the saint as one who has achieved perfect self-control. Francis achieves sainthood not through a rigid repression of the passions, but a joyful acceptance of eros and a deliberate redirection of eros toward union with God, with others, and with all of creation.[71] Thus Francis "achieved in his life the utopia of the Sermon on the Mount through his version of true joy."[72]

The similarities between Boff's and John Paul II's treatments of eros in the Sermon on the Mount are quite striking. They agree that Jesus's ethic is not about prohibition of evil but attraction to the good. In both there is a sense that the Sermon on the Mount penetrates more deeply into the affective nature of the human person, touching on the deepest longing for union with God and with others. Both see eros as primary, as if the entire drama of human life is a tugging at the heart, not an obligation to be fulfilled, but a desire to go the extra mile.

The differences between the two accounts are also instructive. For John Paul II, human eros is essentially responsive: "The moral life presents itself as the response due to the many gratuitous initiatives taken by God out of love for man."[73] Eros is a pull from God, a response to the eternal law, revealed in its perfection in the Sermon on the Mount. We return to God along the well-worn channels of a law that has been revealed in history and inscribed on human hearts. For Boff, eros is essentially creative, not simply responsive. The journey to God is not a turning back, but a leap ahead into newness and creativity. Eros is a push from something innate in human desire.

This difference is manifest in the way each figure views the relationship of freedom and discipline in the moral life. John Paul II looks rather more favorably than Boff upon the idea of self-control. John Paul II stresses: "It is precisely at the price of self-control that man reaches that deeper and more mature spon-

71. Ibid., 20–22, 130–35.
72. Ibid., 139.
73. John Paul II, *Veritatis Splendor* §10.

taneity with which his 'heart,' mastering his instincts, rediscovers the spiritual beauty of the sign constituted by the human body in its masculinity and femininity."[74] As we have seen, Boff does not think that eros should go untamed. But he does think of spontaneity as something to be liberated and channeled, rather than achieved. Eros is a primal force that manifests itself in spontaneity and creativity if it is not hindered. John Paul II thinks of spontaneity as the end result of a long and arduous process of training. John Paul II rejects the idea that Jesus's ethos inhibits spontaneity.[75] But there is no such thing as spontaneity as such. The follower of Jesus participates in "another spontaneity of which the 'carnal man' knows nothing or very little."[76] This other—true—spontaneity happens only gradually: "The ethos of redemption contains in every area—and directly in the sphere of the lust of the flesh—the imperative of self-control, the necessity of immediate continence and of habitual temperance."[77] A Thomistic account of the virtues is in the background here. A virtue is a type of *habitus* for Thomas Aquinas. Acquiring a moral virtue is a timeful process, a skill based on the repetition of good acts.[78] For John Paul II, freedom is a rare achievement that requires self-mastery over time. Boff does not dismiss the necessity of discipline, but he does tend to view freedom as something that will manifest itself spontaneously if we learn to clear away hindrances.

This contrast holds true not only on the individual level, but on the historical level. For John Paul II, the Sermon on the Mount is the culmination in history of a long and patient pedagogy begun by God at creation through the natural law, made explicit in the law on Sinai, and brought to refinement in the Sermon on the Mount. For Boff, by contrast, the Sermon on the Mount is the historical moment when God blew the lid off the creative energies that had been repressed by law. This has

74. John Paul II, *Blessed Are the Pure of Heart*, 188.

75. Ibid., 185.

76. Ibid., 188.

77. Ibid., 194. John Paul II believes that the "value of the nuptial meaning of the body" is the context for Jesus's remarks on adultery in the Sermon on the Mount: "It is a question of this value in the act of self-mastery and temperance, to which Christ refers in the Sermon on the Mount" (195).

78. Thomas Aquinas, *Summa theologiae* I-II Q. 55; I-II Q. 63.2–4.

social implications for Boff. He claims that the working class is the decisive channel for the eruption of eros in human history.[79] The social aspect is muted in John Paul II's discussion of eros. Though he makes clear that his analysis applies to every kind of sin and guilt, his focus is nevertheless on sexual concupiscence. He does not move beyond Jesus's words about adultery in Matthew 5:27–28, but takes them as the key to the Sermon on the Mount. The drama of redemption plays out archetypically between a man and a woman in the marriage relationship. It is there, in mutual self-donation, that the meaning of creation shines most clearly.

Kingdom

Boff begins his book *Ecology and Liberation* with a prologue entitled "A Sermon from the Mount of Corcovado." The Christ of Corcovado is the famous statue that overlooks Guanabara Bay in Rio de Janeiro. Boff imagines the statue coming to life and preaching a new Sermon on the Mount to the city. It is addressed to two groups, the oppressed and the oppressors. Christ addresses the oppressed with compassion, detailing the various types of exploitation that Indians, blacks, peasants, street children, and the earth itself have experienced. Christ identifies with their suffering and identifies them as the suffering servant in history, who liberates with his blood. Christ declares blessed all those who struggle for the liberation of the oppressed and declares that they will form the basis of the kingdom. He does not, however, lay moral demands upon them: "You are all blessed, all you who are poor, hungry, sick, and without hope. You are oppressed and victims of a corrupt society, so how can I expect you to live a life of perfect virtue or upbraid you for all your imperfections?"[80] The same measure of understanding is offered to pre-Colombian peoples who offered human hearts to the sun god: "You will not lack his forgiveness for the wars which you made to ensure the human (but inhuman) sac-

79. Boff, *St. Francis*, 17.
80. Leonardo Boff, *Ecology and Liberation: A New Paradigm* (Maryknoll, NY: Orbis, 1995), 1.

rifices you offered."[81] Such understanding is not offered, however, to the "masters of power, who have sucked the workers' blood for five hundred years";[82] they are subject to curses and destruction should they not heed Christ's dire warnings.

Though it is not a direct commentary on Matthew 5–7, Boff's new Sermon on the Mount says a lot about how he views the original version. The Sermon on the Mount, as the center of Jesus's preaching, is fundamentally about the liberation of the oppressed. Boff begins almost all of his theological reflections by pointing to the destitution and misery of the majority of the world's population. The heart of Jesus's message, Boff says, is the petition of the Lord's Prayer: "Thy kingdom come."[83] In his book on the Lord's Prayer, Boff defines the kingdom of God as a utopia, a comprehensive social project of the realization of all of humankind's hopes.[84] The kingdom cannot be reduced to either a purely political or a purely religious project, nor can it be reduced to something that humans bring about.[85] Boff explicitly rejects the Marxist reduction of utopia to a purely intrahistorical process of building an earthly paradise. The kingdom is an eschatological reality by which earth and history are elevated to their supreme ideal in God.[86] Nevertheless, the kingdom has a concrete social manifestation. According to Boff, the one "infallible criterion" that signals the arrival of the kingdom is when "justice begins to reach the poor, the dispossessed, and the oppressed."[87]

The Sermon on the Mount addresses sin, but for Boff sin is always understood as social and structural. Capitalism is the reigning "system of sin."[88] Boff does not ignore the personal aspect of sin; he quotes Paul's list of sins of the flesh in Galatians 5:19–21. But immediately he adds that flesh-mindedness finds its historical

---

81. Ibid., 3. The Christ of Corcovado also tells the native peoples: "You have the power to raise up the people and give back life to their culture, bringing joy to the aged and praising my holy name: God, Virachocha, and Quetzalcoátl."

82. Ibid., 2.

83. Boff, *Lord's Prayer*, 54.

84. Ibid., 54–55.

85. Ibid., 59, 67.

86. Ibid., 46.

87. Ibid., 61.

88. Ibid., 110.

expression in the mechanisms of society, specifically that which tends to the accumulation of wealth by the few at the expense of the many.[89] The personal aspect of sin is always embedded within a social and historical web of relations. This is why the Sermon from the Mount of Corcovado does not set a high standard of personal virtue for the downtrodden. Personal virtue will change once the heavy burden of structural sin is lifted from the shoulders of the oppressed.

Given the oppressive situation of alienation that thwarts the flourishing of the people, the Sermon on the Mount does not reinforce order but overturns it. According to Boff, in the Sermon on the Mount Christ "breaks" the status quo of "neocapitalist systems" and what passes for justice:

> The preaching of a universal love represents permanent crisis for all social and ecclesiastical systems. Christ announces a principle that checkmates all fetishistic and inhuman subordination to a system, be it social or religious. The norms of the Sermon on the Mount presuppose love, a new person, and one liberated for greater things.[90]

Boff is keen to put the Sermon on the Mount in eschatological context and the "apocalyptic atmosphere" of Jesus's teaching.[91] Jesus comes to announce an unsettling that is coming—and is already here.

The differences in interpretation of the Sermon on the Mount between Boff and John Paul II can largely be traced to the fundamental problem that each addresses. For Boff, it is poverty and human misery. For John Paul II, it is an illusory freedom divorced from truth. *Veritatis Splendor* is directed against "relativism and skepticism."[92] In his apostolic letter *Dilecti Amici*, the pope offers the law, of which the Sermon on the Mount is the "culmination," as the antidote to "any kind of relativism or utilitarianism."[93] In

---

89. Ibid., 99.

90. Boff, *Jesus Christ Liberator*, 71.

91. Boff, *Lord's Prayer*, 81–83; idem, *Jesus Christ Liberator*, 56–61.

92. John Paul II, *Veritatis Splendor* §1.

93. John Paul II, *Dilecti Amici* §6, http://www.vatican.va/holy_father/john_paul_ii/apost_letters/documents/hf_jp-ii_apl_31031985_dilecti-amici_en.html.

his homily from the Mount of the Beatitudes, the pope offers Jesus's words as a call to those tempted to shed their Christian heritage.[94] John Paul II addresses a different problem and a different audience. Boff's Jesus addresses the poor and the oppressed. In *Veritatis Splendor*, Jesus addresses the rich young man. Despite a phrase-by-phrase interpretation of Jesus's encounter with the rich young man in Matthew, John Paul II says nothing about the actual content of the story's punch line—"Go, sell your possessions, and give the money to the poor"—except to say that it is an invitation that applies to everyone, because it brings out the full meaning of the commandment to love one's neighbor.[95]

It is not that John Paul II is unconcerned about poverty and other social ills. His 1995 encyclical *Evangelium Vitae* is a powerful condemnation of the "culture of death" that reigns in the contemporary world and the "war of the powerful against the weak" that is this culture's vehicle.[96] Nevertheless, John Paul II regards social ills as an effect of a deeper crisis, the turning away from the splendor of truth. Near the end of *Veritatis Splendor*, the pope includes a section on social and political renewal. He decries the injustice and corruption that tramples on people's fundamental rights. But he says that "at the bottom" of these situations are causes that are "cultural"; going deeper, he says that the heart of culture is the "moral sense," which in turn is rooted in the "religious sense." This telescoping etiology leads him to contend that upon only the truth can the renewal of society be based.[97] Social ills can be remedied only by a turning of each person away from relativism and toward the truth.

It is significant that the pope speaks in terms of *re*newal. The turning is a *re*turning; moral norms help "*preserve* the human social fabric."[98] It is not without reason that Boff entitled his obituary of John Paul II "The Great Restorer."[99] For John Paul II, what is

---

94. "Homily of John Paul II, Israel—Korazim, Mount of the Beatitudes" §4.

95. John Paul II, *Veritatis Splendor* §18.

96. John Paul II, *Evangelium Vitae* (Boston: St. Paul Books, 1995), §12. *Evangelium Vitae* mentions the Sermon on the Mount in the context of a "refinement" of the Decalogue's declaration of the inviolability of human life; see §§40–41.

97. John Paul II, *Veritatis Splendor* §§98–99.

98. Ibid., §97.

99. Leonardo Boff, "John Paul II: The Great Restorer," *Witness Magazine*, April 15, 2005, http://www.thewitness.org/article.php?id=889.

needed is not a radical change, but a return to the unchanging: "In the end, only a morality which acknowledges certain norms as valid always and for everyone, with no exception, can guarantee the ethical foundation of social coexistence, both on the national and international levels."[100] In the Sermon on the Mount, Jesus drives the law deep into the heart, such that no human sin can shake it loose. John Paul II interprets martyrdom not in the context of apocalyptic, but in the context of the unshakeability of moral norms. The martyr is one who will accept death rather than bend a moral norm. The martyr thereby wards off "in civil society and within the ecclesial communities themselves, the most dangerous crisis which can affect man: the confusion between good and evil."[101] The Sermon on the Mount does not represent, as it does for Boff, "a permanent crisis for all social and ecclesiastical systems." For John Paul II, the Sermon on the Mount represents the kind of moral clarity upon which social stability is based, and the ecclesiastical hierarchy plays a key role in maintaining moral teaching free of ambiguity and compromise.[102]

Conclusion

It would be tempting to conclude by simply chalking up the differences between John Paul II and Boff to the differences in their respective contexts: John Paul II speaks to a Northern audience, Boff to a Southern one. Although that is true, they nevertheless have something to teach one another and, perhaps, us. John Paul II does a much better job than Boff in situating Jesus in his Jewish context. For John Paul II, the Sermon on the Mount does not cut against the grain of the Old Testament, but brings it to its proper fulfillment. John Paul II also has a more nuanced and positive understanding of freedom, one that does not reach its fulfillment in the mere absence of external restrictions. John Paul II rightly understands freedom as the fruit of a timeful process of training

100. John Paul II, *Veritatis Splendor* §97.
101. Ibid., §93.
102. On the magisterium of the church as guardian of moral clarity, see ibid., §§2–3.

in the virtues, which can take place only within a community of virtuous persons. At the same time, we can learn from Boff's placing of the Sermon on the Mount in its eschatological context. Boff is right to point to the centrality of the kingdom in Jesus's message. The kingdom is a social project, brought about by God's grace, that asks us to unthink the necessity of violence and exploitation. The Sermon on the Mount does not necessarily invite us to take liberties with the moral law. It does, however, invite Christians to marshal our creativity to imagine ways to love our enemies and refuse to store up earthly treasure in a world that makes those commands of Jesus seem hopelessly utopian.

John R. W. Stott

Jeffrey P. Greenman

John R. W. Stott (born 1921) has been called "the recognized senior theologian and thinker of world evangelicalism."[1] As a scholarly preacher associated throughout his entire public ministry with a single Anglican church, All Souls', Langham Place in London, Stott's prominence within evangelical circles stems from his stature as a biblical theologian who was able to articulate the central convictions of conservative Protestantism in clear and compelling ways. Alongside American evangelist Billy Graham, Stott has been the most influential figure in the global evangelical movement since World War II. The five-volume History of Evangelicalism series published by InterVarsity Press will conclude with a book entitled *The Global Diffusion of Evangelicalism: The Age of Graham and Stott*.[2] The subtitle points to Stott's worldwide influence, achieved chiefly through his authorship of over forty

---

1. Adrian Hastings, *A History of English Christianity, 1920–1990* (London: SCM, 1991), 651. Restricting his view to England, David Edwards claims that, apart from William Temple, Stott was "the most influential clergyman in the Church of England during the twentieth century"; see David L. Edwards and John R. W. Stott, *Essentials: A Liberal-Evangelical Dialogue* (London: Hodder & Stoughton, 1988), 1.

2. At the time of publication, the first two volumes in this series have appeared: Mark A. Noll, *The Rise of Evangelicalism: The Age of Edwards, Whitefield, and the Wesleys* (Downers Grove, IL: InterVarsity, 2004); and David W. Bebbington, *The Dominance of Evangelicalism: The Age of Spurgeon and Moody* (Downers Grove, IL: InterVarsity, 2005). Brian Stanley is scheduled to write the final volume.

books, his strategic role as a leading architect of key evangelical organizations and conferences, as well as his extensive travels as a preacher and mentor to rising evangelical leaders in the developing world.

Stott is the son of a distinguished London physician. His father's agnostic beliefs did not prevent his mother from taking him to Sunday school. While a teenager at the prestigious Rugby School, Stott experienced a clear but undramatic conversion to Christ. He attended Trinity College, Cambridge, studying modern and medieval languages, then theology at Ridley Hall, earning a double first-class degree. He was ordained in 1945 and served his curacy at the same church where he attended Sunday school, where he became rector in 1950 at what he calls "the tender age" of twenty-nine, and where he has been rector emeritus since 1975.[3] He continues to preach regularly at All Souls'. The congregation has served as his base for an extensive preaching ministry both across Britain and eventually worldwide and has provided support for his writing, which eventually earned him the Lambeth Doctor of Divinity degree for "services to the church as theologian and author." In 2005 Stott was awarded a CBE (Commander of the British Empire) by Her Majesty the Queen "for services to Christian scholarship and the Christian world."

British scholar Alister McGrath suggests that Stott is "an excellent example" of what Antonio Gramsci calls "an organic intellectual," that is, someone "who arises within a community, and who gains authority on account of his or her being seen to represent the outlook of that community."[4] McGrath points out that Stott "possesses no academic or institutional authority worth speaking of, but rightly enjoys enormous status within the worldwide Anglican community (and beyond) on account of his having *earned*

---

3. For a brief account of Stott's career and influence, see Jeffrey P. Greenman, "John R. W. Stott," in *Biographical Dictionary of Evangelicals*, ed. Timothy Larsen (Downers Grove, IL: InterVarsity, 2003), 638–41. For a full treatment, see the two-volume biography by Timothy Dudley-Smith, *John Stott: The Making of a Leader* (Downers Grove, IL: InterVarsity, 1999); and idem, *John Stott: A Global Ministry* (Downers Grove, IL: InterVarsity, 2001).

4. Alister E. McGrath, "*Theologiae proprium subiectum*: Theology as the Critic and Servant of the Church," in *The Bible, the Reformation, and the Church*, ed. W. P. Stephens (Sheffield: Sheffield Academic Press, 1995), 161.

that respect."[5] Stott never held an academic post or became a bishop, the usual institutional roles associated with theological leadership, especially for Anglicans. McGrath rightly identifies Stott's prominence as an instance of "organic authority" within the evangelical movement, understood as "something that *emerges*, not something that is *imposed*."

Billy Graham's global influence stems from his status as the most widely respected and most widely traveled evangelist of his era. Known for his unchallenged personal integrity and for over fifty years of persistent proclamation of salvation through personal faith in Christ, Graham is an iconic figure for a movement dedicated to what historian David Bebbington calls "conversionism."[6] Similarly, Stott's global influence is directly related to his status as the most widely respected and most widely traveled evangelical Bible expositor of his generation. While Stott also conducted dozens of evangelistic missions, particularly on university campuses, he is best known for his exemplary work for over fifty years as an expository preacher. Stott is an iconic figure in evangelicalism largely because evangelicals are characterized by what Bebbington calls "biblicism"—the reverence that evangelicals give to the Bible as the result of their belief "that all spiritual truth is to be found in its pages."[7] Another scholar notes, "No Christian tradition glories more than Evangelicalism in the supremacy of the Bible and the truth it contains."[8] Stott himself has written: "We evangelical people are first and foremost Bible people."[9] Appreciative evangelicals have sometimes compared Stott with John Wesley, who called himself a man of one book, the Bible.

In order to place Stott's treatment of the Sermon on the Mount in its context within evangelicalism, and especially to grasp the significance of his book-length exposition of Matthew 5–7, we need

5. Ibid. (emphasis original).

6. David Bebbington, *Evangelicalism in Modern Britain* (Grand Rapids: Baker, 1989), 5–10.

7. Ibid., 12.

8. Kenneth Hylson-Smith, *Evangelicals in the Church of England, 1734–1984* (Edinburgh: Clark, 1988), 351.

9. John R. W. Stott, *Evangelical Truth* (Downers Grove, IL: InterVarsity, 1999), 65.

to understand both Stott's central role as an expositor as well as his views of Scripture and its interpretation.

Stott as Expositor

In his role as global evangelical statesman, Stott was a prominent figure at many of the most significant evangelical gatherings of the post–World War II era. Not only was Stott a key architect of important events and a leader of influential organizations, but also his typical role at these gatherings was to deliver the keynote sessions focused on substantial Bible teaching. I will highlight three main examples.

First, Stott played a key role as Bible expositor in a series of important evangelical conferences on mission and evangelism. In 1966, Stott delivered the first three Bible studies for the World Congress of Evangelism held in Berlin, Germany. His theme was the Great Commission, and he spoke on John 20:19–23; Matthew 28:16–20; and Luke 24:44–49.[10] In 1974, Stott delivered the key plenary lecture at the International Congress on World Evangelization held in Lausanne, Switzerland (known as the Lausanne Congress) entitled "The Biblical Basis for Evangelism."[11] It is hard to exaggerate the significance of this role. At the outset of his address, he states: "The task assigned to me is to take a cluster of related words in the forefront of recent debate—mission, evangelism, dialogue, salvation and conversion—and attempt to define them biblically."[12] Clearly, at a gathering of 2,300 people from 150 countries aimed at forging a global evangelical consensus concerning evangelism and mission, launching the conference by giving biblical definitions for the key terms in discussion must be seen as a crucial task. Then, fifteen years later, Stott provided the Bible studies for Lausanne II in Manila, formally known as the Second International Congress on

10. Carl F. H. Henry and W. Stanley Mooneyham, eds., *One Race, One Gospel, One Task* (Minneapolis: World Wide Publications), 1.37–56.

11. J. D. Douglas, ed., *Let the Earth Hear His Voice* (Minneapolis: World Wide Publications), 65–78.

12. Ibid., 65.

World Evangelization. He gave three expository addresses, covering Romans 1–5.[13]

Second, Stott was a leading figure in the triennial Student Mission Convention organized by InterVarsity Christian Fellowship, founded in 1946. Popularly known as the Urbana Convention, Stott served in the role of Bible expositor for plenary sessions on five occasions (1964, 1967, 1970, 1976, and 1979) as well as providing two major addresses in 1973.[14]

Third, Stott was a fixture at the Keswick Convention, the oldest Bible convention in the United Kingdom, begun in 1875 as an expression of the holiness movement. A central feature of Keswick has been what is known as the "Bible readings," which are expository addresses that follow consecutively through a section of Scripture. Stott spoke there on seven occasions (1962, 1965, 1969, 1972, 1975, 1978, and 2000). According to a recent study of Keswick's history, Stott's addresses were "invariably marked by lucidity and depth."[15] In 1972, his topic was the Sermon on the Mount.

Stott's View of Scripture and Its Exposition

According to Stott, "the first essential of evangelical Christianity is the revelation of God in the Bible."[16] Throughout his ministry, Stott's doctrine of Scripture has remained consistent. His understanding of Scripture as divine revelation reflects traditional evangelical belief. Stott repeatedly asserts that the Bible is "God's Word written," a definition borrowed from article 20 of the Anglican Thirty-Nine Articles of Religion. He affirms that

13. J. D. Douglas, ed., *Proclaim Christ until He Comes* (Minneapolis: World Wide Publications, 1990), 219–36. Other expositors at that event were Ajith Fernando (Rom. 6–8) and David Penman (Rom. 9–15).

14. After a long absence, Stott was scheduled to return to Urbana to provide the convention's opening night address on the topic of "Radical Christianity" in 2003. Due to illness, he was unable to attend, but a Kenyan colleague read his address verbatim to the audience.

15. Charles Price and Ian Randall, *Transforming Keswick: The Keswick Convention Past, Present, and Future* (Carlisle, U.K.: Paternoster, 2000), 81.

16. John R. W. Stott, *Evangelical Truth* (Downers Grove, IL: InterVarsity, 1999), 67.

the "double authorship of the Bible, namely, that it is the Word of God *and* the word of men, or more strictly the Word of God *through* the words of men, is the Bible's own account of itself."[17] Stott upholds a high view of the Bible's inspiration: "Verbal inspiration means that what the Holy Spirit has spoken and still speaks through the human authors, understood according to the plain, natural meaning of the words used, is true and without error."[18] As we shall see, this view of Scripture's inspiration leads Stott to focus his work as an interpreter and preacher exclusively on the "plain, natural meaning" of the biblical text. The belief that God "still speaks" through Scripture leads him to a commitment to the primacy of expository preaching in the church's ministry.

While the Bible is without error in its teaching and therefore historically reliable, Stott argues that the Bible is not merely an historical record of God's past actions. He says that the Bible "is not a kind of museum in which God's Word is exhibited behind glass like a relic or fossil. On the contrary, it is a living word to living people from the living God, a contemporary message for the contemporary world."[19] According to Stott, the conviction that God still speaks through what he has spoken in the Bible protects against "two opposite errors. The first is the belief that, though it was heard in ancient times, God's voice is silent today. The second is the claim that God is indeed speaking today, but that his Word has little or nothing to do with Scripture." In this context, Stott cites with approval J. I. Packer's assertion that "the Bible is God preaching."[20] According to Packer: "Holy Scripture, the inspired Word (message) of the living God, may truly be described as God preaching—preaching, that is, in the sense of instructing, rebuking, correcting and directing every reader and hearer for the furthering of faith, praise, holiness and spiritual growth."[21]

17. John R. W. Stott, *God's Book for God's People* (Downers Grove, IL: InterVarsity, 1982), 19–20.

18. Ibid., 51.

19. John R. W. Stott, *I Believe in Preaching* (London: Hodder & Stoughton, 1982), 100.

20. Ibid., 103.

21. J. I. Packer, *Truth and Power: The Place of Scripture in the Christian Life* (Downers Grove, IL: InterVarsity, 1996), 123.

This means that the Bible is "God's book for God's people," the title of one of Stott's books about Scripture. As such, Stott advocates the recovery of biblical exposition as an essential feature of the church's life and health. His belief that the Bible is "God preaching" correlates with an elevated view of the importance of human preaching: "The Church is the creation of God by his Word. . . . Not only has he brought it into being by his Word, but he maintains and sustains it, directs and sanctifies it, reforms and renews it through the same Word. The Word of God is the scepter by which Christ rules the Church and the food with which he nourishes it."[22] It follows that the primary responsibilities of a pastor involve preaching, so that the flock are nourished with biblical sustenance. Moreover, Stott argues that "all true Christian preaching is expository preaching." He claims that exposition refers primarily to "the content of the sermon (biblical truth) rather than its style (a running commentary)":

> To expound Scripture is to bring out of the text what is there and expose it to view. The expositor prizes open what appears to be closed, makes plain what is obscure, unravels what is knotted and unfolds what is tightly packed. The opposite of exposition is "imposition," which is to impose on the text what is not there. . . . Our responsibility as expositors is to open it up in such a way that it speaks its message clearly, plainly, accurately, relevantly, without addition, subtraction or falsification.[23]

This account echoes the language used by the prominent Anglican evangelical preacher Charles Simeon (1759–1836), one of Stott's personal heroes. It also corresponds to Packer's account of preaching: "A sermon is an applicatory declaration, spoken in God's name and for his praise, in which some part of the written Word of God delivers through the preacher some part of its message about God and godliness in relation to those whom the preacher addresses."[24] There are also striking similarities between the Simeon-Stott-Packer view and John Calvin's account of the preacher's task:

22. Stott, *I Believe in Preaching*, 109.
23. Ibid., 125–26.
24. Packer, *Truth and Power*, 123.

251

> The task of the preacher of the Word is to expound the scripture in the midst of the worshipping Church, preaching in the expectancy that God will do, through his frail human word, what He did through the Word of His prophets of old, that God by His grace will cause the word that goes out of the mouth of man to become also a Word that proceeds from God Himself, with all the power and efficacy of the Word of the Creator and Redeemer.[25]

Stott fends off the idea that expository preaching boils down to the rehearsal of philological data without concern for addressing matters of "contemporary application." For him, "true biblical preaching goes beyond the elucidation of the text to its application."[26] Stott and Packer consistently affirm that exposition is about what the text means for Christians today, not just what it meant in its original context. Stott develops the idea of preaching as "bridge-building."[27] He contends that preaching involves crossing the "cultural gulf" between the biblical world and the modern world. For Stott, it is "the conveying of a God-given message to living people who need to hear it."[28] Elsewhere he says: "To mount the pulpit and address the congregation without any conviction that we are the bearers of a divine message would be the height of arrogance and folly."[29]

It is worth pausing here to notice the centrality of the word *message* in Stott's account of Scripture and its exposition. For Stott, to say that Scripture is God's word is equivalent to saying it is God's message. In strict terms, Stott's point is that pulpit exposition is not about preaching the Bible, per se, but preaching the content of the Bible's *message*. This is a point where evangelical conversionism and biblicism meet. The divine message of good news in Jesus Christ is at the heart of the entire Bible. Scripture is God's own preaching of a message of salvation, hence, to preach the message of the Bible is

---

25. Cited in O. C. Edwards Jr., *A History of Preaching* (Nashville: Abingdon, 2004), 314.

26. John R. W. Stott, "Paralyzed Speakers and Hearers: The Cure Is Recovery of Bible Exposition," *Christianity Today* 25 (March 13, 1981), 44–45.

27. Stott, *I Believe in Preaching*, chap. 4.

28. Ibid., 137.

29. John R. W. Stott, "Biblical Preaching Is Expository Preaching," in *Evangelical Roots*, ed. Kenneth Kantzer (Nashville: Nelson, 1978), 161.

to proclaim Christ and his salvation. An emphasis upon the Bible's message is a central focus of evangelical thinking. Donald McKim's typology of how preachers use Scripture analyzes neoevangelical preaching as focused on "Scripture as message," over against fundamentalist theology's emphasis upon "Scripture as proposition," Scholastic theology's emphasis on "Scripture as doctrine," or liberal theology's emphasis upon "Scripture as experience."[30]

This way of understanding biblical exposition, and its centrality in the life of the church, is a richly theological conception. It helps explain how an expository preacher such as Stott can become the "the recognized senior theologian and thinker of world evangelicalism." Within this tradition, suggests Packer, "the preacher, rather than the critical commentator or the academic theologian, is the true interpreter of Scripture, for the preacher is the person whose privilege it is to bridge the apparent gap between the Bible and the modern world by demonstrating the relevance of what Scripture says to the lives of those addressed."[31]

1972 Keswick Addresses

In 1972 Stott gave four Bible readings at the Keswick Convention on Matthew 5–7, under the title "Christ's Portrait of a Christian."[32] He also uses the phrase "Jesus' portrait of Jesus' people." Stott began the first address by suggesting that the original setting of the Sermon on the Mount, featuring Jesus with his disciples on the Galilean hills, might even be called "the first Palestinian Keswick Convention"![33] Stott divided the Sermon on the Mount into four sermons:

1. A Christian's character (5:1–16)
   a. Four beatitudes on relationship to God

30. Donald K. McKim, *The Bible in Theology and Preaching*, rev. ed. (Nashville: Abingdon, 1994). From this standpoint, it is perhaps no accident that a popular evangelical paraphrase of the entire Bible by Eugene Peterson is entitled *The Message*.

31. Packer, *Truth and Power*, 125.

32. John R. W. Stott, "Christ's Portrait of a Christian: Studies in Matthew 5, 6, and 7," in *The Keswick Week, 1972*, ed. H. F. Stevenson (London: Marshall, Morgan & Scott, 1972). I am grateful to Tyler Wigg-Stevenson, study assistant to John Stott, for providing a copy of this material.

33. Ibid., 45.

      b. Four beatitudes on relationship to men

      c. Salt and light metaphors: a Christian's double influence in wider community, if he lives by the Beatitudes

   2. A Christian's righteousness (5:17–48)

      a. Christ and the law (5:17–20)

      b. Christians and the law (5:21–48)

   3. A Christian's ambition (6:1–34)

      a. A Christian's "religious life" (distinctly religious practices) (6:1–18)

      b. A Christian's "secular life" (public life in the world) (6:19–34)

   4. A Christian's relationships (7:1–29)

      a. Our brother (7:1–5)

      b. "Pigs and dogs" (those who have "decisively rejected the Gospel") (7:6)

      c. Our heavenly Father (7:7–11)

      d. All men (7:12)

      e. Fellow pilgrims (7:13–14)

      f. False prophets (7:15–20)

      g. Jesus Christ (7:21–29)

The main interpretative patterns in Stott's reading of the Sermon are already in place in these 1972 lectures; there are no major changes of direction in his subsequent work. Over the next few years, Stott expanded his text into a book-length manuscript, most of which was delivered as lectures at Regent College, Vancouver, during the summer of 1975. Indeed, virtually all the key ideas and many of the most memorable phrases from these lectures are worked into his full treatment of the Sermon.

Christian Counter-Culture (1978)

Stott's book *Christian Counter-Culture: The Message of the Sermon on the Mount* appeared in 1978 as part of InterVarsity Press's Bible Speaks Today series, coedited by Stott and J. Alec Motyer.[34] As of

34. John R. W. Stott, *Christian Counter-Culture* (Downers Grove, IL: InterVarsity, 1978). The book subsequently has been retitled *The Message of the Sermon on the*

September 2005, the volume had sold over 150,000 copies in the United States and over 29,000 in the United Kingdom and had been translated into over twenty languages. In their series preface, the coeditors portray the volumes as "Old and New Testament expositions, which are characterized by a threefold aim: to expound the biblical text with accuracy, to relate it to contemporary life, and to be readable." They distinguish their series from commentaries by saying that a "commentary seeks rather to elucidate the text than to apply it, and tends to be a work of reference than of literature." They also distance their series from the sorts of published sermons "that attempt to be contemporary and readable, without taking Scripture seriously enough."

What Stott gives us is a sustained theological reading of the Sermon on the Mount as a cohesive whole. The book's organizing theme is clear from the title: *Christian Counter-Culture*. In the preface he says that if the church accepted Jesus's "standards and values as here set forth, and lived by them, it would be the alternative society he always intended it to be, and would offer to the world an authentic Christian counter-culture."[35]

When it was written, the title would have resonated with the cultural currents flowing through the late 1960s and early 1970s, and especially with Theodore Roszak's acclaimed book *The Making of a Counter-Culture*. The title suggests Stott's diagnosis of the underlying problem facing contemporary Christianity, which is the church's conformity to the world's standards. He writes that young people looking for "meaning, peace, love and reality" should find these in the church, but "too often what they see in the church is not a counter-culture but conformism."[36] He adds: "No comment could be more hurtful to the Christian than the words, 'But you are no different from anybody else.'"[37] Why?

Mount. In addition to this book, Stott wrote seven other books in the Bible Speaks Today series: Galatians (1968), 2 Timothy (1973), Ephesians (U.K. edition 1979; U.S. edition 1980), Acts (1990), 1–2 Thessalonians (1991), Romans (1994), and 1 Timothy and Titus (1996).

35. Stott, *Christian Counter-Culture*, 10.
36. Ibid., 16.
37. Ibid., 17.

For the essential theme of the whole Bible from beginning to end is that God's historical purpose is to call out a people for himself; that this people is a "holy" people, set apart from the world to belong to him and to obey him; and that its vocation is to be true to its identity, that is, to be "holy" or "different" in all its outlook and behaviour.[38]

Stott reads the Sermon on the Mount in light of this overall biblical framework:

Jesus emphasized that his true followers, the citizens of God's kingdom, were to be entirely different from others. They were not to take their cue from the people around them, but from him, and so prove to be genuine children of their heavenly Father. To me the key text of the Sermon on the Mount is 6:8: "Do not be like them."[39]

This is a tremendously important statement. Whereas other interpreters have argued that the structure or shape of the Sermon revolves around the Beatitudes, the Lord's Prayer, conflicts with rival religious leaders, or "the greater righteousness," Stott finds the interpretive key in its pivotal concept of distinctiveness—the spiritual and moral differentness of Jesus's authentic disciples.[40] Stott elaborates on this approach, which puts "do not be like them" at the center for the Sermon:

Right through the Sermon on the Mount this theme is elaborated. Their character was to be completely distinct from that admired by the world (the Beatitudes). They were to shine like lights in the prevailing darkness. Their righteousness was to exceed that of the scribes and Pharisees, both in ethical behaviour and in religious devotion, while their love was to be greater and their ambition nobler than those of their pagan neighbours. There is no single paragraph of the Sermon on the Mount in which the contrast between Christian and non-Christian standards is not drawn. It is

38. Ibid.
39. Ibid., 18.
40. For a helpful overview of rival views of the Sermon's structure, see Warren Carter, *What Are They Saying about Matthew's Sermon on the Mount?* (Mahwah, NJ: Paulist Press, 1994).

the underlying and uniting theme of the Sermon; everything else is a variation of it. . . . The Sermon on the Mount is the most complete delineation anywhere in the New Testament of the Christian counter-culture.[41]

What holds the Sermon on the Mount together is its theological coherence. Stott approaches Matthew 5–7 as a sustained argument that spells out the nature of authentic Christian discipleship. From this perspective, it should not be surprising to find that Stott tells us that the Sermon "forms a wonderfully coherent whole."[42]

Given this approach, Stott emphasizes the applicability of Jesus's teaching to his followers in every age. For Stott, this is not an "impossible ideal" intended merely to call us to repentance or a "higher ideal" reserved for a religious elite or an "interim ethic" that is no longer relevant today:

> The standards of the Sermon are neither attainable by every man, nor totally unattainable by any man. To put them beyond anybody's reach is to ignore the purpose of Christ's sermon; to put them within everybody's is to ignore the reality of man's sin. They are attainable all right, but only by those who have experienced the new birth which Jesus told Nicodemus was the indispensable condition of seeing and entering God's kingdom. For the righteousness he described in the Sermon is an inner righteousness. Although it manifests itself outwardly and visibly in words, deeds and relationships, yet it remains essentially a righteousness of the heart. . . . Only a belief in the necessity and the possibility of a new birth can keep us from reading the Sermon on the Mount with either foolish optimism or hopeless despair. Jesus spoke the Sermon to those who were already his disciples and thereby also the citizens of God's kingdom and the children of God's family. The high standards he set are appropriate only to such. We do not, indeed could not, achieve this privileged status by attaining Christ's standards. Rather by attaining his standards, or at least approximating to them, we give evidence of what by God's free grace and gift we already are.[43]

41. Stott, *Christian Counter-Culture*, 18–19.
42. Ibid., 24.
43. Ibid., 29.

This defense of the Sermon's full applicability incorporates a number of features that typify Stott's general theological outlook, ones that represent evangelicalism's core theological convictions. There is a robust sense of sin as incapacitating people from living according to God's standards, an insistence on the decisive experience of being "born again," the centrality of an "inner" righteousness of the heart for a life that pleases God, the rejection of "works-righteousness" or human achievement that could earn God's approval, and an emphasis on God's "free grace and gift." Given this theological framework, the Sermon on the Mount becomes a manifesto for Christian disciples at all times and in all places.

The Theological Argument of the Sermon on the Mount

Stott's approach to the Sermon traces a cohesive message through the successive chapters, using a reading strategy organized around the core theme of differentness. According to his reading, the Beatitudes are spiritual qualities meant to characterize all of Jesus's followers. There is a logical progression from one beatitude to the next. He sums up his exposition of the Beatitudes by saying:

> The beatitudes paint a comprehensive portrait of a Christian disciple. We see him first alone on his knees before God, acknowledging his spiritual poverty and mourning over it. This makes him meek or gentle in all his relationships, since honesty compels him to allow others to think of him what before God he confesses himself to be. Yet he is far from acquiescing in his sinfulness, for he hungers and thirsts after righteousness, longing to grow in grace and in goodness.
>
> We see him next with others, out in the human community. His relationship with God does not cause him to withdraw from society, nor is he insulated from the world's pain. On the contrary, he is in the thick of it, showing mercy to those battered by adversity and sin. He is transparently sincere in all his dealings and seeks to play a constructive role as a peacemaker. Yet he is not thanked for his efforts, but rather opposed, slandered, insulted and persecuted on account of the righteousness for which he stands and the Christ with whom he is identified.

Such is the man or woman who is "blessed," that is, who has the approval of God and finds self-fulfillment as a human being.

Yet in all this the values and standards of Jesus are in direct conflict with the commonly accepted values and standards of the world. The world judges the rich to be blessed, not the poor, whether in the material or the spiritual sphere; the happy-go-lucky and carefree, not those who take evil so seriously that they mourn over it; the strong and brash, not the meek and gentle; the full not the hungry; those who mind their own business, not those who meddle in other men's matters and occupy their time in do-goodery like "showing mercy" and "making peace"; those who attain their ends even if necessary by devious means, not the pure in heart who refuse to compromise their integrity; those who are secure and popular, and live at ease, not those who suffer persecution.[44]

In summary, says Stott, what the Beatitudes show is that "the culture of the world and the counter-culture of Christ are at loggerheads with each other."[45] Yet, ironically, those who are persecuted by the world are called to serve the world, living out their differentness in the public realm.

Stott turns next to Matthew 5:13–16: "If the beatitudes describe the essential character of the disciples of Jesus, the salt and light metaphors indicate their influence for good in the world."[46] Discussing the phrase *salt of the earth and light of the world*, Stott draws attention to existence of two "distinct communities" here—the church and the world. He says, "Christian saltiness is Christian character as depicted in the beatitudes" and that "if we Christians are indistinguishable from non-Christians, we are useless."[47] When discussing Christians as the "light of the world," Stott argues that this light is conveyed when Christians "allow the light of Christ within us to shine out from us, so that people may see it."[48]

As Stott expounds the social impact of Christians as salt and light, he again refers to the underlying problem of the church's conformity: "The Sermon is built on the assumption that Christians

44. Ibid., 54.
45. Ibid., 56.
46. Ibid., 57.
47. Ibid., 60.
48. Ibid., 62.

are different, and it issues a call to us to *be* different. Probably the greatest tragedy of the church throughout its long and chequered history has been its constant tendency to conform to the prevailing culture instead of developing a Christian counter-culture."[49]

When Stott turns to Matthew 5:17–20, he says: "So far Jesus has spoken of a Christian's character, and of the influence he will have in the world if he exhibits this character and if his character bears fruit in 'good works.' He now proceeds to define this character and these good works in terms of righteousness."[50] This righteousness consists in obedience to God's moral law. Such obedience exceeds the righteousness of the scribes and Pharisees. Stott interprets the "exceeding righteousness" as "greater than Pharisaic righteousness because it is deeper, being a righteousness of the heart" rather than an "external and formal obedience, a rigid conformity to the letter of the law."[51] This is what Stott calls "deep obedience," which is "possible only in those whom the Holy Spirit has regenerated and now indwells."[52] The theme here is the difference between the disciples' authentic experience of "inner righteousness" and worldly attempt to "lower the law's standards and make it easier to obey."[53] Stott proceeds to explain the rest of Matthew 5 as six parallel paragraphs that illustrate the "deeper righteousness" named in 5:20.

Stott summarizes his argument so far. The Beatitudes have described the "essential elements of Christian character." The metaphors of salt and light describe "the influence for good" exerted by Christians who live out the Beatitudes. The Sermon then describes Christian righteousness, which Stott calls "righteousness unlimited. It must be allowed to penetrate beyond our actions and words to our heart, mind and motives, and to master us even in those hidden, secret places."[54] When he turns to the interpretation of Matthew 6, he explains that Jesus moves from "a Christian's moral righteousness to his 'religious' righteousness." Stott finds that in both

49. Ibid., 63.
50. Ibid., 69.
51. Ibid., 75.
52. Ibid.
53. Ibid., 80.
54. Ibid., 125.

spheres, moral and religious, "Jesus issues his insistent call to his followers to be different."[55] Jesus's disciples are to be different from the hypocritical, ostentatious religion of the Pharisees and equally different from the "mechanical formalism of the heathen." Stott argues that "the essential difference in religion as in morality is that authentic Christian righteousness is not an external manifestation only, but one of the secret things of the heart."[56]

Turning to the Lord's Prayer, Stott puts its content into the larger context of the Sermon: "Jesus is always calling his followers to something higher than the attainments of those around them, whether religious people or secular people. He emphasizes that Christian righteousness is greater (because inward), Christian love is broader (because inclusive of enemies) and Christian prayer deeper (because sincere and thoughtful) than anything to be found in the non-Christian community."[57] He interprets the Lord's Prayer as an expression of "the priorities of a Christian" who is "constantly under pressure to conform to the self-centredness of secular culture." He finds that "in the Christian counter-culture our top priority concern is not our name, kingdom and will, but God's."[58] According to Stott, Jesus's teaching on prayer is presented as a "contrast to its non-Christian alternatives. It is *God-centred* (concerned for God's glory) in contrast to the self-centredness of the Pharisees (preoccupied with their own glory). And it is *intelligent* (expressive of thoughtful dependence) in contrast to the mechanical incantations of the heathen."[59]

Stott divides Matthew 6 into two parts: 6:1–18 deals with a Christian's "private life" (giving, praying, fasting), while 6:19–34 is concerned with "public business in the world" (questions of money, possessions, food, drink, clothing, and ambition).[60] Again, Stott finds a unifying theme in this diverse material: "In both spheres also the same insistent summons of Jesus is heard, the call to be different from the popular culture: different from the

55. Ibid., 126.
56. Ibid.
57. Ibid., 143.
58. Ibid., 148.
59. Ibid., 151.
60. Ibid., 153.

hypocrisy of the religious (1–18) and now different also from the materialism of the irreligious (19–34)."[61] Stott finds that Jesus is contrasting the Gentile value system with the alternative lifestyle based on his teachings. There are "two treasures (on earth and in heaven, 19–21), two bodily conditions (light and darkness, 22, 23), two masters (God and mammon, 24) and two preoccupations (our bodies and God's kingdom, 25–34)."[62]

Turning finally to Matthew 7, Stott comments that it is not easy to discern the conceptual links between the "apparently self-contained paragraphs," nor "does the chapter as a whole follow on from the previous chapter with any clear sequence of thought."[63] Nevertheless, Stott finds a connection. He argues that "the connecting thread which runs through the chapter, however loosely, is that of relationships. It would seem quite logical that, having described a Christian's character, influence, righteousness, piety and ambition, Jesus should concentrate finally on his relationships. For the Christian counter-culture is not an individualistic but a community affair, and relations both within the community and between the community and others are of paramount importance."[64]

These relationships are mapped in almost exactly the same way as he had done in his 1972 Keswick lectures. He outlines the chapter as follows:

1. to our brother, in whose eye we may discern a splinter, and whom we have a responsibility to help, not judge (7:1–5)
2. to a group startlingly designated "dogs" and "pigs": they are people all right, but such is their animal nature that we are told not to share God's gospel with them (7:6)
3. to our heavenly Father, to whom we come in prayer, confident that he will give us nothing but "good things" (7:7–11)
4. to everybody in general: the Golden Rule should guide our attitude and behavior toward them (7:12)
5. to our fellow pilgrims, who walk with us along the narrow way (7:13–14)

61. Ibid.
62. Ibid.
63. Ibid., 174.
64. Ibid.

6. to false prophets, whom we are to recognize and of whom we are to beware (7:15–20)
7. to Jesus our Lord, whose teaching we are committed to heed and obey (7:21–27)[65]

Stott pulls together the threads in the book in his conclusion:

> Jesus does not set before his followers a string of easy ethical rules, so much as a set of values and ideals which are entirely distinctive from the way of the world. He summons us to renounce the prevailing secular culture in favour of the Christian counter-culture. Repeatedly during our study we have heard his call to his people to be different from everybody else.[66]

In the last paragraph of the book, he asserts that the Sermon is Jesus's "picture of God's alternative society":

> These are the standards, the values and the priorities of the kingdom of God. Too often the church has turned away from this challenge and sunk into a bourgeois, conformist respectability. At such times it is almost indistinguishable from the world, it has lost its saltness, its light is extinguished and it repels all idealists. For it gives no evidence that it is God's new society which is tasting already the joys and powers of the age to come. Only when the Christian community lives by Christ's manifesto will the world be attracted and God be glorified. So when Jesus calls us to himself, it is to this that he calls us. For he is the Lord of the counter-culture.[67]

We find that Stott has done what he said he would do in the book's opening pages. He has interpreted every paragraph of the Sermon from the vantage point of his unifying theme—the contrast between Christian and non-Christian values and standards.

Stott's Theological Exegesis

From this analysis, it should be clear that Stott interprets the Sermon on the Mount as a cohesive theological argument articulating

65. Ibid., 174–75.
66. Ibid., 210.
67. Ibid., 222.

the nature of authentic Christian discipleship. This is exemplary Anglo-American evangelical theological exegesis, dedicated to enabling the message of Scripture to be heard and obeyed. Stott presents the Sermon as a moral vision, according to which Christians are neither to conform to the world's ways nor withdraw from the world, but live a distinctive way of life as an uncompromised community in the midst of the world.

Unlike Charles Haddon Spurgeon, his evangelical forefather, Stott's account of Matthew 5–7 makes no appeal to categories derived from medieval mysticism, takes no swipes at Wesleyan theology, and refrains from anti-Catholic polemics.[68] He stays close to the text, allowing Scripture to interpret Scripture, looking at the Sermon within the overall canon of Scripture. His method is geared toward expounding the "plain, natural meaning" of the text. What we see in *Christian Counter-Culture* is what we would expect, given his account of expository preaching.

There are close similarities between Stott's exposition and Calvin's method of writing commentaries. According to Richard Gamble, "Calvin makes his commentaries understandable to the dullest student and, as a hermeneutical principle, limits his discussions to the text, unfolding the mind of the biblical author and doing that, in part at least, by refraining from prolonged examination of various exegetical positions taken by others."[69] The same can be said confidently of Stott. Moreover, Stott agrees with Calvin not only that "the chief virtue of an interpreter" is brevity and simplicity, but also in the rejection of allegorical interpretations in the quest for an accurate interpretation of the Bible. Gamble argues that Calvin avoided lengthy references to other writers because "he wants to present the message of Scripture as simply and clearly as possible."[70]

Also, there are clear similarities between Stott's approach and the expository sermons and writings of J. C. Ryle, onetime bishop of Liverpool. According to Packer, "Of all nineteenth-century Anglican evangelicals, Ryle has unquestionably exercised the most

68. See Timothy Larsen's chapter on Spurgeon in this volume.
69. Richard C. Gamble, "*Brevitas et facilitas*: Toward an Understanding of Calvin's Hermeneutic," *Westminster Theological Journal* 47 (1985): 1–17 at 3.
70. Ibid., 7.

widespread and sustained influence."[71] We know that Stott consulted Ryle's 1856 volume on Matthew, for he quotes Ryle's "expository thoughts" on several occasions. Ryle says that he is not writing "a learned critical commentary" and that he is writing for "a mixed company" (i.e., for families and private reading, as well as ministers, but not primarily for scholars). Ryle tells us that he has prepared himself to write through "laborious examination of other men's opinions" and lists forty-four names, including Chrysostom, Augustine, Calvin, and Bucer, as well as a number of Puritan and Victorian biblical interpreters.[72] About 120 years later, Stott says virtually the same things in his own preface of *Christian Counter-Culture*. Like Ryle, Stott draws on the insights of various contemporary exegetes when they enable him to clarify a difficulty presented by the text, but otherwise he does not engage in interpretative arguments. He tells us that he studied about twenty-five commentaries on the passage.[73] What is striking about Stott's use of sources is that, while he seems to have gathered some exegetical insights from a range of commentaries written in the 1950s and 1960s, he relies persistently upon the more theologically oriented writings of Chrysostom, Luther, Calvin, and Bonhoeffer. Stott hardly ever goes more than a few pages without quoting one of those four authorities. There are a few quotations from Augustine and none from John Wesley.

Stott's tone and writing style are strongly reminiscent of Ryle; the chief difference between the two expositions is that Stott provides a continuous verse-by-verse analysis, whereas Ryle does not, preferring to focus on "prominent points" from sections or passages "averaging about twelve verses."[74] Beyond these stylistic similarities, it is possible that Ryle's comments on the Sermon of the Mount have had a strong influence on Stott, although Stott does not explicitly acknowledge a debt to Ryle. Given Stott's unifying theme of differentness, it is interesting to note that Ryle summarizes his own exposition of the Beatitudes by saying: "Let

71. J. I. Packer, "Introduction," in J. C. Ryle, *Matthew: Expository Thoughts on the Gospels* (Wheaton, IL: Crossway, 1993), xiii.

72. Ryle, *Matthew*, xvii.

73. Stott, *Christian Counter-Culture*, 9.

74. Ryle, *Matthew*, xv.

us learn how the principles of Christ are entirely contrary to the principles of the world. It is vain to deny it: they are diametrically opposed."[75] Turning to Matthew 5:13–20, Ryle goes on immediately to write: "These verses teach us the character which true Christians must support and maintain the world."[76] His exposition of the salt and light metaphors sounds like what Stott would eventually write: "Surely, if words mean anything, we are meant to learn from these two metaphors that there must be something marked, distinct and special about our character if we are true Christians."[77] Ryle sums up this section by saying: "There must be a difference of habits, tastes and turn of mind, between us and those who think only of the world."[78] Might Stott have found in Ryle the unifying theme for his own exposition? And might Ryle's account of Jesus's teaching on salt and light shaped Stott's interpretation of that passage, which comes to play such a major role in his thought?

Salt and Light

Not only does Matthew 5:13–14 play a key role in *Christian Counter-Culture*, it is a text that has occupied a central position in Stott's theology. His preferred biblical image for the role of Christians in society, or for the church in the world, has been Jesus's description of his disciples as "salt of the earth" and "light of the world."

Stott's writings on mission and social ethics need to be interpreted in light of the twentieth-century evangelical movement's customary emphasis upon evangelistic preaching and its relative indifference to social and political involvement. It is valuable to see Stott as responding to Carl F. H. Henry's call, in *The Uneasy Conscience of Modern Fundamentalism* (1947), for evangelicals to focus more attention on the social implications of its religious message. For Henry, "despite the orthodox insistence upon revelation and redemption, evangelical Christianity has become increasingly

75. Ibid., 26.
76. Ibid., 27.
77. Ibid., 27–28.
78. Ibid., 28.

inarticulate about the social reference of the Gospel."[79] Consistent with Henry's analysis, Stott spoke of evangelicalism's "temporarily mislaid social conscience." Writing in 1984, Stott offered the following assessment:

> For approximately 50 years (c. 1920–1970) evangelical Christians were preoccupied with the task of defending the historic biblical faith against the attacks of theological liberalism, and reacting against its "social gospel." But now we are convinced that God has given us social as well as evangelistic responsibilities in his world. Yet the half-century of neglect has put us far behind in this area. We have a long way to catch up.[80]

I would argue that Stott was the most influential single individual in changing the evangelical movement's basic stance toward social involvement. In retrospect, it seems clear that only someone of Stott's stature, and only someone marshaling a strong biblical argument, could successfully meet Henry's challenge of articulating the "social reference of the Gospel" in ways that many evangelicals would embrace. As one scholar of British evangelism writes: "John Stott was foremost in demonstrating the Evangelical concern to remain loyal to the revelation of God and yet relevant to the needs and demands of the modern world."[81] Further, my claim is that the key passage in Stott's case for a renewed evangelical social conscience was the Sermon on the Mount. Specifically, his consistent appeal to Matthew 5:13–14 played an important role in reshaping the way that many evangelicals understand the church's mission and its engagement with social and political life. Through Stott's influence, language depicting the church's calling as salt and light has been woven through some of the most important documents of the global evangelical movement and has become commonplace in evangelical discussions of social issues. His own writings rely upon these verses extensively, and he uses those verses in a remark-

79. Carl F. H. Henry, *The Uneasy Conscience of Modern Fundamentalism* (Grand Rapids: Eerdmans, 1947), 26.

80. John R. W. Stott, *Decisive Issues Facing Christians Today* (Old Tappan, NJ: Revell, 1984), xi.

81. Hylson-Smith, *Evangelicals in the Church of England*, 320.

ably consistent way to articulate the Christian's responsibility toward society and to describe the moral witness of the Christian community.

Berlin Congress (1966)

Our survey of Stott's use of these verses in critical contexts goes back to 1966, when Stott gave the Bible studies at the World Congress on Evangelism in Berlin. In his discussion of the Great Commission, Stott stated:

> The commission of the Church . . . is not to reform society, but to preach the Gospel. Certainly, Christ's disciples who have embraced the Gospel, and who themselves are being transformed by the Gospel, are intended to be the salt of the earth and the light of the world (Matthew 5:13–14). That is, they are to influence the society in which they live and work by helping to arrest its corruption and illumine its darkness. They are to love and serve their generation, and play their part in the community as responsible Christian citizens. But the primary task of the members of Christ's Church is to be Gospel heralds, not social reformers.[82]

At this point in his career, Stott defined the mission of the church in terms of its responsibilities for preaching, converting, and teaching. Yet, even as he asserts the primacy of evangelism, he tempers that assertion by appealing to Matthew 5:13–14. Preaching seeks to make disciples; disciples who are transformed by the gospel have a social responsibility; this responsibility involves being salt and light in the world, as "responsible citizens." We see here an early indication of the eventual shape of Stott's own thinking about mission, a direction that would powerfully influence the direction of global evangelism. Without downplaying the priority of evangelism, Stott sought to articulate the importance of Christian social involvement. The biblical basis for this approach was found in Matthew 5:13–14.

82. John R. W. Stott, "The Great Commission," in *One Race, One Gospel, One Task*, ed. Carl F. H. Henry and W. Stanley Mooneyham (Minneapolis: World Wide Publications), 1.50–51.

Lausanne Congress (1974)

In his address at Lausanne Congress in 1974, Stott presents the mission of the church as follows:

> "Mission" is not a word for everything the church does. . . . "Mission" rather describes everything the church is sent into the world to do. "Mission" embraces the church's double vocation to be "the salt of the earth" and "the light of the world." For Christ *sends* the church into the earth to be its salt, and *sends* the church into the world to be its light.[83]

This definition of mission is repeated, virtually word for word, in his 1975 book *Christian Mission in the Modern World*.[84] What is particularly significant here is the shift toward a more holistic understanding of the church's mission. The dominant evangelical view until Lausanne was that mission was synonymous with evangelism. This broadened emphasis was framed in terms of the salt and light metaphors of the Sermon on the Mount.

In his book on mission, Stott goes on to elaborate the "practical implications" of this more holistic view of mission. He connects the church's responsibility to be salt and light with the Protestant doctrine of vocation or calling. Stott affirms that God calls all Christians into his service and that this service is found in professions, commerce, government, or other areas of work:

> When any community deteriorates, the blame should be attached where it belongs: not to the community which is going bad but to the church which is failing in its responsibility as salt to stop it going bad. And the salt will be effective only if it permeates society, only if Christians learn again the wide diversity of divine callings, and if many penetrate deeply into secular society in order to serve Christ there.[85]

83. Douglas, *Let the Earth Hear His Voice*, 65 (emphasis original).
84. John R. W. Stott, *Christian Mission in the Modern World* (Downers Grove, IL: InterVarsity, 1975), 30.
85. Ibid., 32.

The Lausanne Covenant, the document resulting from the global congress, defined evangelism as "the proclamation of the historical, biblical Christ as Savior and Lord, with a view to persuading people to come to him personally and so be reconciled to God."[86] The statement goes on to say: "The results of evangelism include obedience to Christ, incorporation into his church and responsible service in the world." Section 5, entitled "Christian Social Responsibility," which proved quite controversial among evangelicals, reflects Stott's new thinking. This section expressed "penitence" for "having sometimes regarded evangelism and social concern as mutually exclusive." It affirmed that "evangelism and socio-political involvement are both part of our Christian duty." It also said, "When people receive Christ they are born again into his kingdom and must seek not only to exhibit but also to spread its righteousness in the midst of an unrighteous world."

In his exposition and commentary on the Lausanne Covenant, Stott takes up this phrase and explains it with reference to the Sermon on the Mount: "We must seek not only the spread of the kingdom itself, nor only to exhibit its righteousness ourselves, but also to spread its righteousness in the midst of an unrighteous world. How else can we be 'the salt of the earth' (Matt. 5:14)?"[87] Here Stott reverts to his favorite biblical image for the church's moral witness in the world.

Willowbank Report (1978)

The 1974 Lausanne Congress spawned what is known as "the Lausanne movement," which included a series of consultations and publications on issues of mission and evangelism developed through international evangelical collaboration. In 1978 Stott served as consultation chairman for a gathering of thirty-three theologians, missionaries, and evangelical leaders from around the world to study the interaction between gospel and culture. The resulting document, *The Willowbank Report: Consultation on Gospel and*

---

86. John R. W. Stott, ed., *Making Christ Known: Historic Mission Documents from the Lausanne Movement, 1974–1989* (Grand Rapids: Eerdmans, 1996), 20.

87. John R. W. Stott, *The Lausanne Covenant: An Exposition and Commentary*, Lausanne Occasional Paper 3 (Minneapolis: World Wide Publications, 1975), 17.

Culture, makes only one reference to the theme of salt and light. But it is a crucial one deployed strategically to spell out the church's mission in the world. We again see Stott's favorite image used in a key section called "the Church's Influence on Culture":

> [We] base the church's cultural responsibility on Scripture rather than on history. We have reminded ourselves that our fellow men and women are made in God's image, and that we are commanded to honour, love, and serve them in every sphere of life. To this argument from God's creation we add another from his kingdom which broke into the world through Jesus Christ. All authority belongs to Christ. He is lord of both universe and church. And he has sent us into the world to be its salt and light. As his new community, he expects us to permeate society.[88]

Grand Rapids Report (1982)

In 1982 another Lausanne consultation was held, partially as result of the controversy that surrounded the Lausanne Covenant's affirmation of the church's dual responsibility for evangelism and social responsibility. Stott served as chairman of the drafting committee and as final editor for what is known as the "Grand Rapids Report," entitled *Evangelism and Social Responsibility: An Evangelical Commitment*. The document begins with a call to worship and thanksgiving:

> Only if they are rooted in a vertical relationship to God in worship can the church's two ministries of kerygma (proclamation) and diakonia (service) be held in proper balance and tension. Only in this way, too, can evangelism and social responsibility be kept from degenerating into merely human activity and even propaganda. The mission of any church can fall into this trap.[89]

Commenting twenty years later, Stott wrote:

> What many people remember from the report is its statement of a threefold relationship between evangelism and social activity. First,

88. Stott, ed., *Making Christ Known*, 105.
89. Ibid., 174.

Christian social activity is a *consequence* of evangelism, since it is the evangelized who engage in it. Second, it is a *bridge* to evangelism, since it expresses God's love and so both overcomes prejudice and opens closed doors. Third, it is a *partner* of evangelism, so that they are "like the two blades of a pair of scissors or the two wings of a bird."[90]

It turns out that, due to Stott's influence, the "two wings" of evangelism and social action are interpreted with reference to the salt and light metaphors in no less than four places in the Grand Rapids Report, two of which are of major importance. The first instance is in a passage that affirms the Christian's positive, intentional engagement with society—an engagement that goes beyond a merely passive spillover of certain Christian values. The basis for a more active involvement is found in an appeal to Matthew 5:13–14:

The salt, light and yeast metaphors that Jesus employed are more dynamic, since each implies the penetration of the old community by the new. The light shines into the darkness, the salt soaks into the meat, the yeast causes fermentation in the dough. So Jesus intends his followers neither to withdraw from the world in order to preserve their holiness, nor to lose their holiness by conforming to the world, but simultaneously to permeate the world and to retain their kingdom distinctives. Only so can they share the Good News with credibility. Only so can they be effective agents for cultural, social and political change.[91]

Later in the report, the document addresses the role of preaching and teaching in preparing Christians for their social responsibilities. The key biblical image used to describe the laity's role in society is salt and light. The role of church leaders is understood to involve encouraging and educating Christians for active social engagement:

People need help to resist the pressures of secular thought and to take a firm stand on the moral principles of Scripture. So we

90. John R. W. Stott, "Twenty Years after Lausanne: Some Personal Reflections," *International Bulletin of Missionary Research* 19 (April 1995): 50–55 at 52 (emphasis original).
91. Stott, *Making Christ Known*, 189–90.

must help them to discern the moral issues in each question, to understand them and to hold them fast. In addition, they need to be made aware of how the socio-political and legislative processes work, and to have their confidence raised that they need not be the helpless victims either of an evil status quo or of revolutionary destruction, but can be active as society's salt and light in the fight to protect, re-establish or introduce Christian ethical values. This kind of consciousness-raising is particularly important for those church members who are community leaders, opinion formers and decision-makers—for example, parents, teachers, journalists and politicians. In a democracy (in which government depends on the consent of the governed), legislation depends on public opinion. Our Christian responsibility is to get into the public debate about current issues, boldly affirm, practice and argue what the Bible teaches, and so seek to influence public opinion for Christ.[92]

Lay leaders who would be salt and light in and through their various vocations or callings need to be taught, equipped, and encouraged with "the moral principles of Scripture."

From this review of key documents from the Lausanne movement, we see the influence of Stott's insistence upon salt and light as dominant images for the church's mission to the world. Although section 6 of the Lausanne Covenant affirmed that "in the church's mission of sacrificial service evangelism is primary," it is important to see that there was a major shift from "mission as gospel proclamation" at Berlin 1966 to "mission as everything the church is sent into the world to do" at Lausanne 1974. The subsequent Lausanne movement enshrined a new orthodoxy among evangelicals. Through the seminal influence of Stott, mainstream evangelicalism comes to consider evangelism and social involvement as inseparably important expressions of Christian mission, like "two wings of a bird." Careful review of these documents reveals that this megashift was made on the basis of a broader conception of the church's mission as found in Scripture, that the key passage in this broadening was drawn from the Sermon on the Mount, and that the person who made the argument was Stott.

92. Ibid., 202.

Decisive Issues Facing Christians Today (1984 and 1990)

We turn now to Stott's own writings focused on moral and political issues. In 1984, Stott published a study of social ethics entitled *Issues Facing Christians Today*, released in two volumes in the United States under the title *Involvement* and later retitled in its second edition as *Decisive Issues Facing Christians Today*.

The book aims to explore "our Christian calling: to live under the Word in the world."[93] In doing so, the structure of the book itself is revealing. The first part of the book deals with theoretical and theological foundations; the remainder of the book addresses a range of current social concerns (such as nuclear war, environment, global poverty, human rights, work and unemployment, industrial relations, racism, marriage and divorce, abortion, and homosexuality). Chapter 1 champions Christian involvement in social and political life, pointing to examples of eighteenth- and nineteenth-century Anglo-American evangelical social activism found in figures such as Wesley, Wilberforce, and Shaftsbury. It also provides a biblical basis for social concern in five major Christian doctrines: God, human beings, Christ, salvation, and church. In chapter 2, Stott develops the idea of a Christian mind. In chapter 3, he addresses issues of pluralism, making a case for Christian engagement in democratic political processes and joining in public debate with reasoned persuasion rather than coercion or imposition as strategies for Christian engagement.

The final chapter of the book's first part deals with the challenges of "secular alienation" and "Christian pessimism," which Stott believes share a feeling of powerlessness to make a difference in society. Stott responds to this situation with a detailed discussion of Matthew 5:13–16, his favorite image of salt and light, images used by Jesus "to illustrate the influence he expected his disciples to exert in human society."[94] He makes four main points, all of which are rewordings of what he has written in *Christian Counter-Culture*:

93. Stott, *Decisive Issues*, xii.
94. Ibid., 66.

1. "Christians are fundamentally different from non-Christians." He says: "The world is dark, Jesus implied, but you are to be its light. The world is decaying, but you are to be its salt and hinder its decay."[95]

2. "Christians must permeate non-Christian society." He explains: "Although Christians are (or should be) morally and spiritually distinct from non-Christians, they are not to be socially segregated. . . . Christians are not to remain aloof from society, where they cannot affect it, but are to become immersed in its life."[96]

3. "Christians can influence non-Christian society." Salt actually preserves; light actually dispels darkness. "Jesus seems to have meant, Christians can hinder social decay and dispel the darkness of evil."[97] He comments: "Our Christian habit is to bewail the world's deteriorating standards with an air of rather self-righteous dismay. . . . The question to ask is 'Where is the church? Why are the salt and light of Jesus Christ not permeating and changing our society?' It is sheer hypocrisy on our part to raise our eyebrows, shrug our shoulders or wring our hands. The Lord Jesus told us to be the world's salt and light. If therefore darkness and rottenness abound, it is our fault and we must accept the blame."[98]

4. "Christians must retrain their Christian distinctiveness."[99] He explains: "On the one hand, we have to permeate non-Christian society, and immerse ourselves in the life of the world. On the other, while doing so, we have to avoid becoming assimilated to the world. We must retain our Christian convictions, values, standards and lifestyle."[100]

95. Ibid. Cf. Stott, *Christian Counter-Culture*, 63–68.

96. Stott, *Decisive Issues*, 66.

97. Ibid., 67.

98. Ibid. This is also what Stott was saying for years. In 1977, Stott chaired the second National Evangelical Anglican Congress, held at Nottingham. The second paragraph of the final report reads: "We confess our share of blame for the moral corruption of society, because we have not been the 'salt' and 'light' that Christ intends his people to be, and we stand under his judgment for our failure"; Nottingham Statement §A2, http://www.spurgeon.org/~phil/creeds/nott.htm (accessed Jan. 2, 2006).

99. Stott, *Decisive Issues*, 66–68.

100. Ibid., 68.

Much of the same material on salt and light appeared in a 1985 article entitled "Salt and Light: The Christian Contribution to Nation-Building." The article was a lecture given by Stott at a meeting of the Accrediting Council for Theological Education in Africa held in Kenya. He addresses issues in Kenyan society directly: "Will Christians be able so to influence Kenya that the values and standards of Jesus Christ permeate its culture? . . . Will Jesus Christ be lord of Kenyan culture?"[101]

For Stott, Jesus "expected his followers to go out into the world, both in order to preach the gospel and make disciples, and in order to make their society more pleasing to God by being its salt and light."[102] He concludes by saying: "We need to offer ourselves humbly to God, to be his new community in the midst of the old, his salt to hinder social decay, and his light to shine in the darkness and dispel it. There is no better way for Christians to contribute to nation-building."[103]

The Lordship of Christ in South Africa (1990)

During 1988 Stott lectured across the major cities in South Africa at the invitation of Michael Cassidy, founder of Africa Enterprise, an evangelistic ministry. One of the six published lectures was entitled "Developing a Christian Impact on Society." He asked: "Will those who have been evangelized be able to penetrate South African culture in such a way as to influence and change it so that the standards and values of Jesus prevail and permeate the culture?"[104] He says:

> I have no doubt that Jesus Christ does desire that His values and standards prevail because He loves justice and hates evil. And He sent His people into the world both to preach the Gospel and make disciples, on the one hand, and on the other, to sweeten the whole

101. John R. W. Stott, "Salt and Light: The Christian Contribution to Nation-Building," *Evangelical Review of Theology* 9.3 (1985): 267–76.

102. Ibid., 267.

103. Ibid., 276.

104. John R. W. Stott, *The Lordship of Christ in South Africa* (Pietermaritzburg: Africa Enterprise, 1990), lecture 4 (1).

community and make its common life and culture more pleasing in His holy sight. One of the main evidences for this desire of Jesus is the salt and light metaphor in Matthew 5:13–16.[105]

Stott goes on to elaborate the images under four headings, familiar to readers of *Christian Counter-Culture* and *Decisive Issues Facing Christians Today*:

1. "Christians are radically different from non-Christians."
2. "Christians must permeate, penetrate, infiltrate non-Christian communities."
3. "Christians can influence and change non-Christian society" through prayer, evangelism, example, democratic argument, action, and suffering.
4. "Christians must retain their Christian distinctiveness," which means . . .
   a. a greater righteousness (explained with reference to Matt. 5:20)
   b. a wider love (explained with reference to loving enemies in Matt. 5:43–48)
   c. a nobler ambition (explained by reference to the Lord's Prayer in Matt. 6)

He concludes with a call to a double repentance: to "repent of our compromises," citing the edict in Matthew 6:24 that "nobody can serve two masters," and "to repent of our pessimism," even in the face of the horrors of apartheid, because "we know the Gospel is the power of God unto salvation to everyone who believes, and we know Jesus has told us to be the salt and light of the world and salt and light are meant to be effective."[106]

Evangelical Truth (1999)

In his *Evangelical Truth* (1999), the introductory chapter entitled "Evangelical Essentials" distinguishes between fundamentalism

105. Ibid., lecture 4 (1–2).
106. Ibid., lecture 4 (14).

and evangelicalism by enumerating ten contrasting tendencies. One of the tendencies Stott identifies regards the way that these related, but distinct, traditions regard the world and the church's involvement in the world:

> Fundamentalists have tended sometimes to assimilate the world's values and standards uncritically (e.g., in the prosperity gospel) and at other times to stand aloof from it, fearing contamination. By no means all evangelicals escape the charge of worldliness. Nevertheless, at least in theory they seek to heed the biblical injunction not to conform to this world and are also anxious to respond to the call of Jesus to penetrate it like salt and light in order to hinder its decay and illuminate its darkness.[107]

Here Stott makes social engagement as salt and light one of the defining marks of evangelicalism.

From this survey of Stott's writings, we see that the salt and light metaphors, which he articulates thoroughly in the early 1970s, plays a major role in his engagement with social ethics over the next three decades. Let me suggest some reasons why it proved so attractive to Stott:

1. It is an image drawn from a central passage of Scripture, recognized by all Christians, past and present, as carrying central significance. Since the Sermon on the Mount is so well known, the metaphor makes an immediate connection with virtually every Christian.
2. The image comes from Jesus himself and is addressed to disciples on the topic of being a disciple.
3. It is a metaphor that holds together what Stott sees the church so often separating, namely, its responsibilities both for evangelism (being the "light of the world" is possible only as we reflect the light of Christ and his gospel) and social

107. Stott, *Evangelical Truth*, 20.

action (since being the "salt of the earth" means involvement in the fabric of society).

4. It is a metaphor that comes with a warning ("losing our saltiness" or "hiding our light under a bushel") that speaks directly to the threats of assimilation or compromise with the prevailing culture that Stott detects as major hindrances to the church's witness.

5. It gives Stott biblical language for the notion of the Christian's calling to "permeate" or "infiltrate" every aspect of society, like salt rubbed into meat.

6. The image is optimistic, rooted in a distinct identity that is given to Christians through the grace and gift of Jesus. Stott often uses it to encourage Christians in difficult social contexts (such as South Africans struggling against apartheid) when he felt that despair or pessimism needed to be overcome in order for the church to engage faithfully in its social responsibilities.

Conclusion

Stott's work as an interpreter of the Sermon on the Mount provides ample evidence of his unusual skill as a scholarly preacher concerned to strengthen the church's faithfulness to the gospel. He finds his place in the long line of pastor-theologians who were concerned, first and foremost, with the exposition of Scripture. As Wallace Alston reminds us: "In former times, theologians were primarily preachers who wrote theology for the church. They wrote on subjects that would increase the faith and understanding of the members and ministers of the church, using language that people could understand."[108] As someone whose theology stands in the tradition of the Protestant Reformers, the Puritans, and Anglican evangelical thinkers such as Simeon and Ryle, Stott exemplifies the enduring strength of this inheritance from "former times." We have seen that Stott makes a valuable contribution to understand-

---

108. Wallace M. Alston Jr., "The Ministry of Christian Theology," in *Theology in the Service of the Church*, ed. Wallace M. Alston Jr. (Grand Rapids: Eerdmans, 2000), 27.

ing the Sermon on the Mount by offering a cohesive theological account of the biblical text that takes Jesus's call "do not be like them" as its interpretive key. In addition, Stott's interpretation of the salt and light metaphors was an essential part of his key role in reshaping the evangelical movement's understanding of mission and its stance toward social and political involvement in the post–World War II era. In these ways, Stott exemplifies what Packer writes: "The preacher, rather than the critical commentator or the academic theologian, is the true interpreter of Scripture, for the preacher is the person whose privilege it is to bridge the apparent gap between the Bible and the modern world by demonstrating the relevance of what Scripture says to the lives of those addressed."[109]

109. Packer, *Truth and Power*, 125.

The Tradition Alive

" Brazos Press seeks to be faithful to the wide and deep embrace of God, publishing out of and to all the major streams of the historic Christian tradition. "

Brazos Press is grounded in the ancient, ecumenical Christian tradition, understood as living and dynamic. As legend has it, Brazos is the Spanish name explorers gave to a prominent Texas river upon seeing how its winding waters sustained fertile soil in an arid land. They christened this life-giving channel Los Brazos de Dios, "the arms of God."

Our logo connotes a river with multiple currents all flowing in the same direction, just as the major streams of the Christian tradition are various but all surging from and to the same God. The logo's three "streams" also reflect the Trinitarian God who lives and gives life at the heart of all true Christian faith.

Our books are marketed and distributed intensively and broadly through the American Booksellers Association and the Christian Booksellers networks and bookstores; national chains and independent bookstores; Catholic and mainline bookstores; and library and international markets. We are a division of Baker Publishing Group.

Brazos Book Club and Border Crossings

Brazos books help people grapple with the important issues of the day and make Christian sense of pervasive issues in the church, academy, and contemporary world. Our authors engage such topics as spirituality, the arts, the economy, popular culture, theology, biblical studies, the social sciences, and more. At both the popular and academic levels, we publish books by evangelical, Roman Catholic, Protestant mainline, and Eastern Orthodox authors.

If you'd like to join the Brazos Book Club and receive our books upon publication at book club prices, please sign up online at **www.brazospress.com/brazosbookclub**.

To sign up for our monthly email newsletter, Border Crossings, visit **www.brazospress.com**. This email newsletter provides information on upcoming and recently released books, conferences we are attending, and more.

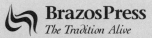

BrazosPress
The Tradition Alive